MW00526913

THE MICHELIN GUIDE

米芝蓮指南

HONG KONG | MACAU

香港 澳門

FACING THE FUTURE TOGETHER
秉持初衷 並肩同行

As this edition of MICHELIN Guide is published, the autumn breeze is giving way to a wintry chill. But in 2020, the hospitality industry has been hit hard, and it feels as though it has experienced a few bleak winters already. While we keep our social distance and put on our masks, the dining scene has been struggling to survive amid constantly shifting policies and regulations. Some operators downsized to stay afloat, while some closed their doors for good.

As soon as the initial peak of the pandemic subsided, our inspectors resumed their routine, visiting every corner of the cities anonymously. Happily, most of the restaurants we selected for our Guide are still up and running, supported by kitchen and service teams who insist on standing their ground and fulfilling their tasks. Despite the seemingly gloomy outlook, our inspectors are glad to reveal some exciting newcomers who are injecting much-needed vigour into the cities and keeping the gastronomic capitals shining bright.

Almost half of our newly listed restaurants have been awarded a Bib Gourmand or a MICHELIN Star. Our picks also cover Ningbo and Latin American cuisines for the first time. On top of that, the team has selected over 10 new accommodation choices, many of which are boutique hotels that promise to make your stay unique and fun. These latest inclusions add to the depth and breadth of our Guide by bringing diversity in both style and levels of comfort.

The MICHELIN Guide has always supported the hospitality industry and will continue to do so, and we sincerely hope that members of the sector can survive through these tough times. We look forward to a time when we can ditch the face coverings and the distancing screens, when we can meet with friends and family freely in our favourite restaurants, and when can once again marvel at every culinary wonder our talent chefs skilfully create.

If you have any comments about our guide, please write to: michelinguide.hongkong-macau@michelin.com

本指南出版之時，秋涼已去，冬意漸濃，可餐飲和酒店業界，在2020年卻彷彿經歷了幾個寒冬。當我們日復日將口罩脫下和戴上之際，餐飲業面臨着不斷轉變的政策，有些因而要縮減規模，個別甚至因而黯然落幕寫下終章。

疫情稍竭時，評審員繼續匿名走訪城中不同角落。我們慶幸指南內大部分餐廳未有被變遷擊潰。書上每一個熟悉的名字，背後都有一群默默努力堅守本業的廚師和服務團隊；縱然經營環境挑戰重重，評審團隊同時發現了業界的新晉成員，為小城的美食風景注入活力，使之持續發光發亮。

本年度新增的餐廳中，近一半獲選必比登甚或星級推介，更首次包羅寧波和拉丁美洲菜系。此外，我們更挑選了逾十家新的住宿選擇，當中不少是別具特色的精品酒店，使指南具備的級別和風格更多元。

米芝蓮指南將持續支持餐飲行業發展。我們期望業界能撐過艱難日子，在不多久的將來，大家可拋開屏風和口罩，無阻地於喜愛的餐廳品嘗廚師們帶來的驚艷滋味。

如對本指南有任何意見，請電郵至：michelinguide.hongkong-macau@michelin.com

CONTENTS
目錄

HONG KONG 香港 P. 20

MACAU 澳門 P.288

THE MICHELIN GUIDE'S COMMITMENTS

Whether they are in Japan, the USA, China or Europe, our inspectors apply the same criteria to judge the quality of each and every restaurant and hotel that they visit. The MICHELIN guide commands a **worldwide reputation** thanks to the commitments we make to our readers – and we reiterate these below:

Our inspectors make regular and **anonymous visits** to restaurants and hotels to gauge the quality of products and services offered to an ordinary customer. They settle their own bill and may then introduce themselves and ask for more information about the establishment.

To remain totally objective for our readers, the selection is made with complete **independence**. Entry into the guide is free. All decisions are discussed with the Editor and our highest awards are considered at an international level.

The guide offers a **selection** of the best restaurants and hotels in every category of comfort and price. This is only possible because all the inspectors rigorously apply the same methods.

All the practical information, classifications and awards are revised and updated every year to give the most **reliable information** possible.

In order to guarantee the **consistency** of our selection, our classification criteria are the same in every country covered by the MICHELIN guide. Each culture may have its own unique cuisine but **quality** remains the **universal principle** behind our selection.

Michelin's mission is to **aid your mobility**. Our sole aim is to make your journeys safe and pleasurable.

承諾

不論身處日本、美國、中國或歐洲,我們的獨立評審員均使用一致的評選方法對餐廳和酒店作出評估。米芝蓮指南在世界各地均享負盛名,關鍵在其秉承一貫宗旨,履行對讀者的承諾:

評審員以匿名方式定期到訪餐廳和酒店,以一般顧客的身份對餐廳和酒店的食品和服務品質作出評估。評審員自行結賬後,在需要時會介紹自己,並會詳細詢問有關餐廳或酒店的資料。

為保證本指南以讀者利益為依歸,餐廳的評選完全是我們獨立的決定。我們不會向收錄在指南內的餐廳收取任何費用,所有評選經編輯和評審員一同討論才作出決定,最高級別的評級以國際水平為標準。

本指南推介一系列優質餐廳和酒店,當中含括不同的舒適程度和價格,這全賴一眾評審員使用一致且嚴謹的評選方法。

所有實用資訊、分類及評級都會每年修訂和更新,務求為讀者提供最可靠的資料。

為確保指南的一致性,每個國家地區均採用相同的評審和分類準則,縱然各地的飲食文化不同,我們評選時的準則完全取決於食物品質和廚師的廚藝。

米芝蓮的目標多年來貫徹始終──致力令旅程盡善盡美,讓您在旅遊和外出用膳時不但安全,且充滿樂趣。

ONCE UPON A TIME, IN THE HEART OF FRANCE...

It all started way back in 1889, in Clermont-Ferrand, when the Michelin brothers founded the Manufacture Française des Pneumatiques Michelin tyre company – this was at a time when driving was considered quite an adventure!

In 1900, fewer than 3,000 cars existed in France. The Michelin brothers hit upon the idea of creating a small guide packed with useful information for the new pioneers of the road, such as where to fill up with petrol or change a tyre, as well as where to eat and sleep. The MICHELIN Guide was born!

The purpose of the guide was obvious: to track down the best hotels and restaurants across the country. To do this, Michelin employed a veritable armada of anonymous professional inspectors to scour every region – something that had never before been attempted!

Over the years, bumpy roads were replaced by smoother highways and the company continued to develop, as indeed did the country's cuisine: cooks became chefs, artisans developed into artists, and traditional dishes were transformed into works of art. All the while, the MICHELIN Guide, by now a faithful travel companion, kept pace with – and encouraged – these changes. The most famous distinction awarded by the guide was created in 1926: the "étoile de bonne table" – the famous star which quickly established itself as the reference in the world of gastronomy!

Bibendum – the famous tyre-clad Michelin man – continued to widen his reach and by 1911, the guide covered the whole of Europe.

In 2006, the collection crossed the Atlantic, awarding stars to 39 restaurants in New York. In 2007 and 2008, the guide moved on to San Francisco, Los Angeles and Las Vegas, and in 2011 it was the turn of Chicago to have its own Michelin guide – The Michelin Man had become truly American!

In November 2007, The Michelin Man took his first steps in Asia: in recognition of the excellence of Japanese cuisine, stars rained down on Tokyo, which was gripped by culinary fever! A guide to Kyoto, Kobe, Osaka and Nara followed, with Yokohama and Shonan then joining Tokyo. Thereafter the Michelin Man set his feet down in Southern China, with the publication in 2009 of a guide to Hong Kong and Macau.

The Red Guide was now firmly on the map in the Far East. The Michelin Man then explored Southeast Asia and China. In 2016 the first editions of MICHELIN Guide Singapore, MICHELIN Guide Shanghai and MICHELIN Guide Seoul were published. The MICHELIN guides collection now covers more than 30 titles in 30 countries, with over 30 million copies sold in a century. Quite a record!

Meanwhile, the search continues... Looking for a delicious cassoulet or pot-au-feu in a typical Parisian bistro, or a bowl of springy wonton noodles in Hong Kong? The Michelin Man continues to span the globe making new discoveries and selecting the very best the culinary world has to offer!

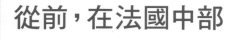

從前，在法國中部

這一切始於1889年，米芝蓮兄弟在法國克萊蒙費朗 (Clermont-Ferrand) 創辦Manufacture Française des Pneumatiques Michelin 輪胎公司──當年駕駛汽車仍被視為一大冒險。

在1900年，法國的汽車總數量少於3,000輛。米芝蓮兄弟靈機一觸，想到為道路駕駛的先驅提供含實用資訊的小指南，如補充汽油或更換輪胎，以至用餐和睡覺的好去處。米芝蓮指南就這樣誕生了！

指南的宗旨非常清晰：搜羅全國各地最好的酒店和餐廳。為達目的，米芝蓮招攬了一整隊神秘專業評審員，走遍全國每一個角落尋找值得推介的酒店和餐廳，這在當時是前所未有的創舉。

多年來，崎嶇不平的道路早已被平順的高速公路取代，米芝蓮公司持續茁壯成長。同時間，全國各地餐飲業的發展亦一日千里：廚子成為大廚、傳統手藝成為藝術，傳統菜餚亦轉化成為藝術傑作。現今米芝蓮指南已成為廣受信賴的旅遊夥伴，不僅與時並進，更致力推動這些轉變。指南中最著名的是早在1926年面世，並迅即成為美食界權威指標的「星級推介」。

由米芝蓮輪胎人必比登為代言人的米芝蓮指南，不斷拓展其版圖，到1911年已覆蓋全歐洲。

2006年，米芝蓮指南系列成功跨越大西洋，授予紐約39家餐廳星級推介。在2007及2008年，米芝蓮指南在三藩市、洛杉磯和拉斯維加斯出版，2011年已拓展至芝加哥，米芝蓮必比登也正式落戶美國。

2007年11月，米芝蓮必比登首次踏足亞洲，在東京廣發星級推介，以表揚日本料理的卓越成就，同時亦掀起美食熱潮。其後，旋即推出京都、神戶、大阪及奈良指南，並繼東京之後推出橫濱和湘南指南。香港和澳門指南亦於2009年推出。

2016年，必比登更涉足新加坡、中國和韓國，推出首本新加坡指南、上海指南和首爾指南，令這本以紅色為標誌的指南，在亞洲地區的覆蓋範圍更見廣泛。

時至今日，米芝蓮指南系列共計超過30本，涵蓋30個國家，一個世紀以來，總銷量超過三千萬冊。這是個令人鼓舞的紀錄！

此時此刻，我們仍然繼續對美食的追尋……是巴黎餐廳的美味雜菜鍋，還是彈牙的雲吞麵？必比登將會努力不懈，發掘全球美食，為你們挑選最出色的佳餚美饌！

STARS

Our famous One ✿, Two ✿✿ and Three ✿✿✿ Stars
identify establishments serving the highest quality
cuisine – taking into account the quality of ingredients,
the mastery of techniques and flavours, the levels of
creativity and, of course, consistency.

✿✿✿   Exceptional cuisine, worth a special journey!

✿✿   Excellent cuisine, worth a detour!

✿   High quality cooking, worth a stop!

BIB GOURMAND

This symbol indicates our inspectors'
favourites for good value. These restaurants
offer quality cooking for $400 or less
(price of a 3-course meal excluding drinks).

PLATE

Good cooking.
Fresh ingredients, capably prepared:
simply a good meal.

THE MICHELIN GUIDE'S SYMBOLS

Michelin are experts at finding the best restaurants and invite you to explore the diversity of the gastronomic universe. As well as evaluating a restaurant's cooking, we also consider its décor, the service and the ambience – in other words, the all-round culinary experience.

Two keywords help you make your choice more quickly: red for the type of cuisine, gold for the atmosphere:

Cantonese • Elegant

FACILITIES & SERVICES

Cash only	
Wheelchair accessible	
Terrace dining	
Interesting view	
Valet parking	
Car park	
Garage	
Private room	
Counter	
Reservations recommended / not accepted	
Non smoking rooms	
Conference rooms	
Indoor / Outdoor swimming pool	
Spa	
Exercise room	
Casino	
Interesting wine list	
New entry in the guide	

HOTEL CLASSIFICATION, ACCORDING TO COMFORT

Particularly pleasant if in red

	Luxury
	Top class comfort
	Very comfortable
	Comfortable
	Quite comfortable

米芝蓮圖標

米芝蓮是追尋最佳餐廳的專家,邀請您共同發掘豐富多元的餐飲世界。在品評餐廳烹調質素同時,我們亦將其裝潢、服務和整體氛圍加入考慮,換言之,是包含味覺、感官和整體用餐經驗的全方位評估。

兩組關鍵詞助你挑選合適的餐廳,紅色為菜式種類;金色是環境氛圍:

粵菜 • 典雅

設施及服務

⑤	只接受現金
♿	輪椅通道
🍴	陽台用餐
←	上佳景觀
🅿	代客泊車
P	停車場
🚗	室內停車場
⚍	私人廂房
🍽	吧檯式
⊘🍴 ⊗🍴	建議訂位 / 不設訂位
⑁	非吸煙房
🛋	會議室
⊠ 🏊	室內 / 室外游泳池
Spa	水療服務
🏋	健身室
⊙	娛樂場所
🍷	供應優質餐酒
N	新增推介

酒店—以舒適程度分類

紅色代表上佳

🏘🏘 🏘🏘	豪華
🏘 🏘	高級舒適
🏘 🏘	十分舒適
🏠 🏠	舒適
🏠 🏠	頗舒適

米芝蓮美食評級分類

星級美食

聞名遐邇的米芝蓮一星✿、二星✿✿和三星✿✿✿推介,推薦的
是食物品質特別出色的餐廳。我們的評級考慮到以下因素:
材料的品質和配搭、烹調技巧和味道層次、
菜餚所展示的創意,少不了的是食物水平的一致性。

✿✿✿ 卓越的烹調,值得專程造訪!
✿✿   烹調出色,不容錯過!
✿   優質烹調,不妨一試!

必比登美食推介餐廳

必比登標誌表示該餐廳提供具品質
且經濟實惠的美食:費用在$400元或以下
(三道菜式但不包括飲料)。

米芝蓮餐盤

評審員萬裏挑一的餐廳,
食材新鮮、烹調用心,菜餚美味。

HONG KONG
香港

Nikada/iStock

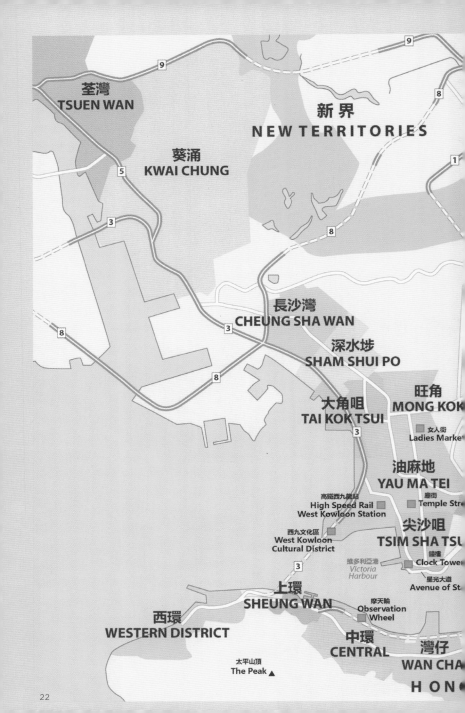

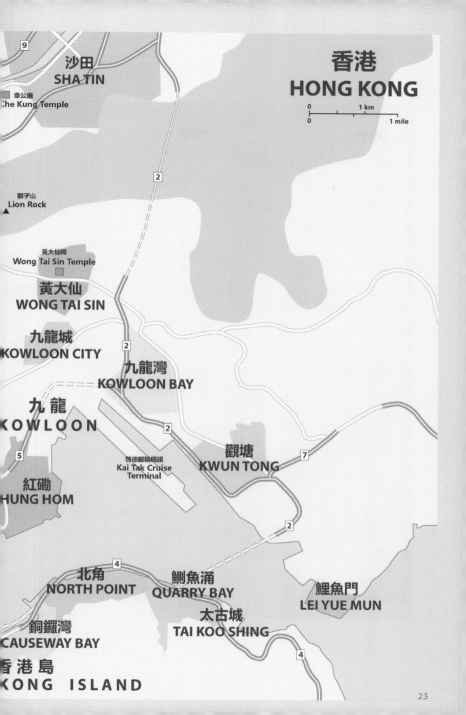

acavalli/iStock

HONG KONG ISLAND

香港島

RESTAURANTS
餐廳

❀ ❀ ❀

CAPRICE

French Contemporary • Elegant

時尚法國菜 • 典雅

Not only is this one of the most glamourous and elegant restaurants in Hong Kong but it also boasts impressive views of the harbour. French cuisine of the highest order features luxurious ingredients, superb techniques and a mastery of flavours and harmony. A stunning wine list accompanies specialities like crab royale, and turbot with sea urchin sauce. The wonderful array of cheeses is another highlight. Dining here is always an amazing experience.

餐室裝潢古典優雅而不失格調，更有迷人海景及貼心專業的服務，在這裏用餐實是非凡享受。先到酒吧呷杯雞尾酒，再享用各式以高級食材輔以精湛烹調技巧所作的法國菜式，每一道都將味道發揮到極致。招牌菜包括多寶魚伴海膽汁和蟹肉拌生蠔及海鮮咔喱；芝士和餐酒的選擇叫人驚歎。

TEL. 3196 8860

**6F, Four Seasons Hotel,
8 Finance Street, Central**
中環金融街8號四季酒店6樓
www.fourseasons.com/hongkong

■ **PRICE** 價錢
Lunch 午膳
Set Menu 套餐 $ 645-895
À la carte 點菜 $ 1,300-2,600
Dinner 晚膳
Set Menu 套餐 $ 1,820
À la carte 點菜 $ 1,300-2,600

■ **OPENING HOURS** 營業時間
Lunch 午膳 12:00-14:30
Dinner 晚膳 18:30-21:00

HONG KONG ISLAND 香港島

MielPhotos2008/iStock

≋ ☺🍴 ⇔

TEL. 2869 8282

**1F, Sino Plaza,
255-257 Gloucester Road,
Causeway Bay**

銅鑼灣告士打道255-257號
信和廣場1樓

www.forumrestaurant1977.com

■ **PRICE** 價錢
Lunch 午膳
Set Menu 套餐 $ 480-550
À la carte 點菜 $ 300-1,000
Dinner 晚膳
À la carte 點菜 $ 500-2,000

■ **OPENING HOURS** 營業時間
Lunch 午膳 11:30-14:30
Dinner 晚膳 18:00-22:30

✿ ✿ ✿

FORUM
富臨飯店

Cantonese • Traditional
粵菜 • 傳統

The iconic dish here, Ah Yat braised abalone, has become as famous as Forum's owner-chef after whom it is named. Indeed, its international fame is such that some even travel from abroad just to taste it – tender and flavoursome abalone slow-cooked in a gourmet broth for days. Try also the braised oxtail, crispy fried chicken and stuffed crab shell with dried scallops. The dining room is spacious and comfortable.

餐廳老闆楊貫一的招牌菜阿一鮑魚赫赫有名，不論是本地食客或世界知名人士皆慕名而至。幕後團隊對此菜式絕不馬虎，採用日本乾鮑燜煮數天而成，且由專人主理。鮑魚以外，其他菜式包括燒汁焗牛尾、脆皮雞和瑤柱焗釀蟹蓋，也展現精湛的烹調技巧。室內裝潢豪華且富時代感，視覺味覺同時得到無比滿足。

L'ATELIER DE JOËL ROBUCHON

French Contemporary •
Contemporary Décor

時尚法國菜 • 時尚

If you want to feel part of the action sit at the counter; if you prefer a more intimate setting then ask for a table in Le Jardin. The signature red and black décor, along with the living garden wall, have become as much a signature in a Joël Robuchon restaurant as the cooking. The contemporary French cuisine is executed to the highest level, using ingredients which are the best available. Expect professional service to match.

乘搭專屬電梯或升降機皆可到達這餐廳。如欲充分感受餐室的氣氛與節奏，開放式廚房前的櫃枱座位無疑是最佳位置；屬意較親密的環境則不妨要求能看到露台的座位。標誌性的紅黑裝潢代表着處理精細的時尚法國菜餚將輪流登場，不論用料或烹調技巧皆無懈可擊，專業的服務令用餐經驗更稱心滿意。

TEL. 2166 9000

Shop 401, 4F, Landmark Atrium,
15 Queen's Road Central, Central

中環皇后大道中15號置地廣場中庭
4樓401號舖

www.robuchon.hk

■ **PRICE** 價錢
Lunch 午膳
Set Menu 套餐 $ 498-758
À la carte 點菜 $ 800-1,800
Dinner 晚膳
Set Menu 套餐 $ 1,280-2,480
À la carte 點菜 $ 800-1,800

■ **OPENING HOURS** 營業時間
Lunch 午膳 12:00-14:30
Dinner 晚膳 18:30-22:00

HONG KONG ISLAND 香港島

✿✿✿

LUNG KING HEEN
龍景軒

Cantonese · Elegant
粵菜 · 典雅

TEL. 3196 8880

4F, Four Seasons Hotel,
8 Finance Street, Central

中環金融街8號四季酒店4樓

www.fourseasons.com/hongkong

■ PRICE 價錢
Lunch 午膳
Set Menu 套餐 $ 660-1,680
À la carte 點菜 $ 500-2,500
Dinner 晚膳
Set Menu 套餐 $ 1,380-2,980
À la carte 點菜 $ 500-2,500

■ OPENING HOURS 營業時間
Lunch 午膳 12:00-14:30
Dinner 晚膳 18:00-21:00

For many, the roast Peking duck alone is reason enough to dine here. However, Chef Chan Yan Tak is a master of Cantonese cuisine and his repertoire is extensive, so consider ordering the Chef's Tasting Menu; wok-fried Wagyu with morels and peppers and simmered lobster in crystal sauce are just two specialities. Superb ingredients, flawless cooking and tantalizing flavour combinations are his hallmarks. Ask for a window table for harbour views.

行政總廚陳恩德的一道北京片皮烤鴨廣受稱頌，然而其經典名菜豈止於此？頂級優質食材、無可挑剔的烹調手法、配搭得天衣無縫的味道，盡皆是其菜式標記。羊肚菌爆澳洲特級和牛柳粒、上湯焗龍蝦球只是其匠心之作中的少數，主廚套餐將是體驗其手藝的最佳選擇。美食當前，即使面朝維港絕景大概也無暇細賞。

HONG KONG ISLAND 香港島

❀ ❀ ❀

8 1/2 OTTO E MEZZO - BOMBANA

Italian • Elegant

意大利菜 • 典雅

Italian films are the second passion, after cooking, of owner-chef Umberto Bombana, which is why he named his restaurant after a Fellini film. Everything they do here oozes Italian charm and passion. Ingredients are the best available and the cooking showcases their true flavours; this, along with the personable and professional service, makes for an unforgettable experience.

店東兼主廚Umberto Bombana熱衷的首推烹飪，其次就是電影，因此餐廳亦以意大利著名導演費里尼的作品「八部半」為名。餐廳無一細節不在展露意大利的熱情和魅力，一絲不苟的選材令菜餚的風味和多變得以完美顯展。無懈可擊的服務，色、香、味俱全的佳餚構成令人難以忘懷的饗宴。

🏖 ◎🍴 &. ⇆ 🍷 **P**

TEL. 2537 8859

**Shop 202, 2F, Alexandra House,
18 Chater Road, Central**

中環遮打道18號歷山大廈2樓202號舖

www.ottoemezzobombana.com

■ **PRICE** 價錢
Lunch 午膳
Set Menu 套餐 $ 780-1,080
À la carte 點菜 $ 1,200-1,600
Dinner 晚膳
Set Menu 套餐 $ 1,780
À la carte 點菜 $ 1,200-1,600

■ **OPENING HOURS** 營業時間
Lunch 午膳 12:00-14:30
Dinner 晚膳 18:30-22:30

■ **ANNUAL AND WEEKLY CLOSING**
休息日期
Closed Sunday 週日休息

◖⫟ ⛨ ✿ ⇔ 🍽 **P**

TEL. 2643 6800

7F, The Landmark Mandarin Oriental Hotel, 15 Queen's Road Central, Central

中環皇后大道中15號
置地文華東方酒店7樓

www.sushi-shikon.com

■ **PRICE 價錢**
Lunch 午膳
Set Menu 套餐 $ 1,800
Dinner 晚膳
Set Menu 套餐 $ 3,500

■ **OPENING HOURS 營業時間**
Lunch 午膳 12:30-14:00
Dinner 晚膳 18:00-22:30

■ **ANNUAL AND WEEKLY CLOSING**
休息日期
Closed Sunday 週日休息

✿✿ ✿✿ ✿✿

SUSHI SHIKON
志魂

Sushi • Classic Décor

壽司 • 經典

The famous sushi-ya moved to this prestigious address in 2019 and had the best Japanese designers and artisans pitching in on every detail, including the karatsu dinnerware. But one thing hasn't changed: long-standing executive chef Kakinuma still leads the same team to deliver the best food with the best skills. The signature Shimane abalone is steamed in sake for seven hours and served with an abalone liver sauce made with a secret recipe.

餐廳遷到現址後，由著名室內設計師、木材及陶瓷職人聯手，雕琢出精緻的用餐環境，同時保持一貫的食物質素。招牌菜清酒蒸鮑魚，烹調時間長達七小時，配合秘製鮑魚肝汁同食，鮮味十足。料理長更選用來自京都、經特別混合的新米，以加強香味、甜度和幼滑度，配合兩種熟成四年的醋，令整體味道更臻極致。

COLLECTION

Fifty Fathoms

BLANCPAIN IS THE GLOBAL MICHELIN GUIDE PARTNER

BLANCPAIN
1735

BLANCPAIN
MANUFACTURE DE HAUTE HORLOGERIE

©Photograph: Laurent Ballesta/Gombessa Project

RAISE AWARENESS,
TRANSMIT OUR PASSION,
HELP PROTECT THE OCEAN

www.blancpain-ocean-commitment.com

26 RUSSELL STREET, CAUSEWAY BAY (852) 2518 9966
THE PROMENADE GALAXY MACAU™, G085, COTAI (853) 2882 3407
SHOPPES AT PARISIAN, SHOP 333B PLACE VENDOME, LEVEL 3 (853) 2882 8581

⌘ ⌘

AMBER

French Contemporary • Elegant
時尚法國菜 • 典雅

There has been a radical revamp at this restaurant helmed by Dutch-born chef Richard Ekkebus. The brightly-lit dining room boasts organic curves, luxury materials and a gold and beige palette. As opposed to the à la carte in the past, it now offers only prix-fixe menus, including a dairy- and gluten-free vegetarian one with reduced salt and sugar. Top-notch ingredients, mostly from Japan, are crafted into light and delicate creations with a modern touch.

這典雅的餐廳以金色和米色為主調，加上名貴皮革座椅、淺色橡木餐桌等，盡顯奢華優雅。主廚以法國菜的技巧，配合日本進口的高質食材，設計出多款套餐。烹飪風格貼合現代飲食潮流：精緻、輕盈、低糖低鹽、不含麩質和奶製品，更提供素食選擇，滿足追求健康的客人。

⌘ ⌘↑ & ⌂ ⌦ **P**

TEL. 2132 0066

7F, The Landmark Mandarin Oriental Hotel, 15 Queen's Road Central, Central

中環皇后大道中15號
置地文華東方酒店7樓

mandarinoriental.com/landmark

■ **PRICE** 價錢
Lunch 午膳
Set Menu 套餐 $ 778-2,088
Dinner 晚膳
Set Menu 套餐 $ 1,548-2,458

■ **OPENING HOURS** 營業時間
Lunch 午膳 12:00-13:45
Dinner 晚膳 18:00-20:45

HONG KONG ISLAND 香港島

TEL. 3185 8388

25F, H Queen's,
80 Queen's Road Central, Central
中環皇后大道中80號H Queen's 25樓
www.arbor-hk.com

■ PRICE 價錢
Lunch 午膳
Set Menu 套餐 $ 598-888
Dinner 晚膳
Set Menu 套餐 $ 1,488-1,888

■ OPENING HOURS 營業時間
Lunch 午膳 12:00-14:30
Dinner 晚膳 18:30-21:30

■ ANNUAL AND WEEKLY CLOSING
休息日期
Closed first day of Lunar New Year
and Sunday 年初一及週日休息

ARBOR

Innovative • Contemporary Décor
創新菜 • 時尚

Its calming Mediterranean colours make this something of an oasis from the bustle of Central. The experienced chef hails from Finland; he uses mostly French techniques in his cooking and sources quality ingredients, mainly from Japan. His sophisticated dishes exhibit typical Nordic precision and deliver intense natural flavours. The service style is quite formal and there's an impressive wine list.

室內設計採用悠閒的地中海風格，讓人暫時遠離中環區的繁囂。祖籍芬蘭、經驗老到的大廚對食材瞭解透徹，秉持對食材的尊重，堅持採用新鮮且大部分皆源自日本的材料。嫻熟的法式烹調技術加上北歐精準細緻的態度，食材的自然滋味不但表露無遺，更得以提升。酒單使人眼前一亮，服務專業周到。

34

❁ ❁

BO INNOVATION

Innovative • Fashionable

創新菜 • 時髦

Alvin Leung celebrates Hong Kong's culture, traditions and people here, from the kitchen façade inspired by the typhoon shelters of Aberdeen Harbour to the graffiti walls which illustrate the journey of this chef. Each vibrant, imaginative and at times 'X-treme' dish comes with its own story and blends strong Chinese techniques with subtle French influences. Ingredients are superb and the flavours are clearly defined and memorable.

靈感來自香港仔避風塘的廚房佈置，記述着主廚研製菜式旅程的牆上塗鴉，甚或是餐廳內各式本地特製食具和古董，通通都是主廚梁經倫獻給香港文化的讚歌。餐點中不乏各式各樣的創作料理，無一不展示香港當代文化，以不一樣的烹調技巧呈現。

🕸 ◐🍴 ⬌ 🚪

TEL. 2850 8371

Shop 8, Podium 1F, J Senses, 60 Johnston Road, Wan Chai

灣仔莊士敦道60號J Senses 1樓平台8號舖

www.boinnovation.com

■ **PRICE** 價錢
Lunch 午膳
Set Menu 套餐 $ 680-960
Dinner 晚膳
Set Menu 套餐 $ 1,880

■ **OPENING HOURS** 營業時間
Lunch 午膳 12:00-14:00
Dinner 晚膳 18:00-21:00

■ **ANNUAL AND WEEKLY CLOSING** 休息日期
Closed Monday to Thursday & Public Holiday lunch; 3 days Lunar New Year and Sunday
週一至週四及公眾假期午膳；農曆新年3天及週日休息

HONG KONG ISLAND 香港島

TEL. 2795 5996
26F, H Queen's,
80 Queen's Road Central, Central
中環皇后大道中80號H Queen's 26樓
www.lecomptoir.hk/ecriture

■ **PRICE** 價錢
Lunch 午膳
Set Menu 套餐 $ 788-1,972
Dinner 晚膳
Set Menu 套餐 $ 1,788

■ **OPENING HOURS** 營業時間
Lunch 午膳 12:00-14:00
Dinner 晚膳 18:30-22:00

■ **ANNUAL AND WEEKLY CLOSING**
休息日期
Closed Sunday 週日休息

ÉCRITURE

French Contemporary •
Contemporary Décor
時尚法國菜 • 時尚

Plenty of creativity went into the design of this understated restaurant from chef Maxime Gilbert, formerly of Amber – and the views are pretty good too. Japan provides many of the ingredients and some of the inspiration, but French techniques bring it all together. To best experience the original and occasionally theatrical cooking, go for the 8-course 'Library of Flavours' menu. Piqniq is their rooftop bar on the floor above.

位於H Queen's頂層的Écriture裝潢簡約而別具特色，窗外有迷人景觀。餐廳採用日本食材以法式手法烹調，包括八道菜的品嘗菜單「Library of Flavours」盡展食材的原汁原味，菜式充滿創意，部分甚至在席前烹調，各種味道配搭使人眼前一亮且難以忘懷。天台酒吧Piqniq是時尚潮流好去處。

KASHIWAYA
柏屋

Japanese • Minimalist

日本菜 • 簡約

The head chef worked for twenty years at the much celebrated, original Kashiwaya restaurant in Osaka before being charged with opening their Hong Kong branch here in Central. It's a predictably discreet, impeccably run operation with around 80% of the menu the same as the original. For the kaiseki cuisine, all the fiercely seasonal ingredients are flown in from Japan, including the soft water for the cooking of the rice.

柏屋在大阪的總店享負盛名,這家首間海外分店於2015年開業,食客可在這兒嘗到正宗的懷石料理。主廚曾於總店效力長達二十年,秉承懷石料理食物精緻、製作嚴謹的宗旨侍客,除了選用最頂尖的時令食材,運用於製作煮物、飯和上湯的軟水亦來自日本。每一道菜式均值得細味品嘗。

TEL. 2520 5218

8F, 18 On Lan Street, Central
中環安蘭街18號8樓
jp-kashiwaya.com/hongkong

■ **PRICE** 價錢
Dinner 晚膳
Set Menu 套餐 $ 1,680-3,980

■ **OPENING HOURS** 營業時間
Dinner 晚膳 18:30-21:00

■ **ANNUAL AND WEEKLY CLOSING**
休息日期
Closed Sunday 週日休息

L'ENVOL

French Contemporary • Elegant

時尚法國菜 • 典雅

TEL. 2138 6818

3F, The St. Regis Hotel,
1 Harbour Drive, Wan Chai

灣仔港灣徑1號瑞吉酒店3樓

www.stregishongkong.com

■ **PRICE** 價錢
Lunch 午膳
Set Menu 套餐 $ 688-898
Dinner 晚膳
Set Menu 套餐 $ 1,388-1,988

■ **OPENING HOURS** 營業時間
Lunch 午膳 12:00-14:30
Dinner 晚膳 18:30-22:30

■ **ANNUAL AND WEEKLY CLOSING**
休息日期
Closed Sunday 週日休息

The restaurant, managed by Chef Olivier Elzer, comes elegantly furnished in marble and wood. Shrewdly prepared, artfully plated dishes coupled with professional and warm service capture the quintessence of French fine dining. Signatures include Hokkaido sea urchin box, and 'la langoustine de Loctudy'. The wine list has 100 different champagnes and the cheese cart boasts over 15 French choices, alongside condiments like Ukrainian honeycomb.

以水晶吊燈、上等木材和雲石，塑造出優雅的用餐環境，開放式廚房更讓人一窺法國主廚的手藝。專業友善的服務團隊，為客人提供精緻難忘的法國菜體驗。不容錯過北海道海膽盒，選用日本海膽及法國小紅蝦，鮮味可口。芝士拼盤包羅超過十五種法國芝士，伴以烏克蘭蜂巢及配料享用。

HONG KONG ISLAND 香港島

✿✿

SUSHI SAITO

鮨・齋藤

Sushi • Traditional

壽司・傳統

Famed chef Takashi Saito and his team artfully and masterfully craft Edomae-style sushi using the finest seasonal seafood. Rice from Akita is cooked in spring water from Kagoshima and dressed in a special blend of vinegar. But before you get to taste his divine creations at the cypress counter, you must first get a seat – and this exclusive sushi-ya seats just 16 guests. Telephone reservations are only accepted on specific days and at specific times.

要一嘗日本大廚齋藤孝司的江戶前壽司，你得先打通只於特定日子開放的訂座熱線。成功的十六位幸運兒，將於以日本柏木鑄造的壽司櫃枱前就座。結合最頂級時令海產、秋田稻米、鹿兒島泉水、特製醬醋和大師熟練技巧的壽司，將逐一登場，每一件都儼如藝術品，讓人禁不住細細端詳品味。

TEL. 2527 0811

45F, Four Seasons Hotel,
8 Finance Street, Central

中環金融街8號四季酒店45樓

www.fourseasons.com/hongkong

■ PRICE 價錢

Lunch 午膳
Set Menu 套餐 $ 1,680
Dinner 晚膳
Set Menu 套餐 $ 3,280

■ OPENING HOURS 營業時間

Lunch 午膳 12:00-12:30
Dinner 晚膳 18:00-20:45

■ ANNUAL AND WEEKLY CLOSING
休息日期

Closed 1-7 January
1月 1日-7日休息

📱♿🔧

TEL. 2668 6488

2F, The Pottinger Hotel,
21 Stanley Street, Central

中環士丹利街21號
中環·石板街酒店2樓

tavie.com.hk

■ **PRICE** 價錢
Dinner 晚膳
Set Menu 套餐 $ 2,580

■ **OPENING HOURS** 營業時間
Dinner 晚膳 18:30-21:00

■ **ANNUAL AND WEEKLY CLOSING**
休息日期
Closed 6 days Lunar New Year and
Wednesday
農曆新年6天及週三休息

✿ ✿

TA VIE
旅

Innovative · Intimate
創新菜 · 親密

The mantra of chef Hideaki Sato is "pure, simple and seasonal". He has a passion for the ingredients and flavours of his native Japan which he brings together with French cooking techniques to create original, creative and sophisticated dishes. His charming wife Hiromi delivers a tasting menu which changes according to season, and is accompanied by an interesting collection of Asian wine and sake. This sweet little restaurant is hidden in the boutique Pottinger hotel.

面積不大的旅藏身於中環·石板街酒店內。日籍大廚佐藤秀明謹遵「純粹、簡約、時令」的信條，以法式烹調手法帶出日本食材的原始滋味，配合創意和精湛純熟的技巧，將之炮製成味道、質感獨特的佳餚。品嘗菜單反映當季食材，並佐以由其妻子精心挑選的亞洲餐酒及日本清酒。

TATE

Innovative · Intimate

創新菜 · 親密

Owner-chef Vicky Lau tells edible stories with an eight-course menu that treads the boundary between French and Chinese cooking in a feminine, sophisticated way. Each dish is an ode to an ingredient, mostly locally sourced, with occasional exceptions such as Hokkaido scallop or Australian Wagyu. Wine flights are predominantly French, but also consider sake. Refined and detailed service echoes the sentiments that the food imparts.

灰褐、淡粉紅、磨砂金三種色調為餐室拼湊出優雅的氛圍，菜式則散發着女性的細膩觸覺。八道菜菜單以法國料理為本，加入大量中式元素，每道菜都精緻得像在歌頌所用的材料。這些優質食材包括本地金橘、北海道帶子及澳洲和牛等。除了餐酒配搭服務，更提供多款雞尾酒和清酒，更添醉人氣息。

©⑪ & ⇧

TEL. 2555 2172

210 Hollywood Road, Sheung Wan

上環荷李活道210號

www.tate.com.hk

■ **PRICE** 價錢

Lunch 午膳
Set Menu 套餐 $ 1,180
Dinner 晚膳
Set Menu 套餐 $ 1,480-1,680

■ **OPENING HOURS** 營業時間

Lunch 午膳 12:00-13:30
Dinner 晚膳 18:00-22:00

■ **ANNUAL AND WEEKLY CLOSING**

休息日期

Closed Tuesday to Thursday lunch, Sunday and Monday

週二至週四午膳、週日及週一休息

HONG KONG ISLAND 香港島

YING JEE CLUB
營致會館

Cantonese • Contemporary Décor
粵菜 • 時尚

TEL. 2801 6882

**Shop G05, 107-108, GF & 1F,
Nexxus Building, 41 Connaught
Road Central, Central**

中環干諾道中41號盈置大廈
地下G05及1樓107-108號舖

www.yingjeeclub.hk

■ **PRICE** 價錢
Lunch 午膳
Set Menu 套餐 $ 430-680
À la carte 點菜 $ 300-1,000
Dinner 晚膳
Set Menu 套餐 $ 880-1,480
À la carte 點菜 $ 500-1,200

■ **OPENING HOURS** 營業時間
Lunch 午膳 11:30-14:30
Dinner 晚膳 18:00-22:00

Rather than gimmicky promotions, the owner prefers to divert his energy and resources into finding quality ingredients and honing the chefs' skills. The tasteful, modern room adorned with marble tables, velvet seats and metallic trim primes the diners for Cantonese classics re-created with finesse. Crispy salted chicken is silky and tender without being overly oily while stir-fried lobster with shallot and scallion boasts juicy meat in thin crisp crust.

裝潢典雅時尚，讓客人在舒適的環境中享用精緻美食。主廚着重選料新鮮，加上熟練的烹調技巧，炮製出細緻傳統的廣東菜。招牌菜脆皮貴妃雞皮脆酥香、口感嫩滑。另外推介肉質鮮嫩中帶香脆的香葱爆乳龍。地下酒吧專售氈酒調製的雞尾酒，也有輕井澤威士忌等較特別的選擇。

AAHARN

Thai • Design
泰國菜 • 型格

The bright yellow walls and contemporary art may not say much about the historic police armoury building Aaharn occupies, but its name cannot be more revealing – it means "food" in Thai. The Australian chef David Thompson oversees the operation and his short but very sweet menu changes seasonally to feature the best ingredients from Thailand. Don't miss their desserts, such as the Thai cupcakes – and on balmy nights ask for a table on the terrace.

餐廳置身歷史建築之中,過去是警察總部的軍械庫,內部裝潢卻充滿現代感和藝術氣息。晚市時段可於陽台用餐,感受悠閒氣氛。泰籍主廚擁有多年經驗,曾學習宮廷料理,特別挑選家鄉的優質食材,炮製出精緻傳統的泰國佳餚。菜單頗為精簡,不妨請服務員推介招牌菜式,但不要忘記預留位置給杯子蛋糕等甜品。

TEL. 2703 9111

**1F, Block 2, Tai Kwun,
10 Hollywood Road, Central**
中環荷李活道10號大館2座1樓
www.aaharn.hk

■ **PRICE** 價錢
Lunch 午膳
Set Menu 套餐 $ 228-416
À la carte 點菜 $ 300-800
Dinner 晚膳
Set Menu 套餐 $ 688
À la carte 點菜 $ 300-800

■ **OPENING HOURS** 營業時間
Lunch 午膳 12:00-14:30
Dinner 晚膳 18:30-22:00

■ **ANNUAL AND WEEKLY CLOSING**
休息日期
Closed Sunday and Monday
週日及週一休息

88 ⓄⓇ ⇌

TEL. 2380 9007

1F, Somptueux Central,
52-54 Wellington Street, Central
中環威靈頓街52-54號
Somptueux Central 1樓

www.andohk.com

■ **PRICE** 價錢
Lunch 午膳
Set Menu 套餐 $ 588-1,216
Dinner 晚膳
Set Menu 套餐 $ 1,288-1,688

■ **OPENING HOURS** 營業時間
Lunch 午膳 12:00-14:30
Dinner 晚膳 18:00-21:00

■ **ANNUAL AND WEEKLY CLOSING**
休息日期
Closed Monday lunch and Sunday
週一午膳及週日休息

ANDŌ

Innovative • Contemporary Décor
創新菜・時尚

Born in Argentina but having honed his skills in Japan, chef-founder Agustin Balbi opened Andō to realise his culinary vision from his unique vantage point. In a minimalistic dining room boasting tasteful details and an open kitchen, his tasting menu takes diners on a personal journey by fusing his ancestral roots with strong Japanese influences. Don't miss the signature Sin Lola, the caldoso rice – also a homage to his grandma.

阿根廷主廚Agustin Balbi於香港開設的首間餐廳，糅合他的西班牙背景，以及在日本的豐富工作經驗和啟發，建立出別樹一幟的風格。品嘗菜單以獨特方式呈現主廚的烹飪歷程，當中的高湯燴飯，是他向祖母致敬之作。用餐環境簡約舒適，並設有偌大的開放式廚房，讓客人得以全情投入享受美食。

ARCANE

European Contemporary •
Contemporary Décor
時尚歐陸菜 • 時尚

Aussie chef Shane Osborn lets diners witness how quality ingredients turn into artistic culinary creations in the open kitchen. Simple recipes are executed with a refined edge which allows authentic flavours to shine through. The affable sommelier is more than happy to pair your food with wine from their extensive cellar covering Europe, Oceania and The Americas - and which includes a lavish Burgundy selection. The reasonably priced lunch set menu is recommended.

開放式廚房讓食客能注視澳洲籍主廚Shane Osborn 烹調時的專注、體會他的熱情，以簡易方式烹調日本海鮮、澳洲牛肉和法國有機雞肉等食材，也反映了他對食材的尊重。讓用餐體驗更完滿，不妨請經驗豐富的侍酒師為您配對餐酒，當中涵蓋勃艮第、大洋洲和美國等地產物。價格合理的午膳套餐值得一試。

TEL. 2728 0178

3F, 18 On Lan Street, Central
中環安蘭街18號3樓
www.arcane.hk

■ **PRICE** 價錢
Lunch 午膳
Set Menu 套餐 $ 458
À la carte 點菜 $ 800-1,200
Dinner 晚膳
À la carte 點菜 $ 800-1,200

■ **OPENING HOURS** 營業時間
Lunch 午膳 12:00-14:30
Dinner 晚膳 18:00-22:30

■ **ANNUAL AND WEEKLY CLOSING**
休息日期
Closed Saturday lunch and Sunday
週六午膳及週日休息

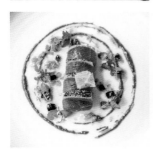

HONG KONG ISLAND 香港島

45

BEEFBAR

Steakhouse • Contemporary Décor

扒房 • 時尚

☎🍴♿⌖

TEL. 2110 8853

**2F, Club Lusitano,
16 Ice House Street, Central**
中環雪廠街16號西洋會所2樓
www.beefbar.hk

■ **PRICE** 價錢
Lunch 午膳
Set Menu 套餐 $ 330-620
À la carte 點菜 $ 450-1,500
Dinner 晚膳
À la carte 點菜 $ 450-1,500

■ **OPENING HOURS** 營業時間
Lunch 午膳 12:00-14:00
Dinner 晚膳 18:30-22:00

■ **ANNUAL AND WEEKLY CLOSING**
休息日期
Closed 3 days Lunar New Year and
Sunday 農曆新年3天及週日休息

This branch of the Monte Carlo-based group boasts stylish décor that blends marble and leather. Quality steaks from the U.S., Japan and Korea, including the bestselling ribeye cap, are broiled then chargrilled to seal in the juices under a lightly charred crust. To start, consider beef tartare prepared tableside or one of the lighter ceviches and tacos. Kobe beef street snacks make interesting bites that show refinement as well as flavour.

這家源自摩納哥的扒房裝潢亮眼，以白色雲石配搭黑色皮革，時尚有型。主打來自美國、日本、韓國等地的頂級牛扒，無論是安格斯牛、和牛或神戶牛，不同部位都被烤至恰到好處。不要錯過大受歡迎的肋眼蓋，外層微微焦脆，內裏則軟嫩多汁。而前菜不妨選擇墨西哥卷餅或席前炮製的牛肉他他等。

CELEBRITY CUISINE
名人坊

Cantonese • Classic Décor

粵菜 • 經典

Having just six tables and a host of regulars makes booking ahead vital at this discreet and colourful restaurant. The short menu is jam-packed with specialities, such as whole superior abalone in oyster sauce, baked chicken with Shaoxing wine and the signature fried rice. The must-try bird's nest-stuffed chicken wing is crispy on the outside, juicy on the inside and each bite bursts with flavour, enlivened by contrasting textures.

小小的餐廳隱藏於蘭桂坊酒店內,但因為菜餚精美,擁有眾多常客,必須提早訂座。餐牌上全是大廚富哥的特選菜式,招牌菜包括頂級鮑魚、招牌炒飯、須提前一天預訂的花雕焗飛天雞等。而最特別的是大廚自創的燕窩釀鳳翼,去骨雞翼裏釀滿燕窩,外層香脆、餡料多汁,口感和味道都十分出眾,不容錯過。

TEL. 3650 0066

1F, Lan Kwai Fong Hotel, 3 Kau U Fong, Central
中環九如坊3號蘭桂坊酒店1樓

■ **PRICE** 價錢
Lunch 午膳
À la carte 點菜 $ 200-400
Dinner 晚膳
À la carte 點菜 $ 350-1,000

■ **OPENING HOURS** 營業時間
Lunch 午膳 12:00-14:30
Dinner 晚膳 18:00-22:00

■ **ANNUAL AND WEEKLY CLOSING**
休息日期
Closed 4 days Lunar New Year
農曆新年休息4天

HONG KONG ISLAND 香港島

47

🕊 ◎♨ ⅃ ⊡

TEL. 2525 9191

**3F, Shanghai Tang Mansion,
1 Duddell Street, Central**

中環都爹利街1號上海灘3樓

www.duddells.co

■ **PRICE** 價錢
Lunch 午膳
Set Menu 套餐 $ 398
À la carte 點菜 $ 450-1,000
Dinner 晚膳
Set Menu 套餐 $ 1,488
À la carte 點菜 $ 450-1,000

■ **OPENING HOURS** 營業時間
Lunch 午膳 12:00-14:30
Dinner 晚膳 18:00-22:30

■ **ANNUAL AND WEEKLY CLOSING**
休息日期
Closed New Year's Day
元旦休息1天

🕸

DUDDELL'S
都爹利會館

Cantonese • Fashionable

粵菜 • 時髦

Duddell's is as much about art as it is about food. Regular art shows and screenings are featured, alongside traditional Cantonese cooking using luxury ingredients. The kitchen team on board since 2020 revamped the menu to include specialities like crispy crab shell stuffed with crabmeat and Hokkaido milk and sautéed Australian M5 beef shank with sand ginger and scallion. Start the evening with a pre-dinner drink in the vibrant bar.

都爹利會館除了滿足喜歡粵菜的客人，也令一眾藝術愛好者感到稱心，皆因餐館會定期舉行藝術展覽、沙龍等活動，布置更時尚得猶如一所藝術館。餐前不妨於閣樓酒吧歇息淺酌，新上任的廚師團隊繼續選用高級矜貴的食材，精緻粵菜推介包括黃金炸釀3.6牛乳蟹蓋及沙薑京葱炒M5和牛金錢腱等。團隊服務周到。

THE DIFFERENCE WE'RE MAKING WITH COFFEE FARMERS IS ONE YOU CAN TASTE.

Exceptional coffee comes from care, for the ecosystem, for the future and for farmers like Don Fernando from Caquetá, Colombia, by supporting them with equipment and training on sustainable practices.

what else?

FOOK LAM MOON (WAN CHAI)
福臨門 (灣仔)

Cantonese • Classic Décor

粵菜 • 經典

Thanks to 70+ years of glorious history, Fook Lam Moon is held dear by its faithful regulars as an institution in classic Cantonese cuisine. Thanks to a stable kitchen team, the food has always been consistently good. Seasonal ingredients – including live seafood that is shipped daily – are cooked in traditional ways. Standouts such as deep-fried crispy chicken, baked stuffed crab shell, and gourmet soup in whole winter melon, are true delights. Some dishes need pre-ordering.

由1948年開業至今，福臨門一直是城中具標誌性的酒家之一。多年來水準保持一致，全賴共事多年、默契十足的團隊。家族第三代秉承父輩烹調粵菜的宗旨，以傳統烹調手法，配合優質食材奉客。時令菜單全年供應，海鮮則每天進貨，確保嘗到真鮮味。招牌菜有釀焗鮮蟹蓋及炸子雞等。部分菜式需預訂，建議致電查詢。

TEL. 2866 0663
35-45 Johnston Road, Wan Chai
灣仔莊士敦道35-45號
www.fooklammoon-grp.com

■ **PRICE** 價錢
Lunch 午膳
À la carte 點菜 $ 400-1,000
Dinner 晚膳
À la carte 點菜 $ 800-2,000

■ **OPENING HOURS** 營業時間
Lunch 午膳 11:30-14:30
Dinner 晚膳 18:00-22:00

■ **ANNUAL AND WEEKLY CLOSING**
休息日期
Closed 2 days Lunar New Year
農曆新年休息2天

HONG KONG ISLAND 香港島

GUO FU LOU
國福樓

Cantonese • Elegant
粵菜 • 典雅

TEL. 3468 8188

The Pavilion at The Murray Hotel,
22 Cotton Tree Drive, Central

中環紅棉路22號美利酒店平台亭樓

www.fooklammoon-grp.com

■ **PRICE** 價錢
Lunch 午膳
À la carte 點菜 $ 400-1,000
Dinner 晚膳
Set Menu 套餐 $ 1,880
À la carte 點菜 $ 800-2,000

■ **OPENING HOURS** 營業時間
Lunch 午膳 12:00-14:30
Dinner 晚膳 18:00-21:30

■ **ANNUAL AND WEEKLY CLOSING**
休息日期
Closed 2 days Lunar New Year
農曆新年休息2天

It may have moved from Wan Chai to Central, but the kitchen team stayed the same so all your favourites are still on the menu. The must-try classic jasmine tea smoked chicken boasts tender juicy flesh layered with depths of flavours. Honey-glazed char siu pork is marinated in a secret seasoning blend, each bite exuding the aroma of Chinese rose wine. Ask about seasonal items and their signature deep-fried sesame balls, only available at dinner.

嚴選頂級食材，呈獻多款精緻手工粵菜，包括採用新鮮清遠雞的茉莉花茶燻雞，以及用傳統秘方製作的蜜汁叉燒。前者茶味芳香，肉質鮮甜嫩滑；後者肉汁豐富，每一口都滲出玫瑰露酒香氣。此外，不妨考慮時令推介，例如夏天獨有、須提前預訂的冬瓜盅。充滿芝麻香、只在晚市供應的燈影煎堆香脆煙韌，萬勿錯過。

HO HUNG KEE (CAUSEWAY BAY)
何洪記 (銅鑼灣)

Noodles and Congee • Friendly

粥麵 • 友善

No discussion about Hong Kong's historic noodle shops would be complete without mentioning Ho Hung Kee, which originally opened in Wan Chai in the 1940s and is famed for its springy wonton noodles and fresh, sweet soup. More elements have been added here at its new address – dim sum and some Cantonese dishes are now served too. For the interior, they've adopted a more contemporary, Western style aesthetic.

何洪記是香港歷史悠久的麵家之一，自四十年代起在灣仔區營業，多年來其招牌雲吞麵憑着麵條彈牙、湯底鮮甜而口碑載道；其粥品也很出色。遷至商場後，設計變得西化，但重視食品質素的經營方針始終不變，更增加了食物種類，除粥麵外，還供應點心和廣式小菜，難怪吸引到新舊客人到此用膳。

TEL. 2577 6028

Shop 1204-1205, 12F, Hysan Place, 500 Hennessy Road, Causeway Bay

銅鑼灣軒尼詩道500號希慎廣場12樓1204-1205號舖

■ **PRICE 價錢**
À la carte 點菜 $ 100-200

■ **OPENING HOURS 營業時間**
11:30-22:45

■ **ANNUAL AND WEEKLY CLOSING 休息日期**
Closed 2 days Lunar New Year
農曆新年休息2天

HONG KONG ISLAND 香港島

TEL. 2570 7088

134 Tung Lo Wan Road, Tai Hang

大坑銅鑼灣道134號

www.imteppanyaki.com

■ **PRICE 價錢**
Lunch 午膳
Set Menu 套餐 $ 320-880
À la carte 點菜 $ 1,000-2,000
Dinner 晚膳
Set Menu 套餐 $ 1,600-1,980
À la carte 點菜 $ 1,000-2,000

■ **OPENING HOURS 營業時間**
Lunch 午膳 12:00-14:00
Dinner 晚膳 18:00-21:45

I M TEPPANYAKI & WINE
鑄・鐵板燒

Teppanyaki・Classic Décor

鐵板燒・經典

Less a meal, more a full multi-sensory experience. Sit at the teppanyaki bar, admire the cooking show and enjoy contemporary Japanese flavours that make great use of prime ingredients like lobster and premium quality Wagyu. You also get to hear all about owner-chef Lawrence Mok's extraordinary triathlon experiences straight from his own mouth while he prepares your food. There is a private room available for small groups.

這間僅設二十個座位的鐵板燒餐廳，由經驗豐富的創辦人兼總廚莫師傅主理。客人可嘗到鮑魚、龍蝦、黑毛和牛等高級食材，不能錯過的有甘鯛魚配海膽忌廉汁，酥脆的魚鱗和幼嫩多汁的魚肉配合得天衣無縫。坐在鐵板燒桌前，食客會看到廚師預備食材的嚴謹態度及對細節的執著。如要親嘗莫師傅手藝，務必提前預訂並註明。

JARDIN DE JADE (WAN CHAI)
蘇浙滙 (灣仔)

Shanghainese • Cosy
滬菜 • 舒適

The first Hong Kong venture from this renowned Shanghai restaurant group is certainly not lacking in grandeur, thanks to its double-height ceiling and striking chandelier. The kitchen naturally focuses on Shanghainese cooking and makes good use of traditional recipes but presents the dishes in a more modern style. High quality ingredients are sourced from the mainland. A seasonal menu is offered to reflect the produce available. Try steamed reeves shad or smoked duck.

作為上海著名餐飲集團的首家香港分店,餐廳的裝潢雅致,特高樓底配上引人注目的吊燈,別具氣派。餐館以時尚包裝演繹傳統上海菜式,味美且外形精緻。集團注重選料,從內地搜羅優質食材,更每季推出時令菜單。推介菜式包括清蒸鰣魚、樟茶鴨和清炒河蝦仁等。

◎🍴 ⇔ 🅿

TEL. 3528 0228

G3-4, GF, Sun Hung Kai Centre, 30 Harbour Road, Wan Chai
灣仔港灣道30號新鴻基中心地下 G3-4號舖

www.jade388.com

■ **PRICE** 價錢
Lunch 午膳
À la carte 點菜 $ 200-400
Dinner 晚膳
À la carte 點菜 $ 200-400

■ **OPENING HOURS** 營業時間
Lunch 午膳 11:30-14:15
Dinner 晚膳 17:30-21:30

HONG KONG ISLAND 香港島

53

KAM'S ROAST GOOSE
甘牌燒鵝

Cantonese Roast Meats • Friendly

燒味 • 友善

For over 70 years, the Kams have been famous for their roast goose and this shop was opened by the third generation. But the goose extravaganza doesn't stop at their juicy roast goose with crispy skin. Try also their silky, melty goose blood pudding or the decadent blanched noodles tossed in goose fat. Other Cantonese barbecue dishes glistening in the window are also worth trying. With only 30 seats, don't be surprised to see a queue.

祖父輩創業至今逾七十年，以家傳秘方炮製的甘氏燒鵝早已遠近馳名，櫥窗前盡是色澤油亮的傳統廣式燒味。金牌燒鵝當然是鎮店之寶，此外，燒乳豬、鵝掌、鵝肝等滷水食品和入口即融的鵝紅亦不容錯過。佐以鵝油製作的太子撈麵香氣四溢，更教人欲罷不能。菜式琳瑯滿目，如果想多嘗幾款，建議偕親友共往。

TEL. 2520 1110

226 Hennessy Road, Wan Chai

灣仔軒尼詩道226號

www.krg.com.hk

■ **PRICE** 價錢
Set Menu 套餐 $ 64-116
À la carte 點菜 $ 100-200

■ **OPENING HOURS** 營業時間
11:30-21:00

■ **ANNUAL AND WEEKLY CLOSING**
休息日期
Closed 3 days Lunar New Year
農曆新年休息3天

HONG KONG ISLAND 香港島

LIU YUAN PAVILION
留園雅敘

Shanghainese • Family

滬菜 • 溫馨

With its authentic Shanghainese cooking and Shanghainese-speaking clientele, it's tempting to think you're in Shanghai. The dining room impresses with understated elegance and the booth seats offering more privacy are especially prized. Specialities include drunken squab whose velvety meat and springy skin exude an intoxicating winey aroma. Stir-fried shrimps, braised pig knuckle and braised 'lion head' meatballs are also not to be missed.

開業多年的留園雅敘環境素淨優雅，擁有不少忠心顧客，當中不乏一眾老上海，侍應亦會親切地以流利上海話為客人點菜。菜單網羅各式正宗滬菜，不論是清炒蝦仁、松子桂魚或紅燒元蹄等經典小菜，還是需預訂的鮑魚紅燒肉和小米刺參雞湯，均呈現上海菜的大器風格。推介花雕醉乳鴿，皮爽肉嫩，吃罷濃郁酒香溢滿口腔。

◎¶ ⇧ ⦆

TEL. 2804 2000

**3F, The Broadway,
54-62 Lockhart Road, Wan Chai**

灣仔駱克道54-62號博匯大廈3樓

■ **PRICE** 價錢
Lunch 午膳
À la carte 點菜 $ 200-300
Dinner 晚膳
À la carte 點菜 $ 250-750

■ **OPENING HOURS** 營業時間
Lunch 午膳 12:00-14:30
Dinner 晚膳 18:00-22:15

■ **ANNUAL AND WEEKLY CLOSING**
休息日期
Closed 3 days Lunar New Year
農曆新年休息3天

HONG KONG ISLAND 香港島

🕸 ⊙ �’ ⅋ ⌂ ⛵

TEL. 2866 0300

PMQ, 35 Aberdeen Street, Central

中環鴨巴甸街35號PMQ

www.louise.hk

■ **PRICE** 價錢
Lunch 午膳
Set Menu 套餐 $ 398-566
À la carte 點菜 $ 750-1,400
Dinner 晚膳
À la carte 點菜 $ 750-1,400

■ **OPENING HOURS** 營業時間
Lunch 午膳 12:00-14:00
Dinner 晚膳 18:30-22:00

■ **ANNUAL AND WEEKLY CLOSING**
休息日期
Closed Monday 週一休息

LOUISE

French Contemporary • Chic

時尚法國菜 • 新潮

Chef Julien Royer, of Odette in Singapore fame, opened this restaurant which spans across two floors with an interior rendered in a 1930s colonial style. The downstairs bar serves an all-day French snacking menu, while the dining room focuses on à la carte fine dining. Pâté en croûte Louise boasts melt-in-the-mouth pastry and a moist, flavoursome filling. Langoustine raviolis and homemade sorbets burst with flavour.

這家由法籍廚師Julien Royer監督的法國餐廳，坐落在極具歷史感的前已婚警察宿舍。室內設計師以復古牆紙、水晶燈飾、木紋餐桌和藤椅，塑造三十年代的殖民地風情。位於地面的酒吧全日提供小食和各式美酒，走到樓上的主餐室，則可享用法式冷肉批、海螯蝦意大利餃及自製雪葩等用料上乘、賣相精緻的菜餚。

MAN HO
萬豪金殿
Cantonese • Elegant
粵菜 • 典雅

After a major makeover in 2019, Man Ho now welcomes guests with a sophisticated interior inspired by a Chinese garden. Cascading glass chandeliers shaped like morning glory are set nicely against marble moon gates and camellia enamel art. The young but experienced head chef takes a creative approach to Cantonese classics, as manifested in specialities like honey-glazed barbecued Iberico pork loin, and pan-fried fish maw in almond milk chicken broth.

翻新後以中式庭園為主題，牽牛花吊燈充滿特色。設貴賓廂房，適合商務宴客。菜單包括自家製點心、生猛海鮮和精緻粵菜，傳統與創新兼備。貴妃叉燒選用西班牙黑毛豬，肉質纖細，香味濃郁；杏仁濃湯煎花膠外脆內軟；艇皇花膠鮮魚湯新鮮香甜，但每天限量供應，建議預訂。不妨以世界各地的美酒搭配佳餚。

TEL. 2810 8366

3F, JW Marriott Hotel, Pacific Place, 88 Queensway, Admiralty

金鐘金鐘道88號太古廣場
JW萬豪酒店3樓

www.jwmarriotthongkong.com/dining

■ **PRICE** 價錢
Lunch 午膳
Set Menu 套餐 $ 1,580
À la carte 點菜 $ 300-1,300
Dinner 晚膳
Set Menu 套餐 $ 1,580
À la carte 點菜 $ 300-1,300

■ **OPENING HOURS** 營業時間
Lunch 午膳 12:00-14:30
Dinner 晚膳 18:00-22:00

HONG KONG ISLAND 香港島

MAN WAH
文華廳

Cantonese • Classic Décor

粵菜 • 經典

TEL. 2825 4003

25F, Mandarin Oriental Hotel,
5 Connaught Road Central, Central
中環干諾道中5號文華東方酒店25樓
www.mandarinoriental.com/
hongkong

This elegant restaurant is always full whatever the time of day. The chef, who has been at the helm since 2018, puts his emphasis on precision, finesse and robust flavours and these are reflected in his dim sum, barbecue meats and stir-fries. It has been closed for a makeover since Aug 2020 and will unveil a new look in spring 2021.

■ **PRICE** 價錢
Lunch 午膳
Set Menu 套餐 $ 628-748
À la carte 點菜 $ 500-1,600
Dinner 晚膳
Set Menu 套餐 $ 1,488
À la carte 點菜 $ 500-1,600

不論午市或晚市，文華廳均座無虛席，氣氛熱鬧卻不失高雅。黃師傅精細處理每道菜式，不論點心、燒味或小菜，皆展露扎實的傳統粵菜烹調技巧。餐廳於2020年8月展開大規模翻新，並將於2021年春季重開。

■ **OPENING HOURS** 營業時間
Lunch 午膳 12:00-14:30
Dinner 晚膳 18:30-21:00

HONG KONG ISLAND 香港島

MANDARIN GRILL + BAR
文華扒房+酒吧

European Contemporary • Elegant
時尚歐陸菜 • 典雅

This stylish room designed by the late Sir Terence Conran features a glass-fronted kitchen and an ornate ceiling covered in fan-shaped sculptural relief, reminiscent of the hotel's logo. Grill house classics, such as steak tartare and house-smoked salmon, are given a modern spin, while starters and desserts show imagination and a light hand from the well-versed team. There is also a good selection of chargrilled steaks, some great for sharing.

室內設計出自已故名家Sir Terence Conran的手筆，優雅而明亮，天花上的扇形圖案呼應着酒店的標誌，充滿巧思。提供多款以木炭燒烤的扒類，適合共享。此外，也提供牛肉他他、煙三文魚等經典菜式，以及選料上乘、令人垂涎三尺的精緻歐陸美食。建議留點空間，一嘗各式甜品，全面體會廚房的創意和功架。

TEL. 2825 4004

1F, Mandarin Oriental Hotel,
5 Connaught Road Central, Central
中環干諾道中5號文華東方酒店1樓
www.mandarinoriental.com/
hongkong

■ **PRICE** 價錢
Lunch 午膳
Set Menu 套餐 $ 598-698
Dinner 晚膳
Set Menu 套餐 $ 1,288-1,988

■ **OPENING HOURS** 營業時間
Lunch 午膳 12:00-14:30
Dinner 晚膳 18:00-21:00

■ **ANNUAL AND WEEKLY CLOSING**
休息日期
Closed Saturday lunch 週六午膳休息

HONG KONG ISLAND 香港島

TEL. 2368 1223

GF, World Wide Commercial Building, 34 Wyndham Street, Central
中環雲咸街34號世界商業大廈地下
www.newpunjabclub.com

■ **PRICE 價錢**
Lunch 午膳
À la carte 點菜 $ 600-800
Dinner 晚膳
À la carte 點菜 $ 600-800

■ **OPENING HOURS 營業時間**
Lunch 午膳 12:00-14:00
Dinner 晚膳 18:00-22:30

■ **ANNUAL AND WEEKLY CLOSING**
休息日期
Closed Monday lunch 週一午膳休息

NEW PUNJAB CLUB
Indian • Vintage
印度菜 • 復古

This tandoor grill restaurant serving cuisine from Northern India is named after a social club founded during the British era – the owner's father is still a member. The décor is also reminiscent of that era with red leather banquettes and the owner's art collection. Lamb tomahawk is the signature dish on the menu, along with samosa chaat (crushed samosa with yoghurt and crispy noodles) and paneer kulcha (an Indian cheese).

這家餐廳供應北印度美食，嗜肉的饕客會找到眾多以Tandoor土窯爐烤製的菜式，咖喱則只屬配角。選用斧頭扒炮製的羊扒是招牌菜，以乳酪混和咖喱蓉及脆麵而成的咖喱角亦不俗；更有由印度進口的芝士。菜式分量較大，適合多人分享。紅色皮沙發及掛畫盡顯英式風格。建議網上訂座，須以信用卡確認。

60

OCTAVIUM

Italian · Chic

意大利菜 · 新潮

A dining concept by Umberto Bombana of 8½ Otto e Mezzo fame, Octavium displays meticulous attention to detail – handmade Venetian glasses, Italian designer furniture and a wall covered in Norwegian tree bark. The same level of care and precision also goes into the food. For mains, try Carabineros shrimp linguine, or Mayura tenderloin. Round it out with tiramisu.

如果喜歡自然風格，必定會被這裏的環境吸引。除了充滿格調的意大利傢具，牆身更採用挪威樹皮作裝飾，令人放鬆心情。餐廳由意籍主廚Bombana開設，廚師團隊亦已合作多年，確保風味正宗。菜單隨食材供應而轉換，招牌菜包括西班牙紅蝦扁意粉、Marango里脊肉。最後來一客提拉米蘇，更加圓滿。

TEL. 2111 9395

**8F, One Chinachem Central,
22 Des Voeux Road Central, Central**
中環德輔道中22號華懋中心一期8樓
www.octavium.com.hk

■ **PRICE** 價錢
Lunch 午膳
Set Menu 套餐 $ 380-780
À la carte 點菜 $ 900-1,200
Dinner 晚膳
Set Menu 套餐 $ 988-1,488
À la carte 點菜 $ 900-1,200

■ **OPENING HOURS** 營業時間
Lunch 午膳 12:00-14:30
Dinner 晚膳 18:30-22:00

■ **ANNUAL AND WEEKLY CLOSING**
休息日期
Closed 4 days Lunar New Year and Sunday 農曆新年4天及週日休息

HONG KONG ISLAND 香港島

PANG'S KITCHEN
彭慶記

Cantonese • Simple
粵菜 • 簡樸

A household name since 2001, this restaurant wins the hearts of many with its traditional and homely Cantonese cooking. Try the baked fish tripe in a claypot or stir-fried glutinous rice. Unlike places that serve snake soup in autumn and winter only, here it's available all year round. Fried fish head in claypot with scallion and ginger uses the lower jaws of bighead carp, available in a limited quantity daily. Reservations are recommended.

彭慶記自2001年開業以來一直服務跑馬地居民，並以家常小菜和傳統菜式打響名堂，家喻戶曉的菜式包括缽仔焗魚腸、生炒糯米飯及太史五蛇羹等。以大魚下巴配以薑葱烹煮、名為「薑葱魚鏢煲」的菜式為特別之作，食材由老闆每天親自採購，限量供應。座位數量不多，建議提前訂座。

○▯

TEL. 2838 5462

25 Yik Yam Street, Happy Valley
跑馬地奕蔭街25號

■ **PRICE 價錢**
Set Menu 套餐 $ 98
À la carte 點菜 $ 250-500

■ **OPENING HOURS 營業時間**
11:00-21:45

■ **ANNUAL AND WEEKLY CLOSING**
休息日期
Closed 3 days Lunar New Year
農曆新年休息3天

HONG KONG ISLAND 香港島

PETRUS
珀翠

French • Elegant
法國菜 • 典雅

Heavy drapes at the windows, thick carpets and elegantly laid tables give this restaurant the look of a grand Parisian salon – but here you also get fabulous harbour views. The French cooking, however, shows a certain modernity; the menu is ingredient-led with the luxury ingredients coming from as far as France or sometimes no further than Hong Kong Island. The wine cellar is notable too and includes 45 vintages of Château Pétrus dating back to 1928.

璀璨奪目的水晶吊燈、高貴的絨布簾幕與一絲不苟的餐桌佈置，讓餐廳披上了奢華的巴黎沙龍外觀，窗外美不勝收的海景更是錦上添花。餐單上供應的是經典法國菜，廚師團隊繼續搜羅來自法國及全球各地的名貴材料，並以出色的技巧演繹。酒窖內的佳釀多不勝數，包括自1928年起產自珀翠酒莊的多個年份葡萄酒。

TEL. 2820 8590

56F, Island Shangri-La Hotel, Pacific Place, Supreme Court Road, Admiralty

金鐘法院道太古廣場
港島香格里拉酒店56樓

www.shangri-la.com/island

■ **PRICE 價錢**
Lunch 午膳
Set Menu 套餐 $ 488-688
Dinner 晚膳
Set Menu 套餐 $ 1,088-1,588

■ **OPENING HOURS 營業時間**
Lunch 午膳 12:00-14:00
Dinner 晚膳 18:30-21:30

HONG KONG ISLAND 香港島

◎⏁ ⬦ ♿
TEL. 2817 8383

Shop 8, UG Level, Sino Plaza,
255 Gloucester Road, Causeway Bay

銅鑼灣告士打道255號
信和廣場UG層8號舖

www.roganic.com.hk

■ **PRICE 價錢**
Lunch 午膳
Set Menu 套餐 $ 280-980
Dinner 晚膳
Set Menu 套餐 $ 680-980

■ **OPENING HOURS 營業時間**
Lunch 午膳 12:00-14:00
Dinner 晚膳 18:30-21:00

■ **ANNUAL AND WEEKLY CLOSING**
休息日期
Closed Monday 週一休息

ROGANIC

European Contemporary • Design
時尚歐陸菜 • 型格

A sister establishment to its namesake in London, Roganic is the brainchild of British chef Simon Rogan. The low-ceilinged room is spacious, with plants on the shelves and fridges to grow micro-herbs. The chefs make seemingly simple dishes that burst with flavours and amazing textures, a nod to their philosophy and ethos. The lunch menu offers great value, while the 6- and 9-course tasting menus come with choices of mains and dessert.

英國大廚Simon Rogan的首家海外分店，延續崇尚自然有機的風格，不僅在天花、餐廳各處放滿植物，更選用大量本地的新鮮蔬果。午市套餐價格相宜，另有六道菜及九道菜的嘗味餐單，讓人充分體驗具Rogan特色的味道和口感。客人可以在吧檯享用甜品和美酒。餐廳另設實驗廚房Aulis，提供使用豪華食材、多達二十道菜的套餐。

LEADING A HEALTHIER FUTURE

AIA is committed to helping people live Healthier, Longer, Better Lives. This is our purpose that sits at the heart of everything we do. Our products and policies don't just protect lives but help make lives healthier, longer and better. Every single day.

HEALTHIER, LONGER, BETTER LIVES

Contact your financial planner

AIA Customer Hotline **2232 8888** | aia.com.hk

AIA Hong Kong and Macau | AIA_HK_MACAU

"EATING MY GREENS, WHY WOULD I DO THAT?"

For me, it's just part of a balanced diet.
That's my why.

LiveWithVitality

David Beckham
AIA Global Ambassador

If you have the why, we can help with the how.
AIA Vitality Hotline 2232 8282 | aia.com.hk/aiavitality
AIA Hong Kong and Macau   AIA HK MACAU

RÙN
潤

Cantonese • Elegant
粵菜 • 典雅

Chef Hung has worked in many 5-star hotel restaurants and values food quality and shrewd techniques more than anything else. Seasonal ingredients from around the world are painstakingly prepared the traditional way and then plated with modern refinement. Alongside classic Cantonese fare, vegan and non-gluten set menus take care of different dietary needs. Ask the wine and tea sommeliers for their advice; be sure to try their custom-brewed floral tea.

雖然是粵菜餐廳，但室內設計走歐陸路線，既舒適又優雅。以傳統烹調技巧，配合來自世界各地的優質食材，並加入創意元素，從擺盤到味道都一絲不苟。當中不乏時令菜式，不僅選取當季材料，口味亦配合其時節，例如夏天餐單會比較清新。另外提供素食、無麩質套餐。同時備有侍酒師和茶師，令用餐體驗更圓滿。

TEL. 2138 6808

2F, The St. Regis Hotel,
1 Harbour Drive, Wan Chai

灣仔港灣徑1號瑞吉酒店2樓

www.stregishongkong.com

■ **PRICE** 價錢
Lunch 午膳
Set Menu 套餐 $ 588
À la carte 點菜 $ 300-1,500
Dinner 晚膳
Set Menu 套餐 $ 788
À la carte 點菜 $ 500-1,500

■ **OPENING HOURS** 營業時間
Lunch 午膳 12:00-14:30
Dinner 晚膳 18:00-22:30

HONG KONG ISLAND 香港島

65

RYOTA KAPPOU MODERN

Japanese • Contemporary Décor
日本菜 • 時尚

TEL. 2628 1899

21F, 18 On Lan Street, Central
中環安蘭街18號21樓

www.ryota.hk

■ **PRICE** 價錢
Lunch 午膳
Set Menu 套餐 $ 580-780
Dinner 晚膳
Set Menu 套餐 $ 1,580-2,080

■ **OPENING HOURS** 營業時間
Lunch 午膳 12:00-14:30
Dinner 晚膳 18:00-21:00

■ **ANNUAL AND WEEKLY CLOSING**
休息日期
Closed 5 days Lunar New Year and
Sunday 農曆新年5天及週日休息

Floor-to-ceiling windows let in natural light and allow expansive views, while designer furniture and artisan tableware exude style. Only seasonal kappo-style set menus are offered. Donabe, hot pot for one cooked à la minute, features only ingredients in season. The chef's favourite Omi Wagyu Katsu with black truffle and egg confit was inspired by sukiyaki and its flavours are in perfect harmony. Ask for the counter seats to see the kitchen in action.

老闆兼主廚以豐富經驗和日本食材，為客人帶來割烹風格的日式美食。由落地玻璃透進來的自然光，加上名家設計的傢具和陶瓷餐具，提供了獨特的視覺享受。建議坐在圍繞開放式廚房的板前位置，好好欣賞廚師功架。午市菜單相對簡樸，晚市則包括多款招牌套餐。和牛黑松露溫泉蛋的靈感來自壽喜燒，卻充滿創新元素，值得一試。

HONG KONG ISLAND 香港島

SUMMER PALACE
夏宮

Cantonese • Luxury

粵菜 • 豪華

There's a timeless, exotic feel to this room whose decoration of gilt screens, golden silk wall coverings and lattice panels is inspired by the palace in Beijing. The menu is a roll-call of Cantonese classics; double-boiled soups are a speciality; dim sum is a highlight; and signature dishes include marinated pig's trotters with spicy ginger, braised '20-head' Yoshihama abalone in oyster sauce, and deep fried crispy chicken. They also offer a good selection of teas.

以北京故宮為設計靈感，高聳的餐室以大紅色餐椅配以傳統中式屏風、金色絲綢畫作及雕塑，加上華麗的水晶吊燈，營造出迷人情調。菜單羅列各款傳統廣東名菜，招牌菜包括沙薑豬腳仔、蠔皇吉品鮑魚、脆皮炸子雞等，燉湯也是其專長，部分需提早預訂。午市時點心是不俗的選擇，茗茶選項也相當可觀。

TEL. 2820 8552

5F, Island Shangri-La Hotel, Pacific Place, Supreme Court Road, Admiralty

金鐘法院道太古廣場
港島香格里拉酒店5樓
www.shangri-la.com/island

■ **PRICE** 價錢
Lunch 午膳
À la carte 點菜 $ 300-1,500
Dinner 晚膳
À la carte 點菜 $ 300-1,500

■ **OPENING HOURS** 營業時間
Lunch 午膳 11:30-14:00
Dinner 晚膳 18:00-21:00

HONG KONG ISLAND 香港島

88 ⏀⏀ ⓒ ⏚

TEL. 5599 8133

Shop 1, GF, The Oakhill,
16 Wood Road, Wan Chai
灣仔活道16號萃峯地下1號舖

www.takumibymori.com

■ **PRICE 價錢**
Dinner 晚膳
Set Menu 套餐 $ 2,080

■ **OPENING HOURS 營業時間**
Dinner 晚膳 18:30-21:30

■ **ANNUAL AND WEEKLY CLOSING**
休息日期
Closed 3 days Lunar New Year and
Sunday 農曆新年3天及週日休息

TAKUMI BY DAISUKE MORI

Innovative • Elegant
創新菜 • 典雅

Named after its executive chef from Japan, this restaurant features a dark marble counter against greyish-blue panelling. Chef Mori specialises in French haute cuisine made with seasonal Japanese produce. The seafood-heavy prix-fixe 9-course menu also includes his acclaimed chargrilled Hida beef tenderloin, and can be enjoyed with excellent wine pairings. There are only 11 counter seats around the open kitchen so reservations are recommended.

開放式廚房屹立於店中央,配以柔和燈光、黑底白紋雲石吧枱,充滿時尚感,更能夠讓全店十一個座位都欣賞到烹調過程。日籍主廚採用來自家鄉的時令食材,創造出富有個人風格的菜式。套餐包括招牌菜炭燒飛驒和牛,以及多款新鮮海產,並會根據季節轉變。餐酒質素尤佳,非常適合配搭美食。建議訂座。

THE CHAIRMAN
大班樓

Cantonese • Cosy

粵菜 • 舒適

Showing respect for the mostly organic ingredients from small suppliers and local fishermen, the kitchen team puts its heart and soul into making elegant creations such as steamed crab with aged Shaoxing wine layered with flavours and showing astute precision. Labour-intensive dishes like crispy chicken stuffed with shrimp paste need pre-ordering. Service is pleasant and reassuring; ask servers about the daily specials not on the menu.

專於粵菜的大班樓受不少老饕支持，全因其以精挑細選食材見稱，貨源來自小型供應商和本地漁民，大部分都是有機產品。推介菜式有雞油花雕蒸大花蟹，傳統功夫菜如香煎百花雞件配魚露，更需要提前預訂。主餐牌以外，不時設有特別時令推介，不妨向服務員查詢。甜點方面可以一嘗生磨杏仁茶，滋潤味美。

📶🍴 ⇄

TEL. 2555 2202
18 Kau U Fong, Central
中環九如坊18號
www.thechairmangroup.com

■ **PRICE** 價錢
Lunch 午膳
Set Menu 套餐 $ 288
À la carte 點菜 $ 500-800
Dinner 晚膳
À la carte 點菜 $ 500-800

■ **OPENING HOURS** 營業時間
Lunch 午膳 12:00-14:00
Dinner 晚膳 18:00-22:00

■ **ANNUAL AND WEEKLY CLOSING**
休息日期
Closed 3 days Lunar New Year
農曆新年休息3天

VEA

Innovative • Trendy

創新菜 • 前衛

TEL. 2711 8639

**30F, The Wellington,
198 Wellington Street, Central**

中環威靈頓街198號
The Wellington 30樓

www.vea.hk

■ **PRICE** 價錢
Dinner 晚膳
Set Menu 套餐 $ 1,680

■ **OPENING HOURS** 營業時間
Dinner 晚膳 18:45-20:45

■ **ANNUAL AND WEEKLY CLOSING**
休息日期
Closed Sunday 週日休息

An impressive counter and open kitchen dominate the room and this is where you'll want to sit to watch chef Cheng and his team in action. An experience it most certainly is, thanks to an 8-course tasting menu that features ingredients from around the globe. The creative and original dishes stimulate all the senses while also paying respect to the history of Hong Kong, as well as the chef's childhood memories.

開放式廚房和櫃枱座位佔據着餐室主要位置，安坐此處將能讓你一睹廚師團隊揮灑自如的烹調過程。八道菜的品嘗菜單採用來自世界各地的食材，以西式手法烹調；菜式設計創意十足，靈感除了取材自主廚的童年回憶外，更蘊含了香港文化在其中。用餐前可先到酒吧淺酌一杯同樣富創意的雞尾酒。

XIN RONG JI
新榮記

Taizhou • Traditional

台州菜 • 傳統

Taizhou cuisine emphasises the natural flavours of ingredients, which are only sparingly seasoned with aromatics. Wild-caught yellow croaker from the East China Sea is the speciality here; other recommendations include deep-fried conger eel and braised radish and seasonal offerings are also available. The elegant dining room is traditionally styled and decorated with bonsai plants; tables are made from one piece of solid wood.

秉承待人為本的信念，新榮記把台州口味帶來香港。烹調上着重原汁原味，在烹煮過程中僅以薑、葱、蒜配合簡單調味料，帶出食材自身味道。餐廳推崇東海海鮮，堅持採用優質新鮮的食材；推介家燒黃魚、黃金脆帶魚，以及從台州運抵、經多重功夫烹煮的家燒蘿蔔。貼心的服務團隊令用餐體驗更為美滿。

TEL. 3462 3518

GF & 1F, China Overseas Building, 138 Lockhart Road, Wan Chai

灣仔駱克道138號
中國海外大廈地下及1樓

www.xinrongji.cc

■ **PRICE** 價錢
Lunch 午膳
À la carte 點菜 $ 500-1,000
Dinner 晚膳
À la carte 點菜 $ 500-1,000

■ **OPENING HOURS** 營業時間
Lunch 午膳 12:00-14:30
Dinner 晚膳 18:00-22:00

■ **ANNUAL AND WEEKLY CLOSING**
休息日期
Closed 3 days Lunar New Year
農曆新年休息3天

HONG KONG ISLAND 香港島

88 **圀॥** **ᴴ**

TEL. 2547 9237

154-158 Wing Lok Street, Sheung Wan

上環永樂街154-158號

www.yardbirdrestaurant.com

■ **PRICE 價錢**
Dinner 晚膳
À la carte 點菜 $ 350-500

■ **OPENING HOURS 營業時間**
Dinner 晚膳 18:00-23:15

YARDBIRD N

Yakitori • Chic

雞肉串燒 • 新潮

Yardbird moved here in 2018 and since then, reservations aren't accepted so arrive early and expect to queue. The main draw is no doubt the 20-plus types of yakitori skewers made with local 'three-yellow' chicken from beak to tail, grilled over binchotan charcoal. Rare cuts like thyroid and ventricle can be hard to find elsewhere, as are the crispy meatballs with tare and egg yolk. Check out the extensive list of Japanese whisky.

搬到現址後依然人流不絕，而且不設訂座，須耐心等候。其二十多款串燒選用本地三黃雞，除了常見的雞胸、雞翼、雞皮等，也提供雞心房、甲狀腺等珍奇部位。特別推介伴以醬油和蛋黃的雞肉丸，其表面烤至香脆且帶備長炭的誘人香氣。酒品種類繁多，包羅日本威士忌、清酒及雞尾酒。

YAT LOK
一樂燒鵝

Cantonese Roast Meats • Simple

燒味 • 簡樸

This family business has been run by the Chu's since 1957 and in this location since 2011. The signature roast geese glistening behind the window are marinated with a secret recipe and go through over 20 preparatory steps before being chargrilled to perfection. Char siu pork uses pork shoulder from Brazil for melty tenderness. Roast pork belly and soy-marinated chicken are also recommended. Expect to share a table with others.

一樂早於1957年開業，後於2011年遷至現址，一直由店東朱氏夫婦打理。掛在窗前的鎮店招牌脆皮燒鵝油光亮澤，乃根據朱先生的家族秘方醃製，在其自設工場經二十多道工序燒製，色香味俱佳。每次只出爐十隻，因此得靠運氣才可嘗到特定部位。店內燒味均以炭爐燒烤，其中化皮燒腩仔和蜜汁叉燒別具水準。

🛑 🚫🍴

TEL. 2524 3882

34-38 Stanley Street, Central
中環士丹利街34-38號

■ **PRICE** 價錢
À la carte 點菜 $ 70-360

■ **OPENING HOURS** 營業時間
10:00-21:00

■ **ANNUAL AND WEEKLY CLOSING**
休息日期
Closed 10 days Lunar New Year and Wednesday
農曆新年10天及週三休息

HONG KONG ISLAND 香港島

ZEST BY KONISHI
French Contemporary • Intimate
時尚法國菜 • 親密

TEL. 2715 0878
28-29F, 18 On Lan Street, Central
中環安蘭街18號28-29樓
zestbykonishihk.com

■ **PRICE** 價錢
Lunch 午膳
Set Menu 套餐 $ 420-1,070
Dinner 晚膳
Set Menu 套餐 $ 1,680
À la carte 點菜 $ 800-1,400

■ **OPENING HOURS** 營業時間
Lunch 午膳 12:00-14:30
Dinner 晚膳 18:30-21:30

■ **ANNUAL AND WEEKLY CLOSING**
休息日期
Closed Sunday 週日休息

With a name that embodies freshness and seasonality, this restaurant extends across two levels, with a bar and reception on the upper, and soothing and intimate dining room on the lower. The colour scheme is soft and muted, juxtaposing neutrals with occasional popping hues. Featuring mostly Japanese and some French ingredients, the prix-fixe menu changes according to season, usually with both seafood and meat as the main course.

佔地兩層，到埗後可於上層欣賞風景並享用雞尾酒，然後才到樓下品嘗當代法式美食。室內設計色調柔和，帶有自然氣息，裝飾用的木塊和草綠色的地氈，令人放鬆心情。主廚強調不時不食的概念，並採用來自日本、法國和本地的食材，非常新鮮。於午、晚餐時段皆有供應的套餐，主菜同時包括海鮮和肉類。

ZHEJIANG HEEN
浙江軒

Zhejiang • Traditional

浙江菜 • 傳統

The oversized Xihu picture on its wall is hard to miss. Run by a group of Hongkongers of Zhejiang descent, this traditionally furnished three-storey restaurant features exposed brick walls and wooden beams, dotted by Chinese artwork. On the menu, Zhejiang and Shanghainese specialities brush shoulders. Make sure you pre-order 'snatched tiger tails' – seared swamp eel in brown sauce that shows exquisite knife work and has a springy texture.

由浙江人經營，佔地三層，外牆是大幅浙江風景圖，室內則採用大紅柱子、木製傢具、鮮花圖案地氈等中式元素，配以名貴掛畫，呈現古典風情。食材同樣優質，炮製出多款浙江及上海美食。搶虎尾爽口彈牙、刀功精細，值得提早預訂。廚師引以為傲的清蒸鰣魚也甚為推薦，更有為素食人士而設的特選菜式。

TEL. 2877 9011

1-3F, Kiu Fu Commercial Building, 300-306 Lockhart Road, Wan Chai

灣仔駱克道300-306號
僑阜商業大廈1-3樓

www.zhejiangheen.com

■ **PRICE** 價錢
Lunch 午膳
À la carte 點菜 $ 200-500
Dinner 晚膳
À la carte 點菜 $ 400-800

■ **OPENING HOURS** 營業時間
Lunch 午膳 11:30-14:30
Dinner 晚膳 18:00-22:30

■ **ANNUAL AND WEEKLY CLOSING**
休息日期
Closed 3 days Lunar New Year
農曆新年休息3天

HONG KONG ISLAND 香港島

📞🍴🔄♿
TEL. 2156 1883

**GF, The Mercer Central,
29 Jervois Street, Sheung Wan**
上環蘇杭街29號尚圜地下
zuicho-kappo.com

■ **PRICE** 價錢
Lunch 午膳
Set Menu 套餐 $ 1,200
Dinner 晚膳
Set Menu 套餐 $ 1,800

■ **OPENING HOURS** 營業時間
Lunch 午膳 12:00-12:30
Dinner 晚膳 18:00-20:30

■ **ANNUAL AND WEEKLY CLOSING**
休息日期
Closed 5 days Lunar New Year and
Sunday 農曆新年5天及週日休息

ZUICHO Ⓝ
瑞兆

Japanese • Minimalist

日本菜 • 簡約

Zuicho serves just one omakase multicourse Kappo menu that changes monthly. The head chef worked in revered establishments in Tokyo for years and all ingredients are shipped from Japan. The highlight is Satsuma beef fillet; it is steeped in a special marinade, before being slow-cooked and deep-fried and served with tempura of uni wrapped in shiso leaf and an array of sea salts.

主廚曾於銀座工作，與當地漁販關係良好，優質食材每天由日本直送到港。只提供一款廚師發辦套餐，同時會因應當日貨源製作一道額外菜式，供客人選擇添加。招牌菜是來自鹿兒島薩摩的牛腰脊，炸脆後多汁且肉味濃郁，配搭用紫蘇葉包着的海膽天婦羅及不同海鹽享用。清酒備有不同份量，服務員會細心講解並作推介。

ANCIENT MOON
古月

Singaporean and Malaysian •
Friendly

星馬菜 • 友善

It was Singaporean and Malaysian street food enjoyed whilst travelling that inspired owners Fanni and Lico to open their fun little place. The small menu lists about 12 items and avoids serving the more standard dishes. Instead, it's one of the few places to offer Malaysian chilli pan mee (a flavoursome white noodle dish with dried fish and chilli sauce) and Singaporean bak kut teh, made with pork ribs and garlic.

藏身於鬧市中，古月的位置確是有點隱蔽，你須從書局街進入方能找到。看着牆上帶有地方特色的卡通繪畫，不難猜中這裏提供的是星、馬兩地美食。餐單貴不貴多，當中多是在香港較少見，甚或是首家供應的菜式，包括以胡椒和生蒜作湯底的新加坡肉骨茶及配自製辣椒乾進食非常惹味的馬來西亞板麵等。

TEL. 3568 4530
Shop A, 29 Kam Ping Street,
North Point
北角錦屏街29號A舖

■ **PRICE** 價錢
Set Menu 套餐 $ 50-90
À la carte 點菜 $ 50-100

■ **OPENING HOURS** 營業時間
12:00-21:15

■ **ANNUAL AND WEEKLY CLOSING**
休息日期
Closed 5 days Lunar New Year,
Sunday and Public Holidays
農曆新年5天、週日及公眾假期休息

HONG KONG ISLAND 香港島

BA YI
巴依

Xinjiang · Friendly
新疆菜 · 友善

TEL. 2484 9981

43 Water Street, Sai Ying Pun
西營盤水街43號

■ **PRICE** 價錢
Lunch 午膳
À la carte 點菜 $ 100-200
Dinner 晚膳
À la carte 點菜 $ 200-300

■ **OPENING HOURS** 營業時間
Lunch 午膳 12:00-14:30
Dinner 晚膳 18:00-21:30

■ **ANNUAL AND WEEKLY CLOSING**
休息日期
Closed 2 weeks Lunar New Year and
Monday 農曆新年兩週及週一休息

Despite being somewhat out of the way, lamb-lovers gather here in numbers for items such as stewed lamb and mutton skewers, prepared by the Xinjiangese kitchen team. The signature roasted lamb leg is big enough to share between two and needs pre-ordering. Besides lamb, it's also worth trying the chicken stew with potato and chilli, as well as the Ketik yoghurt drink. The dining room still features the map of the Silk Road on a stretched canvas.

開業多年，標誌性的巨型絲路圖始終佔據着店中央的顯著位置。同是新疆人的廚師團隊與店主合作無間，一直堅守着同一使命：為客人提供地道而優質、價錢相宜的正宗新疆菜，當中不乏羊肉特色菜，如手抓肉、羊肉串燒和足夠二人享用、需預訂的烤羊腿等。此外，大盤雞和酸奶也值得一試，店主更不時加入新菜式。

BRASS SPOON (WAN CHAI)

Vietnamese • Simple

越南菜 • 簡樸

The chef has barely had time to draw breath since he opened his small shop selling pho, Vietnam's national dish. He learnt to cook in France, where his family had a Vietnamese restaurant, and chose this small street to recreate the feeling you get when you come across a little ramen shop in Tokyo. He uses US Angus beef and Danish pork and, for the noodles' soup base, slow-cooks beef shank bone for more than 16 hours.

這小小的越式河粉店選址於一條寧靜小街上，源於店東對日本街頭小巷拉麵店的嚮往。於法國習廚的主廚兼店東注重細節，堅決不用味精，湯底以牛小腿骨熬煮逾十六小時而成，味道濃郁；客人可揀選不同級別的美國牛肉，也可自選配料。餐單也提供各種越式小食，如春卷和蒸粉卷等。不設訂座，建議提早前往輪候。

TEL. 2877 0898

Shop B, GF, 1-3 Moon Street, Wan Chai

灣仔月街1-3號地下B舖

■ **PRICE** 價錢
À la carte 點菜 $ 90-220

■ **OPENING HOURS** 營業時間
12:00-18:45

■ **ANNUAL AND WEEKLY CLOSING**
休息日期
Closed Public Holidays and Sunday
公眾假期及週日休息

○🍴

TEL. 2803 7177

420-424 Queen's Road West, Western District

西環皇后大道西420-424號

■ **PRICE 價錢**
Lunch 午膳
Set Menu 套餐 $ 45-55
À la carte 點菜 $ 200-400
Dinner 晚膳
À la carte 點菜 $ 200-400

■ **OPENING HOURS 營業時間**
Lunch 午膳 11:30-14:30
Dinner 晚膳 17:30-21:30

■ **ANNUAL AND WEEKLY CLOSING**
休息日期
Closed 4 days Lunar New Year
農曆新年休息4天

(😳)

CAFÉ HUNAN (WESTERN DISTRICT)
書湘門第 (西環)

Hunanese • Neighbourhood

湘菜 • 親切

The Hunanese chef honed his skills at his mother's restaurant, so he is passionate about his home-town cooking. Ingredients such as chillies and smoked pork are sourced directly from farmers in Hunan. The speciality braised pork elbow entails four complicated cooking steps spanning over 10 hours to develop layered flavours and the right texture. Stir-fried pork with Youxian beancurd and spicy organic cauliflower are also worth trying.

來自湖南的廚師從小已在母親的菜館幫忙，奠定了扎實的廚藝基礎。他熱衷烹調風味正宗的湖南菜，店內使用食材大部分來自湖南，例如從農戶採購而來的煙燻臘肉和各種辣椒。推介菜式包括經四個工序以十小時製作的霸王肘子，還有攸縣香乾炒肉和乾鍋有機花菜。部分菜式設不同辣度供選擇。

Tablet Hotels
THE HOTEL EXPERTS AT THE MICHELIN GUIDE

The MICHELIN Guide is a benchmark in gastronomy.
With Tablet, it's setting the same standard for hotels.

Tablet and Michelin have combined to launch an exciting new selection of hand-picked hotels. A pioneer in online curation, and part of the MICHELIN Group since 2018, Tablet is your source for booking the world's most unique and extraordinary hotels — places where you'll find a memorable experience, not just a room for the night.

Tablet features thousands of hotels in over 100 countries — and a team of experts ready to assist with every step of your journey.

Book your next hotel stay at **TabletHotels.com**.

CHIUCHOW DELICACIES (NORTH POINT)
潮樂園 (北角)

Chiu Chow • Neighbourhood

潮州菜 • 親切

Velvety sliced goose steeped in signature spiced marinade strikes the perfect balance between lean meat and fat. Oyster omelette is generously loaded with the plump juicy bivalves and eggy goodness, while the crisp edges contrast nicely with the gooey centre. Call to ask about dishes that need pre-ordering and be aware you may have to share a table with strangers when it's busy. The other branch on the same street is permanently closed.

樓高兩層，但繁忙時段仍須拼桌。招牌菜滷水鵝片肥瘦適中，鵝味濃郁，不含味精的滷汁令肉質更嫩滑。蠔仔粥、蠔餅及韭菜豬紅等都大受歡迎。煎蠔餅用料十足，蠔仔帶有鮮味，外層煎得金黃香脆，外脆內嫩。此外還供應較罕見的潮式生醃蟛蜞，值得一試。要注意部分菜式需預訂，建議致電查詢。

TEL. 3568 5643

Shop 4, GF, Gain Yu Building, 96 Wharf Road, North Point
北角和富道96號僑裕大廈地下4號舖

■ **PRICE** 價錢
À la carte 點菜 $ 50-250

■ **OPENING HOURS** 營業時間
11:00-22:30

■ **ANNUAL AND WEEKLY CLOSING**
休息日期
Closed 3 days Lunar New Year
農曆新年休息3天

HONG KONG ISLAND 香港島

CIAK - ALL DAY ITALIAN

Italian • Contemporary Décor

意大利菜 • 時尚

The name helpfully explains what to expect – fresh Italian food, any time of the day. Most ingredients are imported from Italy, including the flour and mineral water used to make the wild yeast bread. Pasta and sausages really stand out, as do the 10" pizzas that come in an array of toppings. Or you can opt for half-and-half for twice the pleasure in one pie. From time to time it hosts wine pairing dinners that oenophiles should not miss.

店名All Day Italian,寓意全日均可在此嘗到意式美食,其中麵包和麵條均自家製作,廚師選材嚴謹,除特地由意大利進口麵粉和礦泉水,更自行培養麵種。十吋薄餅設有多款口味,更可自選雙拼組合,點餐更具彈性,其中豬肉腸仔拼蘑菇芝士薄餅值得一試。愛杯中物的不妨留意餐廳不定期舉行的葡萄酒晚宴。

TEL. 2116 5128

Shop 265, 2F, Cityplaza,
18 Taikoo Shing Road, Tai Koo Shing

太古太古城道18號
太古城中心2樓265號舖

www.ciakconcept.com

■ PRICE 價錢
Set Menu 套餐 $ 268-398
À la carte 點菜 $ 350-750

■ OPENING HOURS 營業時間
11:30-21:30

CONGEE AND NOODLE SHOP
粥麵館

Noodles and Congee • Simple

粥麵 • 簡樸

Hidden in a glass office tower, this simple shop may have no ambiance or character to speak of, but guests come for the creamy congee made by a chef with over 30 years of experience. Bestsellers include fresh crab congee and chicken congee with abalone. Regulars also customize with their favourite ingredients such as fish belly and beef. Expect to sit on plastic chairs and share a table with strangers.

隱藏在充滿藝術氣息的嘉里中心內，店內裝潢卻不講究，食客全是慕粥品之名而來。為了品嘗逾三十年經驗老師傅精心炮製的傳統靚粥，客人都不介意坐塑膠椅及跟陌生人拼桌。暢銷粥品有原味蟹皇粥及鮑魚滑雞粥，但食客通常會自選配粥材料，炸醬魚片頭撈麵或福丸湯米等麵食也是不錯的選擇。

🖫 ✍️ ⛶ **P**

TEL. 2750 0208

Shop 2A, 2F, Kerry Centre,
683 King's Road, Quarry Bay

鰂魚涌英皇道683號
嘉里中心2樓2A號舖

■ **PRICE** 價錢
Set Menu 套餐 $ 35-75
À la carte 點菜 $ 50-150

■ **OPENING HOURS** 營業時間
10:30-20:00

■ **ANNUAL AND WEEKLY CLOSING**
休息日期
Closed 4 days Lunar New Year and Saturday
農曆新年4天及週六休息

HONG KONG ISLAND 香港島

TEL. 6809 9771

49 Hollywood Road, Central

中環荷里活道49號

cornerstonehk.net

■ **PRICE** 價錢
Set Menu 套餐 $ 188
À la carte 點菜 $ 300-400

■ **OPENING HOURS** 營業時間
11:30-22:00

■ **ANNUAL AND WEEKLY CLOSING**
休息日期
Closed Sunday dinner 週日晚膳休息

CORNERSTONE

European Contemporary • Friendly

時尚歐陸菜 • 友善

Owner-chef Shane Osborn of Arcane fame calls it an 'Australian café' – in fact, it feels more like a hip bistro with its faux-industrial décor. The small menu is a tapestry of global culinary cultures, including Aussie, European and Asian favourites. Though it changes a few times each month to keep things fresh, dishes are always competitively priced and loaded with big flavours and pleasing textures. Online reservations only.

簇新而現代化的小餐館，佇立在蘇豪區之中，裝潢以灰色作主調，內外都充滿型格。儘管老闆的定位是澳洲餐廳，卻選用來自世界各地的優質食材，菜式具有歐洲和亞洲元素，無論是味道還是口感都十分出色，而且服務員親切友善，價錢也物有所值。餐單每月更新數次，為常客保持新鮮感。只接受網上訂座。

DIN TAI FUNG (CAUSEWAY BAY)
鼎泰豐 (銅鑼灣)

Shanghainese • Cosy
滬菜 • 舒適

Worry not – the xiao long bao are good enough to justify the long queueing time. The group's executive chef visits here frequently to ensure quality. Ingredients are still sourced from the same suppliers and the same team has been running the kitchen all these years. Other standouts are double-boiled chicken soup and braised beef brisket noodle soup. This efficiently run branch is bigger than the one in Tsim Sha Tsui.

鼎泰豐在銅鑼灣的分店多年來備受追捧，歸功於餐廳始終如一的水準，供應商合作良久，而行政總廚蔡師傅每月專程從台灣到店巡查，監察出品及服務，難怪很多時都需要輪候入座。小籠包固然是重點所在，原盅雞湯和紅燒牛肉湯麵也蠻受歡迎。餐廳還為初次光顧的客人提供進食小籠包的說明，非常周到。

TEL. 3160 8998
Shop G3-G11, GF,
68 Yee Woo Street, Causeway Bay
銅鑼灣怡和街68號地下G3-G11號舖
www.dintaifung.com.hk

■ **PRICE** 價錢
À la carte 點菜 $ 200-400

■ **OPENING HOURS** 營業時間
11:30-22:00

■ **ANNUAL AND WEEKLY CLOSING**
休息日期
Closed 4 days Lunar New Year
農曆新年休息4天

HONG KONG ISLAND 香港島

EIGHT TREASURES
八寶清湯腩

Noodles · Simple

麵食 • 簡樸

TEL. 2889 8366

Shop B, GF, Wing Wah Building, 124 Electric Road, Tin Hau

天后電氣道124號榮華大廈地下B舖

■ **PRICE** 價錢
À la carte 點菜 $ 50-150

■ **OPENING HOURS** 營業時間
10:00-22:00

■ **ANNUAL AND WEEKLY CLOSING**
休息日期
Closed 5 days Lunar New Year and Wednesday
農曆新年5天及週三休息

This family-run noodle shop moved from Hung Hom to this address in 2018 and gained a loyal following soon after. Beef lovers adore its signature beef brisket in a tonic broth simmered with eight herbs (hence the name) and beef bones for over 10 hours. Or, top your soup or tossed noodles with boneless short ribs, inside skirt, outside skirt or a combo of all three. Beef honeycomb tripe, sinew, tongue and beef balls are also excellent alternatives.

經歷兩次搬遷，於2018年搬到現址後依然座無虛席，需要拼桌。鎮店之寶是以藥膳作湯底的清湯腩。清湯底依古法秘方，以當歸等八種食材，每天花上十數小時熬製，味道清甜。除了一般牛腩，可選坑腩、爽腩和崩沙腩，如果想同時品嘗到它們的不同口感，推介清湯蘿蔔牛寶麵。此外還有金錢肚和手打牛丸等配料。

ENG KEE NOODLE SHOP
英記麵家

Noodles • Neighbourhood

麵食 • 親切

This family-run shop has been feeding hungry locals with Cantonese noodle soup since 1994. It prides itself on its signature beef brisket – braised one night ahead and steeped in a spiced marinade overnight for silky tenderness and deep flavours. Their oven-grilled char siu is made with pork shoulder and pork neck and has a juicy, springy texture thanks to the fine marbling. The deep-fried wontons also earn unanimous praise.

於1994年開業的英記一直以帶住家風味的潮式和廣東麵食服務食客。以牛坑腩製作的招牌牛腩每天晚上就開始燜煮，以滷水浸泡過夜後，開店前再燜煮，是以軟腍入味。用焗爐烹調的自家製叉燒除了選用脢頭肉，也以豬頸肉製作，因其肥瘦分佈比例使油分均勻滲透，吃起來肉爽且多汁。淨牛腩、叉燒湯麵和炸雲吞深受食客歡迎。

TEL. 2540 7950

GF, 32 High Street, Sai Ying Pun

西營盤高街32號地下

■ **PRICE** 價錢
À la carte 點菜 $ 45-110

■ **OPENING HOURS** 營業時間
09:00-18:30

■ **ANNUAL AND WEEKLY CLOSING**
休息日期
Closed 7 days Lunar New Year
農曆新年休息7天

HONG KONG ISLAND 香港島

○🍴 ⇕

TEL. 2578 4898

62-68 Java Road, North Point

北角渣華道62-68號

■ **PRICE 價錢**
Lunch 午膳
À la carte 點菜 $ 100-200
Dinner 晚膳
À la carte 點菜 $ 200-400

■ **OPENING HOURS 營業時間**
Lunch 午膳 11:30-14:45
Dinner 晚膳 18:00-21:30

■ **ANNUAL AND WEEKLY CLOSING**
休息日期
Closed 4 days Lunar New Year
農曆新年休息4天

😋

FUNG SHING (NORTH POINT) Ⓝ
鳳城 (北角)

Shun Tak · Traditional

順德菜 · 傳統

This long-standing heavyweight in Shun Tak cuisine has a traditionally furnished look and is spread over two floors. Guests come for dim sum in the morning while Cantonese favourites and painstakingly prepared Shun Tak specialities are served at lunch and dinner. Try fatty pork crabmeat fritters, Daliang-style scrambled egg white with milk, and crispy fried chicken, all showing astute techniques. Call ahead to ask about dishes that need pre-ordering.

作為香港著名的順德菜館，擁有傳統茶樓格局，供應早茶、順德手工菜和傳統粵菜，並設有龍鳳禮堂，不同需求均得到滿足。菜單選擇眾多，每款都盡顯扎實的功夫，招牌菜包括金錢蟹盒、大良炒鮮奶、脆皮炸子雞等。當中，炸子雞是新鮮生炸，確保皮脆肉嫩，口感一流。但部分菜式須提前預訂，建議致電查詢。

HOP SZE
合時小廚

Cantonese • Friendly

粵菜 • 友善

This small, bustling joint near Sai Wan Ho MTR station is always crowded – reservations are a must and many items need pre-ordering, such as tea-marinated chicken, and roasted pigeon. Regulars also come for Cantonese classics such as claypot dishes and wok-fried items that exhibit nice 'wok hei'. Those after a pleasant surprise should ask about the secret, off-the-menu items. Warm and friendly service makes for a pleasant meal.

鄰近西灣河鐵路站，交通便利。室內設計簡潔舒適，服務親切友善，深受附近街坊支持。以傳統粵菜為主，各式小炒和煲仔菜式均鑊氣十足，另有不少隱藏菜式未有列於餐牌上，可向店員查詢。餐廳必須訂座，建議同時預留熱門菜式，例如使用新鮮雞製作的茶皇雞，以及可選擇原隻上桌的燒乳鴿。

📞🍴

TEL. 2569 0862

GF, Lai Wan Building,
39 Shau Kei Wan Road, Sai Wan Ho

西灣河筲箕灣道39號麗灣大廈地下

■ **PRICE** 價錢
Lunch 午膳
À la carte 點菜 $ 250-350
Dinner 晚膳
À la carte 點菜 $ 350-500

■ **OPENING HOURS** 營業時間
Lunch 午膳 12:00-14:30
Dinner 晚膳 18:00-22:00

■ **ANNUAL AND WEEKLY CLOSING**
休息日期
Closed 2 days Lunar New Year
農曆新年休息2天

HONG KONG ISLAND 香港島

KAU KEE
九記
Noodles • Neighbourhood
麵食 • 親切

TEL. N/A
21 Gough Street, Central
中環歌賦街21號

■ **PRICE** 價錢
À la carte 點菜 $ 55-100

■ **OPENING HOURS** 營業時間
12:30-22:30

■ **ANNUAL AND WEEKLY CLOSING**
休息日期
Closed 10 days Lunar New Year,
Public Holidays and Sunday
農曆新年10天、公衆假期及週日休息

Kau Kee has been trading since the 1930s and has consequently built up such a huge following that you'll probably have to line up in the street first to eat here. It's all very basic and you'll have to share your table but the food is delicious. Beef noodles are the speciality; different cuts of meat with a variety of noodles in a tasty broth or spicy sauce. Try the milk tea too.

開業於三十年代的九記深得食客支持，每天自十二時起，即使店舖還未正式營業，來自世界各地的食客都已整裝待發在門外輪候，午膳時間尤其擠擁。店內陳設簡單，進餐時要和其他人共用餐桌。歷久不衰的食物當然要數清湯牛腩，而咖喱牛腩亦不乏老饕捧場，配上更能掛湯的伊府麵，滋味無窮。

KWAN KEE CLAY POT RICE (QUEEN'S ROAD WEST)
坤記煲仔小菜（皇后大道西）

Cantonese · Neighbourhood

粵菜 · 親切

Its gigantic red sign, typical greasy spoon style interior and traditional stir-fries all point to an authentic Hong Kong culinary experience. Claypot rice is only served at night and features a three-rice blend enrobed in the oil brushed on the bottom of the pot. The rice is chewy and fragrant, with a crispy crust at the bottom perfectly scorched from the right amount of heat and time. Their signature white eel claypot rice is the top choice.

親切而熟悉的飯店大門帶着滿滿的地道香港風味，飯店供應的是傳統港式小炒，晚上亦可點選煲仔小菜及煲仔飯。其馳名煲仔飯用上了三種米混合而成，均勻地塗在瓦煲底的油滲透於飯內，米飯吃起來特別香滑軟糯；控制得宜的時間與火候令飯焦變得十分香脆。不妨一試其招牌白鱔飯。

TEL. 2803 7209

Shop 1, GF, Wo Yick Mansion,
263 Queen's Road West,
Sai Ying Pun

西營盤皇后大道西263號
和益大廈地下1號舖

■ **PRICE** 價錢
Lunch 午膳
À la carte 點菜 $ 40-80
Dinner 晚膳
À la carte 點菜 $ 80-120

■ **OPENING HOURS** 營業時間
Lunch 午膳 11:00-14:30
Dinner 晚膳 18:00-23:30

■ **ANNUAL AND WEEKLY CLOSING**
休息日期
Closed 7 days Lunar New Year and Sunday lunch
農曆新年7天及週日午膳休息

HONG KONG ISLAND 香港島

©🍴

TEL. 2156 9328

2-3F, 40-50 Des Voeux Road West, Sheung Wan

上環德輔道西40-50號2-3樓

■ **PRICE** 價錢
À la carte 點菜 $100-350

■ **OPENING HOURS** 營業時間
06:00-22:00

■ **ANNUAL AND WEEKLY CLOSING**
休息日期
Closed 3 days Lunar New Year
農曆新年休息3天

😊

LIN HEUNG KUI
蓮香居

Cantonese • Traditional
粵菜 • 傳統

This huge two-floor eatery opened in 2009 with the aim of building on the success of the famous Lin Heung Tea House in Wellington Street. It's modest inside but hugely popular and the dim sum trolley is a must, with customers keen to be the first to choose from its extensive offerings. The main menu offers classic Cantonese dishes with specialities such as Lin Heung special duck. Don't miss the limited offered pig's lung soup with almond juice. The pastry shop below is worth a look on the way out.

蓮香居於2009年開業，樓高兩層，延續威靈頓街蓮香樓的輝煌成績。樸素的內部裝潢掩不住鼎沸的人氣，以傳統點心車盛載着各式各樣經典點心，讓人急不及待從中選擇心頭好，限量供應的川貝杏汁白肺湯不能錯過。菜單上羅列了傳統廣東菜及懷舊小菜，如蓮香霸王鴨。離開時不妨逛逛樓下的中式餅店。

MEGAN'S KITCHEN
美味廚

Cantonese • Cosy

粵菜 • 舒適

Those who like a little privacy while they eat will appreciate the booth seating with sliding screens – the restaurant underwent a renovation in 2016. The choice of Cantonese dishes is considerable and includes specialities like steamed minced beef with dried mandarin peel – and all dishes come with complimentary rice, soup and dessert. The restaurant is also known for its hotpots, which are made with good quality ingredients.

在廣東菜和火鍋中難以選擇？美味廚讓你不再苦惱。這兒除了有各式廣東小菜如陳皮蒸手剁牛肉和美味煲仔飯外，火鍋亦同樣聞名，更有海鮮、和牛、不同口味的自製肉丸等火鍋配料。點選小菜奉送湯、白飯和甜品，經濟實惠。餐廳內的卡座設備齊全，拉下布幕即成私密度高的私人廂座。

☺🍴⇔🛏

TEL. 2866 8305

5F, Lucky Centre,
165-171 Wan Chai Road, Wan Chai
灣仔灣仔道165-171號樂基中心5樓
www.meganskitchen.com

■ **PRICE** 價錢
Lunch 午膳
Set Menu 套餐 $ 68-228
À la carte 點菜 $ 200-500
Dinner 晚膳
À la carte 點菜 $ 200-500

■ **OPENING HOURS** 營業時間
Lunch 午膳 12:00-14:30
Dinner 晚膳 18:00-23:00

HONG KONG ISLAND 香港島

PO KEE
波記

Cantonese Roast Meats •
Neighbourhood

燒味 • 親切

Po Kee is familiar to anyone who's lived in Western District as it's been a feature here for over 40 years and for many local residents a bowl of rice noodles (Lai Fan) with roasted duck leg remains a cherished childhood memory. To prepare his own roast meats, the owner built a factory behind the shop when he moved to the current address. Regulars know to come before 2pm which is about the time the pork sells out each day. Pre-ordering is allowed.

波記在西環屹立四十多年，一碗美味的燒鴨腿瀨粉是不少居民的童年回憶。店內多款燒味均在店舖後的自家工場製作，很受區內居民歡迎，燒肉往往在下午二時前售罄；而要一嘗其燒鵝，最好在四時前到達，否則可能會掃興。客人亦可預訂各款燒味，店主會因應取貨時間而燒製。

TEL. N/A

425P Queen's Road West, Western District

西環皇后大道西425P號

■ **PRICE** 價錢
À la carte 點菜 $ 40-100

■ **OPENING HOURS** 營業時間
11:30-19:30

■ **ANNUAL AND WEEKLY CLOSING**
休息日期
Closed Sunday 週日休息

HONG KONG ISLAND 香港島

😊

PUTIEN (CAUSEWAY BAY)
莆田 (銅鑼灣)

Fujian • Friendly
閩菜 • 友善

The original restaurant was founded in Singapore in 2000 and named after a coastal city in Fujian province – the owner's home town. This branch comes with an easy-going atmosphere and its Fujian cuisine is respectful of tradition, with the focus on natural flavours. There's much to recommend, like stewed yellow croaker, seaweed with shrimps, and braised pig intestine; and don't miss their homemade chilli sauce – a perfect match for fried bean curd.

莆田於2000年在新加坡開業，後擴展至香港，老闆以其家鄉福建內的城市為餐廳命名，堅守忠於原味、鮮味自然的原則，做出一道道美味菜式；無論是清鮮嫩滑的燜黃花魚、回味悠長的九轉小腸，以至香酥的炒芋頭等都令人留下深刻印象，自家秘製的辣椒醬更是非試不可。

Ⓒ🍴 ♿ 🔧

TEL. 2111 8080

Shop A, 7F, Lee Theatre Plaza,
99 Percival Street, Causeway Bay

銅鑼灣波斯富街99號
利舞臺廣場7樓A舖

■ **PRICE** 價錢
Lunch 午膳
À la carte 點菜 $ 150-300
Dinner 晚膳
À la carte 點菜 $ 150-300

■ **OPENING HOURS** 營業時間
Lunch 午膳 11:30-14:45
Dinner 晚膳 17:30-21:45

TEL. 2885 0638

3 Caroline Hill Road, Causeway Bay

銅鑼灣加路連山道3號

■ **PRICE** 價錢
Lunch 午膳
À la carte 點菜 $ 85-120
Dinner 晚膳
À la carte 點菜 $ 85-120

■ **OPENING HOURS** 營業時間
Lunch 午膳 12:00-14:30
Dinner 晚膳 18:00-22:00

■ **ANNUAL AND WEEKLY CLOSING**
休息日期
Closed 2 days Lunar New Year
農曆新年休息2天

RAMEN JO (CAUSEWAY BAY)
拉麵Jo (銅鑼灣)

Ramen • Simple

拉麵 • 簡樸

Named after the owner's favourite manga character, this lively noodle joint serves pork char siu ramen in 10 different flavours alongside gyoza dumplings and other specials. Try the ox's tongue with scallion. From the mild miso-based variety to the fiery spicy type, the rich and flavourful pork bone broth simmered for over 16 hours is the soul of every bowl. Those ordering dipping noodles are given a card illustrating the dipping steps in comic form.

店子名稱源自東主心愛的漫畫人物。餐單內提供十款拉麵，以及餃子、葱花牛舌等小食。其豬骨湯底花上十六小時熬製而成，濃而不膩，配上特製的麵條和醬汁，令人回味無窮。若點選沾麵，服務員會給你一張「沾麵食法」卡片，其上是以漫畫形式展示的正確沾麵進食方法。

SAMSEN (SHEUNG WAN)
泰館

Thai • Exotic Décor
泰國菜 • 異國風情

Readers may recognize the name it shares with a noodle shop in Wan Chai – yes, this is a spinoff by the same owner-chef, Adam Cliff. While it shares almost the same menu as the Wan Chai branch, certain exclusive dishes stand out. For instance, its signature 11-spice Northern Thai curry takes up to eight hours to make and is the perfect companion to egg noodles or roti bread. Friendly service and vibrant atmosphere are also pluses.

和泰麵隸屬同一老闆,共享同一英文店名,連裝潢風格也十分統一:懷舊海報、木製桌椅、從天花懸垂下來的綠色植物,充滿泰國風情。但這裏的菜單更加豐富,其中泰北咖喱使用十一種香料,每天經八小時烹調而成,配以雞蛋製作的麵條,香濃可口,與新鮮製作的煎餅更是絕配。甜品如甜煎餅、芒果糯米飯也十分出色。

🚫🍴
TEL. 2234 0080
GF, 23 Jervois Street, Sheung Wan
上環蘇杭街23號地下
www.samsenhk.com

■ **PRICE** 價錢
Lunch 午膳
À la carte 點菜 $ 150-350
Dinner 晚膳
À la carte 點菜 $ 150-350

■ **OPENING HOURS** 營業時間
Lunch 午膳 12:00-14:00
Dinner 晚膳 18:30-22:30

HONG KONG ISLAND 香港島

SAMSEN (WAN CHAI)
泰麵

Thai • Exotic Décor
泰國菜 • 異國風情

This casual Thai noodle shop next to the historic Blue House is aptly named after an area in Bangkok where the Chinese traded with the Thais. Rattan blinds, bare concrete walls and distressed wood furniture give off a street-stall vibe. The signature boat noodles are not to be missed – the flavoursome broth alone takes 6 hours to make. Those with a sweet tooth can round things off with pandan coconut dumplings served in warm salted coconut cream.

位於著名的藍屋旁邊，以復古風格裝飾：舊傢具、古老小販檔陳設、泰式鐵標牌，充滿懷舊泰式風情。熱愛泰菜的主廚旨在透過湯河及街頭小吃，讓香港人品嘗地道泰國風味。超過六成食材每天由當地直送到店。招牌船麵不容錯過，湯底於早上開始製作，經六小時熬製，滋味濃郁。愛好甜品的話不妨一試班蘭椰子湯圓。

⚛ 🖕

TEL. 2234 0001

68 Stone Nullah Lane, Wan Chai
灣仔石水渠街68號地下
www.samsenhk.com

■ **PRICE** 價錢
Lunch 午膳
Set Menu 套餐 $ 138
À la carte 點菜 $ 200-400
Dinner 晚膳
À la carte 點菜 $ 200-400

■ **OPENING HOURS** 營業時間
Lunch 午膳 12:00-15:00
Dinner 晚膳 18:30-23:00

SANG KEE
生記

Cantonese • Neighbourhood

粵菜 • 親切

Having stood here proudly for over 40 years, Sang Kee is a true symbol of Wan Chai and remains refreshingly impervious to modernisation. The owner insists on buying the seafood herself each day and the Cantonese dishes are prepared using traditional methods. You'll find yourself thinking about their classic dishes like fried snapper, fried minced pork with cuttlefish, and braised fish with bitter melon long after you've sampled them.

現在許多粵菜餐廳都以雷同的裝潢和新派菜單作招徠,令生記這類傳統酒家讓人感到特別親切!開業逾四十年,店主一直堅持每天親自採購優質海鮮,以傳統烹調方式製作一道道經典廣東菜:用時令材料炮製的乾煎海鱲,家常菜如土魷煎肉餅和涼瓜燜魚等,令人回味無窮。

TEL. 2575 2236

**1-2F, Hip Sang Building,
107-115 Hennessy Road, Wan Chai**

灣仔軒尼詩道107-115號
協生大廈1-2樓

www.sangkee.com.hk

■ **PRICE 價錢**
Lunch 午膳
Set Menu 套餐 $ 69-83
À la carte 點菜 $ 100-200
Dinner 晚膳
À la carte 點菜 $ 200-500

■ **OPENING HOURS 營業時間**
Lunch 午膳 12:00-14:00
Dinner 晚膳 18:00-22:00

■ **ANNUAL AND WEEKLY CLOSING**
休息日期
Closed 2 days Lunar New Year
農曆新年休息2天

HONG KONG ISLAND 香港島

🛋 🚫🍴

TEL. 2578 8135

Shop A, GF, 298 Electric Road,
North Point
北角電氣道298號地下A舖

■ **PRICE** 價錢
Set Menu 套餐 $ 74-158
À la carte 點菜 $ 50-150

■ **OPENING HOURS** 營業時間
11:40-22:30

SHE WONG LEUNG
蛇王良

Cantonese • Neighbourhood
粵菜 • 親切

In business for over 20 years, this shop is famous for its snake soup. While most people consume snake soup only in winter, the owner formulates a different herbal base for every season to make it a healthy tonic all year round. The shop also sells home-style fare according to the season, like glutinous rice and lamb stew in winter. Double-boiled soups are popular, but need pre-ordering. The adventurous should try the snake wines.

店舖雖小，但開業超過二十年，一年四季皆供應蛇羹。招牌蛇羹除了雞絲、木耳絲等材料，曾修讀中醫課程的店東也會因應氣候，以藥材配搭蛇肉，達到補而不燥的效果。此外提供多款蛇酒、龜板湯及滋補燉湯，滿足不同食客的需求，不過以珍貴藥材入饌的燉湯須提前預訂。冬天可以一嘗期間限定的羊腩和臘味糯米飯。

SHEK KEE KITCHEN
石記廚房

Cantonese • Simple

粵菜 • 簡樸

During the day ordinary 'Cha Chaan Teng' fare is served but at night this dining hotspot specialises in home-style Cantonese dishes. The owner-chef sources the freshest ingredients from wet markets daily and regulars also call him directly to pre-order certain dishes, including the signature fried chicken with toasted garlic which needs a day's notice. The pan-fried hand-minced cuttlefish patties are springy and flavourful.

於日間供應茶餐廳食物，晚間搖身一變，成為主打家庭式廣東小菜的菜館。大廚兼東主每天會親自往街市選購最新鮮的食材，部分熟客更會直接致電預訂當晚的菜式。石記風沙雞需要提前一天預訂。香煎手打墨魚餅充滿嚼勁、味道鮮美，不容錯過。菜單經常更新，特設每日精選小炒，冬季更少不了合時的煲仔飯。

⇔ ◎❙❙

TEL. 2571 3348

GF, 15-17 Ngan Mok Street, Tin Hau

天后銀幕街15-17號地下

■ **PRICE** 價錢
Lunch 午膳
Set Menu 套餐 $ 52-60
À la carte 點菜 $ 100-300
Dinner 晚膳
À la carte 點菜 $ 200-500

■ **OPENING HOURS** 營業時間
Lunch 午膳 11:30-15:00
Dinner 晚膳 18:00-22:00

HONG KONG ISLAND 香港島

SHEUNG HEI CLAYPOT RICE
嚐囍煲仔小菜

Cantonese • Friendly
粵菜 • 友善

TEL. 2819 6190

GF, 25 North Street, Western District
西環北街25號地下

■ **PRICE** 價錢
Lunch 午膳
Set Menu 套餐 $ 40-52
À la carte 點菜 $ 40-60
Dinner 晚膳
À la carte 點菜 $ 80-100

■ **OPENING HOURS** 營業時間
Lunch 午膳 06:00-16:00
Dinner 晚膳 18:00-06:00

■ **ANNUAL AND WEEKLY CLOSING**
休息日期
Closed 4 days Lunar New Year
農曆新年休息4天

Claypot rice is cooked-to-order over a charcoal stove here and this gives it a characteristic smokiness and a crispy crust at the bottom. Order the one with eel and pork ribs for a rich fish aroma and luscious pork grease that coats every grain. You can also order Cantonese bite-size munchies here. New items are added to the menu monthly; claypot rice and dishes are available after 6pm.

即點即煮的炭烤煲仔飯叫人再三回味，米飯以炭火烹煮，烹調過程中香氣充斥店舖每一角落，飯熟後的焦香又是另一種風味。推介白鱔排骨飯，能吃到鱔的香味之餘，排骨內的油分滲進飯內令米飯更香軟。煲仔小菜及煲仔飯只在晚上六時後供應，款式每月增加，食客也可點選點心佐餐。午市提供碟頭飯及小菜。

SHUGETSU RAMEN (CENTRAL)
麵鮮醬油房周月 (中環)

Ramen • Simple

拉麵 • 簡樸

The queues form early for the ramen here, with many of the customers coming for the Tsukemen ramen, as well as the Abura and special soup ramen. The shop makes its own noodles – which you can have thick or thin – but it is the sauce at the base of the slow-cooked soup that really makes the difference: it's fermented for 18 months in a 100-year-old wooden basket and adds richness and depth.

周月與別不同之處，在其以醬油為湯底的神髓：採用逾一百四十年歷史的愛媛縣梶田商店特製的醬油，配合沙丁魚粉、鯖魚粉及海帶長時間慢火熬製，味道更醇厚豐富。與日本店一樣，香港店設有製麵房，每天新鮮製造兩款粗幼不同的麵條。除了湯拉麵外，還供應沾麵。

TEL. 2850 6009
5 Gough Street, Central
中環歌賦街5號

■ **PRICE** 價錢
À la carte 點菜 $ 90-150

■ **OPENING HOURS** 營業時間
11:30-20:30

■ **ANNUAL AND WEEKLY CLOSING**
休息日期
Closed New Year's Day and first day of Lunar New Year
元旦及年初一休息

⊘🍴 ㅡ

TEL. 2336 7888

30 Hoi Kwong Street, Quarry Bay

鰂魚涌海光街30號

■ **PRICE** 價錢
À la carte 點菜 $ 90-150

■ **OPENING HOURS** 營業時間
12:00-20:30

■ **ANNUAL AND WEEKLY CLOSING**
休息日期
Closed Sunday, New Year's Day and
first day of Lunar New Year
週日、元旦及年初一休息

😊

SHUGETSU RAMEN (QUARRY BAY)
麵鮮醬油房周月 (鰂魚涌)

Ramen • Simple

拉麵 • 簡樸

This was the second branch of Shugetsu to open
in Hong Kong. It's the freshly made noodles and
the soy sauce base that make them so popular.
The broth is prepared with sardines, mackerel
and kelp, and soy sauce that is produced by a
longstanding factory in Ehime. The popular
choice is Tsukemen, for which they use thick
noodles to absorb the sauce's taste more easily –
you decide how large a portion you want.

這是周月在香港的第二間分店,以鮮製麵條和醬油湯
為賣點,湯底用放在百年木桶內經十八個月發酵而成
的醬油,加上沙丁魚粉、鯖魚粉及海帶煮成,美味且味
道特別。除了湯拉麵外,沾麵也頗受歡迎,選用的麵條
較粗但掛湯力強,能盡吸醬汁精華。食客可選擇麵的
分量。

SING KEE (CENTRAL)
星記 (中環)

Cantonese • Classic Décor
粵菜 • 經典

The second branch of Sing Kee is a bright, tidy spot serving classic Cantonese food – something that's proving increasingly hard to find in Central. You'll find only traditional recipes using chicken, pork and seafood here, free of gimmicks or fancy presentation. Many specialities need pre-ordering, like chicken with ginger in clam sauce, or almond juice with fish maw and pig's lung. Come at lunch to take advantage of some reasonable prices.

想在中環區找到提供樸實高質的傳統粵菜且環境乾淨整潔的餐館,星記便是你的選擇。選用新鮮肉類如豬、雞及生猛海鮮等食材,加上扎實的烹調技術,自然不乏支持者。午市提供一系列價錢實惠的小菜,甚得中環人士歡心。建議預訂燉湯如杏汁花膠燉豬肺。

TEL. 2970 0988

2F, 1 Lyndhurst Tower,
1 Lyndhurst Terrace, Central
中環擺花街1號一號廣場2樓
www.singkeedining.com

■ **PRICE** 價錢
Lunch 午膳
Set Menu 套餐 $ 85
À la carte 點菜 $ 100-200
Dinner 晚膳
À la carte 點菜 $ 200-400

■ **OPENING HOURS** 營業時間
Lunch 午膳 11:30-14:15
Dinner 晚膳 18:00-22:15

HONG KONG ISLAND 香港島

SISTER WAH
華姐清湯腩
Noodles • Simple
麵食 • 簡樸

The legendary Sister Wah is no longer at the helm but her sons are running the shop just like she used to. Its signature beef brisket in clear soup uses fresh local beef which is braised in a stock with over 10 different herbs. Other items on the brief menu include homemade dumplings with pork and white cabbage, drunken chicken and Dan Dan noodles. With only six tables, it gets filled up as soon as it opens.

這間家庭式經營的小店，現由華姐大兒子主理，招待工作則由弟弟打點。馳名牛腩的製作每天早上八時便開始，用上150斤肉味香濃的本地新鮮牛腩燜煮；清湯底以十種以上香料秘製，難怪營業時間剛到就吸引了不少食客光顧。除了清湯牛坑腩，也不要錯過菜肉雲吞及以白滷水浸上幾小時的醉雞。

TEL. 2807 0181
Shop A1, 13 Electric Road, Tin Hau
天后電氣道13號A1號舖

■ **PRICE** 價錢
À la carte 點菜 $ 40-70

■ **OPENING HOURS** 營業時間
11:00-22:45

■ **ANNUAL AND WEEKLY CLOSING**
休息日期
Closed 7 days Lunar New Year
農曆新年休息7天

HONG KONG ISLAND 香港島

SUN YUEN HING KEE
新園興記

Cantonese Roast Meats •
Neighbourhood

燒味 • 親切

Located next to Sheung Wan market, this traditionally styled, simple but well maintained barbecue shop has been run by the same family since the mid-1970s. Over the years they've built up an appreciative following so the small place fills quickly. The appetising looking suckling pigs are not the only draw: roast pork, duck and pigeon all have their followers, as do the soft-boiled chicken, the homemade sausages and the preserved meats.

這間家族經營的燒味店自七十年代中已坐落於上環街市旁，格調傳統簡單，多年來累積了不少忠實顧客，小小的店子裏往往座無虛席。燒味每日新鮮現做，且份量十足，經濟實惠。其中燒腩和燒肉是熱門選擇，而白切雞、臘腸及臘肉等亦十分吸引。外賣燒味以斤兩作計算，深受街坊歡迎。

⌷ S ⊘⫪

TEL. 2541 2207

327-329 Queen's Road Central, Sheung Wan

上環皇后大道中327-329號

■ **PRICE** 價錢
À la carte 點菜 $ 40-150

■ **OPENING HOURS** 營業時間
08:00-19:30

HONG KONG ISLAND 香港島

©⑪ ⇔

TEL. 2893 0822

**9F, Causeway Bay Plaza 2,
463-483 Lockhart Road,
Causeway Bay**

銅鑼灣駱克道463-483號
銅鑼灣廣場第二期9樓

www.taiwoorestaurant.com

■ **PRICE** 價錢
À la carte 點菜 $ 150-500

■ **OPENING HOURS** 營業時間
11:00-01:30

■ **ANNUAL AND WEEKLY CLOSING**
休息日期
Closed first day of Lunar New Year
年初一休息

😀

TAI WOO
太湖海鮮城

Cantonese • Neighbourhood

粵菜 • 親切

One of the district's most famous names, Tai Woo moved to these more comfortable surroundings in 2011 and, while the restaurant may be smaller than before, business is better than ever, with over 1,000 customers served every day. What hasn't changed is the quality of the service or the cooking – along with a menu of Cantonese seafood dishes, such as fish fried rice with ginger, are favourites like sesame chicken baked in salt.

自八十年代開業,太湖一直是區內馳名的酒家。2011年遷到更舒適的現址後,食物質素和服務依然維持一貫的高水準,難怪每天有逾千食客光顧。餐館精於烹調海鮮菜式,更設有不同時令海鮮優惠,讓饕客能大飽口福;此外廣東菜式亦值得細味,招牌菜包括芝麻鹽焗雞及薑米鮮魚炒飯等。

TAK KEE
德記

Chiu Chow • Neighbourhood
潮州菜 • 親切

It started out as a street-side hawker stall in the 1990s and still retains the casual, vibrant vibe. The second-generation hands-on owner shops for groceries every day and sometimes helps the experienced chefs with kitchen chores. Pork tripe and peppercorn soup is a culinary highlight, using peppers from Malaysia and Indonesia. Regulars also come for its spiced marinated goose liver, crispy chitterlings stuffed with glutinous rice and oyster omelette.

於1990年開業，早期為大牌檔，現由第二代經營。店東凡事親力親為，每天親自到菜市場採購新鮮食材，間或會在廚房幫忙潮州老師傅打點廚務。這兒的胡椒豬肚湯獨特之處是採用馬來西亞和印尼兩種胡椒，滷水大鵝肝、脆皮糯米釀大腸及馳名蠔仔餅深得食客喜愛。傳統荷包鱔，需最少八位或以上才接受預訂。

TEL. 2819 5568

GF, 3G Belcher's Street, Western District
西環卑路乍街3號G地舖

■ **PRICE** 價錢
Lunch 午膳
À la carte 點菜 $ 100-150
Dinner 晚膳
À la carte 點菜 $ 150-300

■ **OPENING HOURS** 營業時間
Lunch 午膳 11:00-15:00
Dinner 晚膳 17:30-22:30

■ **ANNUAL AND WEEKLY CLOSING**
休息日期
Closed Monday 週一休息

HONG KONG ISLAND 香港島

TASTY (CENTRAL)
正斗粥麵專家 (中環)

Noodles and Congee • *Classic Décor*

粥麵 • 經典

Be prepared to queue and share a table because over 1,000 customers a day, many of whom work in IFC, crowd into this Tasty. They mostly come for the trademark shrimp wonton or the much-loved beef and rice noodle stir fry; congee with prawns and dim sum are also recommended from the vast choice on offer. The last redecoration left the interior looking a lot more contemporary.

坐落於機鐵站上蓋,這家繁忙的店子每天接待逾千個顧客,當中除了在IFC工作的上班族,也有不少是為了一嘗港式風味而來的遊客。繁忙時間到訪,便要做好排隊和拼桌的準備。招牌鮮蝦雲吞麵和乾炒牛河都是店內受歡迎之選。此外,生猛大蝦粥及精美點心亦值得一試。

⭐⚐ ♿ **P**

TEL. 2295 0101

**Shop 3016-3018, 3F, IFC Mall,
1 Harbour View Street, Central**

中環港景街1號
國際金融中心商場3樓3016-3018號舖

www.tasty.com.hk

■ **PRICE** 價錢
À la carte 點菜 $ 60-200

■ **OPENING HOURS** 營業時間
11:00-22:45

TIM HO WAN (NORTH POINT)
添好運 (北角)

Dim Sum • Simple

點心 • 簡樸

Diners have been coming in droves since the day this branch opened. The soberly furnished dining room is always packed so expect to see a queue outside at peak times. The atmosphere is typical of a local tea house and hums with general contentment. There are over 20 dim sum choices on the menu that changes monthly. Don't miss the shrimp dumplings with springy filling enrobed in translucent skin. The famous crispy baked BBQ pork buns never disappoint.

簡約裝潢不減食客到訪的興致,這家點心專門店除了深受北角區街坊歡迎外,亦有不少客人慕名而至,每當繁忙時段總會大排長龍。餐單每月更新,二十多款點心及甜品中,晶瑩蝦餃皮薄剔透,恰如其名,鎮店之寶酥皮焗叉燒包更是不容錯過。店內氣氛與一般本地茶樓無異,熱鬧而略為擁擠。

TEL. 2979 5608

2-8 Wharf Road, North Point

北角和富道2-8號

■ **PRICE** 價錢
À la carte 點菜 $ 50-100

■ **OPENING HOURS** 營業時間
10:00-21:30

■ **ANNUAL AND WEEKLY CLOSING**
休息日期
Closed 3 days Lunar New Year
農曆新年休息3天

HONG KONG ISLAND 香港島

TEL. 2882 3268
7 Heard Street, Wan Chai
灣仔克街7號

■ **PRICE** 價錢
Set Menu 套餐 $ 57-92
À la carte 點菜 $ 50-100

■ **OPENING HOURS** 營業時間
11:00-22:00

TRUSTY CONGEE KING (WAN CHAI)
靠得住 (灣仔)

Noodles and Congee · Simple

粥麵 · 簡樸

As suggested by its name, you can really trust the quality of the food served in this long-standing congee shop. The menu has become more versatile in recent years with congee, noodles and snack sets available. All congee is cooked in fish broth that gives an extra dimension of flavour. Many rave about the pork liver and scallop congee, sticky rice dumpling with salted egg yolk and pork, and poached grass carp skin.

位於灣仔多年的靠得住出品一如其名,從不令人失望。其粥品採用魚湯作粥底,是餐廳一大特色,不容錯過的有心肝寶貝粥、鹹肉粽和爽脆鯇魚皮。食物的種類愈來愈多元化,精選套餐有不同的配搭,不妨試試炸雲吞。2017年翻新後餐室簡潔光亮。

TSIM CHAI KEE (WELLINGTON STREET)
沾仔記 (威靈頓街)

Noodles · Friendly

麵食 · 友善

The long lunchtime queue happens for a reason – the noodles here are bouncy and the broth is flavoursome. Only three toppings are offered – springy dace balls, wontons generously filled with pork and shrimps, and sliced beef with a robust meaty flavour and tender texture. You can even choose a combination of any two or all three toppings. Expect to share a table with strangers when it's busy or eat outside of peak times to beat the crowd.

開業逾廿年，裝潢簡潔但舒適。招牌菜雲吞、鮮鯪魚球和鮮牛肉各有特色：鯪魚球自家製作，帶魚鮮味；雲吞皮薄餡足，爽口彈牙；鮮牛肉則口感嫩滑，牛味濃郁。配搭用豬骨、大地魚和羅漢果等熬煮而成的湯頭，鮮甜味美。想同時品嘗三種美食，可選擇至尊三寶麵。午市需要排隊及拼桌，建議在非繁忙時間光顧。

🍴 ✕🍴

TEL. 2850 6471

98 Wellington Street, Central
中環威靈頓街98號

■ **PRICE** 價錢
À la carte 點菜 $ 35-60

■ **OPENING HOURS** 營業時間
09:00-21:15

■ **ANNUAL AND WEEKLY CLOSING**
休息日期
Closed 4 days Lunar New Year
農曆新年休息4天

WANG FU (CENTRAL)
王府 (中環)

Dumplings · Simple
餃子 · 簡樸

Wang Fu is famous for its Pekingese dumplings – among the 10-plus handmade dumplings on the menu, the green onion mutton one stands out most. Apart from dumpling soups, it also serves fried dumplings with light charred crispy skin and juicy fillings. Try also the tomato and egg dumpling, only available after 2 pm. If you fancy more variety, check out their noodles and cold appetisers as well, or ask about the daily special.

王府早年已立戶於威靈頓街，其北京水餃遠近馳名，超過十款餃子每天由人手新鮮包製。除了泡煮水餃外，店內亦有供應煎餃，餃子外皮煎至略帶焦脆，內餡仍保留着肉汁，份外味美。羊肉京葱餃和花素餃不容錯過，各款涼菜小吃亦別具京川風味。別忘了留意店家的是日精選，當中或會有一些新口味。

🍴   🚫🍴

TEL. 2121 8006

65 Wellington Street, Central
中環威靈頓街65號

■ **PRICE** 價錢
À la carte 點菜 $ 50-100

■ **OPENING HOURS** 營業時間
11:00-22:00

■ **ANNUAL AND WEEKLY CLOSING**
休息日期
Closed 3 days Lunar New Year
農曆新年休息3天

WHAT TO EAT
吃什麼

Taiwanese • Friendly

台灣菜 • 友善

Two Taiwanese mums have revived the old name of their first bento shop. The menu is now bigger, but the food is just as good and the service just as warm and homely. The egg crepe roll is made with ingredients imported from Taiwan and the beef shin in the noodle soup is braised for more than five hours in a spiced broth. Taiwanese veggies such as citron daylily and vegetable fern are hard to find elsewhere.

兩位台灣媽媽開店之路雖歷歷波折，但初心不變：希望讓客人安然坐下好好享用簡單的餐點，感受當中濃濃的人情味。其中牛肉麵的牛肉燜煮逾五小時，美味依然，有牛肋、牛腱或半筋半肉選擇；麵條經特別調配，在本地現做；招牌蛋餅的蛋皮由台灣進口。多款小吃及時令台灣土產均值得一試。

TEL. 2810 9278

Shop A, GF, Carfield Commercial Building, 75-77 Wyndham Street, Central

中環雲咸街75-77號
嘉兆商業大廈地下A舖

■ **PRICE** 價錢
Lunch 午膳
À la carte 點菜 $ 65-250
Dinner 晚膳
À la carte 點菜 $ 65-250

■ **OPENING HOURS** 營業時間
Lunch 午膳 12:00-15:00
Dinner 晚膳 18:00-21:00

■ **ANNUAL AND WEEKLY CLOSING**
休息日期
Closed Public Holidays, Monday dinner and Sunday
公眾假期、週一晚膳及週日休息

HONG KONG ISLAND 香港島

115

TEL. 2834 9963
50 Hennessy Road, Wan Chai
灣仔軒尼詩道50號
www.yixinrestaurant.com

■ **PRICE** 價錢
Lunch 午膳
À la carte 點菜 $ 200-400
Dinner 晚膳
À la carte 點菜 $ 400-600

■ **OPENING HOURS** 營業時間
Lunch 午膳 11:30-15:00
Dinner 晚膳 18:00-22:00

■ **ANNUAL AND WEEKLY CLOSING**
休息日期
Closed 2 days Lunar New Year
農曆新年休息2天

YIXIN
益新

Cantonese • Contemporary Décor
粵菜 • 時尚

North Point was the original location for this family-run restaurant when it opened in the 1950s. It's moved a few times since then but is now firmly ensconced here in Wan Chai. Run by the 3rd generation of the family, a sense of continuity also comes from the head chef who has been with the company over 50 years! The Cantonese food is traditional, with quite a few Shun Tak dishes; specialities include roasted duck Pipa-style, and smoked pomfret.

早於五十年代於港島區開業，輾轉搬至灣仔現址，現由第三代經營。除了地面的主廳和客房外，地庫還有一個裝潢時尚的餐室。益新一向以傳統粵菜馳名，餐單上不乏耗功夫製作的懷舊菜式，吸引不少客人在此舉行宴會。琵琶鴨、金錢雞及古法煙鯧魚等都是常客所愛。另設有預訂菜譜，可向店員查詢。

YUAN IS HERE
(WESTERN DISTRICT) Ⓝ
阿元來了（西環）

Taiwanese • Neighbourhood

台灣菜 • 親切

Decorated with memorabilia and evincing a night market buzz, this Taiwanese street food shop moved here from Sai Ying Pun in 2019. The owner and chef hail from Taiwan and make sure every bite they serve is as authentically Taiwanese as it could be. The signature braised minced pork rice has great depth and a melty texture. Deluxe seafood omelette is a variation of the oyster fritter, with shrimps and scallops. Round it out with taro balls for dessert.

老闆和廚師均來自台灣，為了保持原汁原味，部分材料由家鄉直送。裝潢也充滿台灣元素，令食客仿如置身當地。阿元魯肉飯是店裏的招牌菜式，手切魯肉肥而不膩、香氣十足。蒜泥白肉酸辣開胃。豪華海鮮煎則在傳統蚵仔煎中加上蝦仁和帶子，口感更豐富。同時提供數十款台式飲品，不妨來一份九份芋圓作飯後甜點。

🈂️ ⓢ 🍴

TEL. 3579 2460

GF, 31 North Street, Western District
西環北街31號地下

■ **PRICE** 價錢
À la carte 點菜 $ 40-90

■ **OPENING HOURS** 營業時間
11:00-22:30

yipengge/iStock

BOMBAY DREAMS

Indian • Contemporary Décor

印度菜 • 時尚

Tucked away on the 4th floor of an unremarkable building is something of an institution – this Indian restaurant has been operating here since 2002. The jars of spices that line the shelves tell you this is a kitchen which takes spicing seriously. There's a great value lunch buffet but go for the à la carte for original, well-crafted dishes with an emphasis on northern India – specialities from the tandoor are a highlight.

雖位於商業大廈內，但自2002年開業以來，這間印度餐廳一直不乏捧場客。靠牆的架上放滿了各式各樣的香料瓶，盡顯印度風味。午市供應自助餐，食物種類豐富，價格實惠，深得上班族喜愛。自選餐單上羅列正宗印度菜式，如欲一嘗廚師的拿手菜不容錯過，其中以北印度泥爐炭火(Tandoor)烹調的菜式更是非試不可。

TEL. 2971 0001

4F, Carfield Commercial Building, 75-77 Wyndham Street, Central

中環雲咸街75-77號嘉兆商業大廈4樓

www.diningconcepts.com

■ **PRICE** 價錢

Lunch 午膳
Set Menu 套餐 $ 178
À la carte 點菜 $ 250-400
Dinner 晚膳
À la carte 點菜 $ 250-400

■ **OPENING HOURS** 營業時間

Lunch 午膳 12:00-15:00
Dinner 晚膳 18:00-23:00

HONG KONG ISLAND 香港島

☏❚❙ ⬭

TEL. 2593 2593

9F, LKF Tower, 33 Wyndham Street, Central
中環雲咸街33號蘭桂芳大廈9樓
www.carbone.com.hk

■ **PRICE** 價錢
Lunch 午膳
Set Menu 套餐 $ 398
À la carte 點菜 $ 600-1,200
Dinner 晚膳
À la carte 點菜 $ 600-1,200

■ **OPENING HOURS** 營業時間
Lunch 午膳 12:00-14:30
Dinner 晚膳 18:00-23:30

■ **ANNUAL AND WEEKLY CLOSING**
休息日期
Closed Sunday lunch 週日午膳休息

❚❙❘

CARBONE
Italian-American • Classic Décor
美國意大利菜 • 經典

A nod to Manhattan's American-Italian diners circa 1950s, this colourful place celebrates the era in everything from the floor tiles and chandeliers, to the cutlery and servers' uniforms. In the same line of thought, the menu embraces classics like pastas and steaks. Try Tasmanian lamb tomahawk with a nicely charred crust and juicy tender meat. Let the team know if you're celebrating a special occasion – you may be in for a sweet surprise.

踏入餐廳彷彿走進了五十年代的紐約，天花的吊燈、牆上的木窗框、色彩明艷的地磚，全都帶濃厚的懷舊氣氛。供應美國意大利菜，除了各式意粉，還有多種扒類供選擇，其中來自塔斯曼尼亞的帶長骨羊斧頭扒外層香口，鬆軟多汁。甜品亦不容錯過，侍應會推着載有意大利芝士蛋糕、檸檬芝士蛋糕等甜品的餐車供客人挑選。

CASTELLANA

Italian • Contemporary Décor
意大利菜 • 時尚

This little gem partly owned by celebrity chef Marco Sacco serves authentic Piedmontese dishes, with truffles at the forefront (including white ones when in season). The lunch menu is great value, while the tasting menus cover all parts of Piedmont. Most of the wines are also from Piedmont, with Barolo and Barbaresco to the fore. The service is formal, structured and thoughtful and though slightly claustrophobic, the dining room is neatly decorated.

老闆來自意大利的皮埃蒙特，致力帶來正宗家鄉菜以及出色的服務。雖然餐廳空間有限，但裝飾雅致，佔據整面牆的酒櫃也非常亮麗，當中大部分佳釀來自皮埃蒙特、巴羅洛和巴巴萊斯科。松露菜式是焦點所在，在白松露季節甚至有專屬菜單。午餐價格相宜，嘗味菜單包括了皮埃蒙特的各種地方菜，值得一試。

TEL. 3188 5028

10F, Cubus, 1 Hoi Ping Road, Causeway Bay
銅鑼灣開平道1號Cubus 10樓
www.castellanahongkong.com

■ **PRICE** 價錢
Lunch 午膳
Set Menu 套餐 $ 298-498
À la carte 點菜 $ 600-1,000
Dinner 晚膳
Set Menu 套餐 $ 980-1,280
À la carte 點菜 $ 600-1,000

■ **OPENING HOURS** 營業時間
Lunch 午膳 11:45-14:30
Dinner 晚膳 18:00-22:00

■ **ANNUAL AND WEEKLY CLOSING**
休息日期
Closed Sunday 週日休息

HONG KONG ISLAND 香港島

🍴○

CHILLI FAGARA
麻辣燙

Sichuan • Trendy

川菜 • 前衛

○🍴

TEL. 2796 6866

GF, 7 Old Bailey Street, Central

中環奧卑利街7號地下

www.chillifagara.com

■ **PRICE** 價錢
Lunch 午膳
Set Menu 套餐 $ 108-168
À la carte 點菜 $ 200-400
Dinner 晚膳
À la carte 點菜 $ 300-500

■ **OPENING HOURS** 營業時間
Lunch 午膳 11:30-14:30
Dinner 晚膳 17:00-22:15

■ **ANNUAL AND WEEKLY CLOSING**
休息日期
Closed 4 days Lunar New Year
農曆新年休息4天

The name will be known to all fans of Sichuan cooking as this is their second site and replaced the original one in Graham Street which closed in 2016. It's quite a large space and is moodily dark at night. Dishes are classified 'Ma', 'La' and 'Tang' according to their level of spiciness – it's best to end with a 'La' dish. Chilli crab always delivers, but you won't regret ordering the glazed beef with caramelised garlic and ginger-infused sauce.

店如其名，裝潢離不開火辣辣的紅色，昏暗的燈光為店內增添氣氛。為免白行一趟，請預訂座位。以麻、辣、燙作為分類的主餐單，供應的是辣度不同的四川小菜，以及一系列素菜選擇。建議從辣度較低的燙菜單開始，嗜辣者不妨挑戰一下辣菜單。麻菜單的霸王登格斯辣蟹和辣菜單的薑焗蒜片牛肉均不能錯過。

CHINA TANG (CENTRAL)
唐人館 (中環)

Cantonese · Design

粵菜 • 型格

This handsome restaurant was conceived and designed by the late Sir David Tang as a sister to the London branch, and mixes traditional Chinese art with contemporary Western design. Tables are set closely together and there are several private rooms. Dishes from Beijing, Sichuan and Canton feature and dim sum is popular. The chef has introduced a more modern element to the menu.

由已故鄧永鏘爵士構思及設計，是其繼倫敦唐人館後又一傑作。人手刺繡的牆紙、獨特的鏡飾、古董燈飾及線裝中式排版菜譜，中式傳統藝術與西方美學結合得天衣無縫，流露出典雅貴氣。菜單涵蓋粵、京、川等地美食及精製南北點心：老北京傳統掛爐烤鴨、唐人館叉燒和琉璃蝦球等，滋味無窮。

TEL. 2522 2148

Shop 411-413, 4F, Landmark Atrium, 15 Queen's Road Central, Central

中環皇后大道中15號
置地廣場中庭4樓411-413號舖

www.chinatang.hk

■ **PRICE** 價錢
Lunch 午膳
À la carte 點菜 $ 300-1,000
Dinner 晚膳
À la carte 點菜 $ 800-1,200

■ **OPENING HOURS** 營業時間
Lunch 午膳 12:00-14:30
Dinner 晚膳 18:00-22:30

■ **ANNUAL AND WEEKLY CLOSING**
休息日期
Closed 3 days Lunar New Year
農曆新年休息3天

HONG KONG ISLAND 香港島

📞🍴 🚻

TEL. 6896 3172

29-31 Bridges Street, Sheung Wan

上環必列者士街29-31號

■ **PRICE** 價錢
Dinner 晚膳
Set Menu 套餐 $ 2,600

■ **OPENING HOURS** 營業時間
Dinner 晚膳 19:00-22:00

■ **ANNUAL AND WEEKLY CLOSING**
休息日期
Closed Sunday 週日休息

🍴🍽

DAIGO BY MORI TOMOAKI
醍醐

Sushi • Minimalist

壽司 • 簡約

This restaurant moved here in 2019 – keep an eye out for the wooden door next to a cement wall with no sign. Hidden inside you'll find seating for just 8 people at a counter and an experienced Japanese-Chinese owner-chef ready to dish up the best fish flown in from Japan, meticulously prepared his own way. Omakase only. Reservations are mandatory via an online app.

原址位於天后，搬遷後取名「醍醐」，形容極致的美味。餐廳外只有灰色的弧形水泥牆和一扇木門，沒有顯示店名。室內僅設八個座位，不設電話訂座，需經應用程式預約。主廚是中日混血兒，擁有多年經驗，選用每天由日本運到的新鮮食材，製作出傳統壽司。只提供廚師發辦套餐。

DENG G
鄧記

Sichuan • Cosy

川菜 • 舒適

The chef who once helmed the famous Deng Ji Shi Yuan in Shanghai opened this restaurant in 2016. The Sichuanese menu is divided into eight sections, categorised by taste profiles such as sweet and sour, Yuxiang or Wula. The classic mouth-watering chicken is served with two dressings on the side; you can pay extra for an upgrade with local chicken which is more flavourful. Finish on a sweet note with fried rice cake in brown sugar syrup.

源自上海的鄧記食園,提供經典四川菜。餐單甚有心思,把菜式分為糖醋味、魚香味、糊辣味等八個種類,方便瀏覽。建議來一客口水雞,可選擇質素較好的本地平原雞,味道濃郁而且油脂分佈平均,並附有兩款醬汁。飯後不妨試試甜品紅糖糍粑,或者淺嘗一杯中國酒。餐廳設有兩個包廂,歡迎查詢。

TEL. 2609 2328

**2F, Weswick Commercial Building,
147-149 Queen'S Road East,
Wan Chai**

灣仔皇后大道東147-149號
威利商業大廈2樓

www.elite-concepts.com

■ **PRICE** 價錢
Lunch 午膳
Set Menu 套餐 $ 68-98
À la carte 點菜 $ 100-500
Dinner 晚膳
À la carte 點菜 $ 300-500

■ **OPENING HOURS** 營業時間
Lunch 午膳 12:00-14:30
Dinner 晚膳 18:00-22:30

FARM HOUSE
農圃

Cantonese • Cosy

粵菜 • 舒適

The aquarium running the entire length of one wall of this modern dining room certainly catches the eye. But it's the quality food made with fresh, top-notch ingredients that wins the hearts of the regulars. The famous fried chicken wing stuffed with sticky rice is the must-try item. Baked sea whelk stuffed with foie gras, and steamed rice with chicken, abalone and dried scallops are also well-executed. Service is friendly and thoughtful.

飯店裝潢時尚，巨型水族箱延伸整道牆，非常引人注目。年中無休的農圃一直堅持以新鮮、優質的特級食材烹調粵菜，著名菜式有古法糯米雞翼、鵝肝焗釀響螺和瑤柱鮑魚雞粒飯等。配合細心周到的服務團隊，令用餐經驗更稱心滿意。飯店更出售鮑魚及海參等處理步驟繁複的食品。

TEL. 2881 1331

**1F, China Taiping Tower,
8 Sunning Road, Causeway Bay**

銅鑼灣新寧道8號中國太平大廈1樓

www.farmhouse.com.hk

■ **PRICE** 價錢
Lunch 午膳
À la carte 點菜 $ 200-900
Dinner 晚膳
À la carte 點菜 $ 300-900

■ **OPENING HOURS** 營業時間
Lunch 午膳 11:00-14:45
Dinner 晚膳 18:00-22:30

HONG KONG ISLAND 香港島

🍴○

FRANTZÉN'S KITCHEN

Scandinavian • Neighbourhood

北歐菜 • 親切

With just a handful of tables and counter seats, this small restaurant in the heart of Central is the world-renowned chef Björn Frantzén's first venture outside Sweden. The food sees Nordic roots combine with Asian influences, but his iconic French toast remains true to its origins. Staff cope well with the busy dinner hours. The wine list is small but well-chosen, with exceptional by-the-glass selections, along with Swedish craft beers.

東主Björn Frantzén在瑞典以外首家分店，主打斯堪的納維亞菜。小巧簡潔的空間，藏身在陡峭的住宅區街道上。吧檯位置可以看到瑞典和香港廚師炮製美食的身影。菜式糅合了北歐和亞洲特色，但招牌菜法式多士保留了原有的風味。此外，還提供精選葡萄酒、瑞典進口的手工啤酒，以及多款斯堪的納維亞產品。

📞🍴 ⛟

TEL. 2559 8508
11 Upper Station Street, Sheung Wan
上環差館上街11號
www.frantzenskitchen.com

■ **PRICE 價錢**
Lunch 午膳
Set Menu 套餐 $ 350-650
Dinner 晚膳
Set Menu 套餐 $ 788-1,088
À la carte 點菜 $ 500-800

■ **OPENING HOURS 營業時間**
Lunch 午膳 12:00-15:30
Dinner 晚膳 17:45-22:00

■ **ANNUAL AND WEEKLY CLOSING**
休息日期
Closed Sunday and Monday
週日及週一休息

HONG KONG ISLAND 香港島

♨ ⑪ ♿ 🏠 ✿

TEL. 2511 8912

**Shop 1, GF, Tower 1 Starcrest,
9 Star Street, Wan Chai**

灣仔星街9號星域軒1座地下1號舖

www.giandorestaurant.com

■ **PRICE** 價錢
Lunch 午膳
Set Menu 套餐 $ 298-348
À la carte 點菜 $ 400-1,000
Dinner 晚膳
À la carte 點菜 $ 400-1,000

■ **OPENING HOURS** 營業時間
Lunch 午膳 12:00-14:30
Dinner 晚膳 18:00-22:00

■ **ANNUAL AND WEEKLY CLOSING**
休息日期
Closed Monday 週一休息

🍴⚬

GIANDO

Italian • Cosy
意大利菜 • 舒適

Italian chef Gianni Caprioli owns several restaurants in Hong Kong but this one, minutes from Wan Chai but tucked away in a quiet corner, is his jewel. The look inside is smart and sophisticated, with the booths along one side being the prized seats. Expect to see dishes from all over Italy, with strozzapreti – hand-twisted pasta – and Milanese-style veal chop being two specialities. They have a real passion for wine too – Italian, naturally.

意籍廚師Gianni Caprioli名下餐廳眾多，此店可視為其珍寶，自有其因由。位處鬧市中的寧謐一隅，別有洞天，室內設計精巧富心思；餐單中意大利各地區口味俱備，配上招牌的自製捲意粉及米蘭式小牛扒，視、味覺均感受到濃厚的意式風情。酒單由身兼侍酒師的釀酒師設計，包羅意國佳釀，不妨細酌一番。

HANARE

Japanese • Contemporary Décor
日本菜 • 時尚

You have to walk through Yakiniku Jumbo to get to this eight-seater helmed by Koya Takayuki, who worked in some of the top kaiseki kitchens in Japan. All seats at the marble counter face the grill, separated by bincho charcoal. Two Wagyu-heavy 9-course omakase menus feature different cuts, all of which are meticulously sliced and prepared in a myriad of ways such as yukke, sushi, teriyaki and noharayaki. A must-visit place for beef lovers.

踏入餐廳，就會看到面向廚房的八個座位，配以黑色大理石餐桌，風格簡約得宜。以牛肉為主題，採用廚師發辦形式，按當季最優質的食材，定期轉換午市及晚市的兩款套餐。主廚曾於東京學師，擅於切割牛肉，並利用不同部位，分別製作成壽司、刺身或招牌菜野原燒，定能滿足肉食者的需求。

TEL. 6136 0898

Shop 302, Man Yee Building,
68 Des Voeux Road Central, Central
中環德輔道中68號萬宜大廈302號舖
globallink.com.hk/hanare

■ **PRICE** 價錢
Lunch 午膳
Set Menu 套餐 $ 1,280
Dinner 晚膳
Set Menu 套餐 $ 1,980

■ **OPENING HOURS** 營業時間
Lunch 午膳 12:00-13:30
Dinner 晚膳 18:00-21:00

■ **ANNUAL AND WEEKLY CLOSING**
休息日期
Closed Sunday 週日休息

HANSIK GOO
Korean • Cosy
韓國菜 • 舒適

'Hansik' means Korean food and 'Goo' refers to the famous chef Mingoo Kang. But 'sikgoo' also means family, befitting the modern home-style comfort food the chef champions. The seasonally-driven tasting menu delivers familiar flavours and subtle twists, with yukhoe, Wagyu beef tartare, being the gastronomic highlight. Guests can order add-on dishes to share and the extensive list of Korean rice wine is also worth checking out.

室內設計富現代感，簡約而舒適。儘管食材來自世界各地，在調味和呈現方式上，主廚致力還原傳統韓國風味，希望打破客人對韓國菜的既有印象。店名有「家」的寓意，食物也適合多人分享。除了隨季節變更的套餐，還可以加配其他菜式，不要錯過用和牛製作的招牌肉膾。其酒吧提供香港較少見的韓國米酒。

TEL. 2798 8768
2F, 8 Lyndhurst Terrace, Central
中環擺花街8號2樓
www.hansikgoo.hk

■ **PRICE** 價錢
Dinner 晚膳
Set Menu 套餐 $ 780-1,500

■ **OPENING HOURS** 營業時間
Dinner 晚膳 18:00-22:30

■ **ANNUAL AND WEEKLY CLOSING**
休息日期
Closed Sunday 週日休息

HONG KONG ISLAND 香港島

¶|O

HO LAND
何必館

Cantonese · Cosy

粵菜 • 舒適

Born into a chef family, Chef Lau worked in many famous Cantonese restaurants before starting Ho Land in 2020. The menu includes no-frills, impeccably executed classics such as roast suckling pig, and scrambled egg with crabmeat and shrimps. Traditional gems rarely found elsewhere, such as honey-glazed grilled chicken liver and gezha (deep-fried chicken offal custard) need pre-ordering. With only a few tables, reservations are recommended.

總廚劉師傅出生於廚師世家，擁有豐富粵菜經驗，並找來合作多年的廚房班子，炮製出實而不華的傳統粵菜。當中，蜜汁燒鳳肝、雞子戈渣等功夫菜較為罕見，值得提前預訂。乳豬、蟹肉桂花炒蝦絲等菜式也不容錯過。飯後來一客香甜煙韌的豆沙蘋葉角，加倍滿足。為方便自駕人士，晚上有代客泊車服務。建議訂座。

TEL. 2383 8112

4F, The Broadway,
54-62 Lockhart Road, Wan Chai
灣仔駱克道54-62號博匯大廈4樓

■ **PRICE** 價錢
Lunch 午膳
À la carte 點菜 $ 300-800
Dinner 晚膳
À la carte 點菜 $ 500-1,000

■ **OPENING HOURS** 營業時間
Lunch 午膳 11:30-14:30
Dinner 晚膳 18:00-23:00

HONG KONG ISLAND 香港島

HONG KONG ISLAND 香港島

◎ ⑪ ⎈ ⌂ ⎏ ⌁

TEL. 2477 7717

3F, H Queen's,
80 Queen's Road Central, Central
中環皇后大道中80號H Queen's 3樓
ichu.com.hk

■ **PRICE** 價錢
Lunch 午膳
Set Menu 套餐 $ 218-298
À la carte 點菜 $ 300-1,000
Dinner 晚膳
À la carte 點菜 $ 300-1,000

■ **OPENING HOURS** 營業時間
Lunch 午膳 12:00-14:15
Dinner 晚膳 18:00-22:15

🍴◯

ICHU
Peruvian • Trendy
秘魯菜 • 前衛

This is the first Asian venture of chef Martínez, who helms the famed restaurant 'Central' in Peru; in fact, key members from there were relocated to Hong Kong to ensure his vision is replicated here. The interior is inspired by Peru's landscape and the chef's cooking. Popular dishes include pez limon (yellow tail with yuzu vinaigrette and corn) and soft shell crab causa (deep fried soft shell crab with cold acidic mash potato). Don't miss the aperitivos.

秘魯廚師Virgilio Martinez於亞洲的首家餐廳，廚房、酒吧和服務團隊均曾於秘魯店效力多年，新任秘魯主廚將當地多樣化的特產融入菜式，確保風味不變。酒單側重南美風味，雞尾酒Aperitivos與生醃前菜是不錯的配搭。以秘魯為題的大型抽象畫作高懸於餐室，中央懸浮的樹木及電梯旁的雕像更使人眼前一亮。

INVOLTINI

Italian • Friendly

意大利菜 • 友善

The young chef, an alumnus of both Otto e Mezzo and CIAK, attracts a loyal following with his fresh pasta, made daily in-house. Italian eggs and flour are used in the dough which is rested overnight to give the noodles a lovely al dente texture. The signature tagliolini with springy carabineros red prawns boasts a rich sauce loaded with seafood flavours.

裝潢簡約而優雅，建議選擇開放式廚房旁的座位，欣賞烹調過程。招牌菜是選用意大利原材料、每天新鮮製作的意粉，廚師於前一晚製作麵糰，讓其休息一晚後才製成麵條，口感特佳。特別推介紅蝦意大利幼麵，彈牙的麵條掛上濃濃醬汁，配搭鮮甜的原隻加勒比海紅蝦，滋味無窮。餐廳更販售新鮮意粉禮盒。

TEL. 2658 2128

**11F, The L. Square,
459-461 Lockhart Road,
Causeway Bay**

銅鑼灣駱克道459-461號
The L. Square 11樓

www.involtiniconcept.com

■ **PRICE** 價錢
Lunch 午膳
À la carte 點菜 $ 350-700
Dinner 晚膳
À la carte 點菜 $ 350-700

■ **OPENING HOURS** 營業時間
Lunch 午膳 12:00-14:30
Dinner 晚膳 18:00-21:30

■ **ANNUAL AND WEEKLY CLOSING**
休息日期
Closed 4 days Lunar New Year
農曆新年休息4天

IPPOH
一宝

Tempura • Minimalist

天婦羅 • 簡約

TEL. 2468 0641

39 Aberdeen Street, Central

中環鴨巴甸街39號

www.ippoh.com

■ **PRICE** 價錢
Lunch 午膳
Set Menu 套餐 $ 480-1,100
Dinner 晚膳
Set Menu 套餐 $ 1,380-1,680

■ **OPENING HOURS** 營業時間
Lunch 午膳 12:00-14:00
Dinner 晚膳 18:00-21:30

■ **ANNUAL AND WEEKLY CLOSING**
休息日期
Closed New Year's Day, 4 days Lunar
New Year and Wednesday
元旦、農曆新年4天及週三休息

Now run by the fifth generation, this family business rooted in Osaka still strictly follows the traditional rules of making tempura. The owner-chef insists on battering and frying every morsel himself without delegating his duty. Seafood is flown in daily from Osaka and Toyosu fish market and they use flavourless safflower oil, so as not to overpower the ingredients' natural tastes. The sauce is made to a secret recipe. Omakase is the best way to go. Bookings are essential.

大廚兼東主是這家餐館的第五代傳人，時令的日本海產從大阪和東京豐洲市場空運抵達，放入輕純的紅花油中以明火烹調，並配上每天鮮製的醬汁佐吃。水準多年來始終如一，除因為規模不大有助保持穩定，亦因為大廚堅持親自烹調每件天婦羅。建議點選廚師套餐，可盡嘗最時令的食材。由於座位不多，必須提前預訂。

🍴⊖

JING ALLEY
井巷子

Sichuan • Cosy

川菜 • 舒適

The chef's modern Sichuanese fare is made with ingredients from around the world: duck blood curd from Chengdu, chillies from Yunnan, pork from Japan, chitterlings from Spain... The signature water-boiled black pearl fish uses a green chilli and pork bone stock that doesn't look red or oily like traditional ones; the freshwater fish with springy flesh also adds to the texture and flavour. The chitterlings with mixed chillies are addictively tasty.

於2019年開業的四川餐廳，主廚曾於成都受訓，擅長運用世界各地的食材，包括宮崎快樂豬、西班牙豬大腸，甚至北韓青椒乾，糅合現代烹調風格，帶來不一樣的川菜體驗。招牌菜包括成都清湯水煮黑珍珠，以豬骨湯取代紅油湯底，既清爽，也能在麻辣之餘品嘗到魚肉的鮮甜。小菜如混椒肥腸亦非常出色。

⊘🍴 ⇧

TEL. 2868 9801

**GF, Dawning House,
145 Connaught Road Central,
Sheung Wan**

上環干諾道中145號多寧大廈地下

■ **PRICE** 價錢
Lunch 午膳
Set Menu 套餐 $ 70-130
À la carte 點菜 $ 300-800
Dinner 晚膳
À la carte 點菜 $ 300-800

■ **OPENING HOURS** 營業時間
Lunch 午膳 11:30-15:00
Dinner 晚膳 18:00-23:30

HONG KONG ISLAND 香港島

135

Ⓕ ♿ 🛏 🅿

TEL. 2643 6811

7F, The Landmark Mandarin Oriental, 15 Queen's Road Central, Central

中環皇后大道中15號
置地文華東方酒店7樓

www.kappo-rin.com

■ **PRICE 價錢**
Lunch 午膳
Set Menu 套餐 $ 1,800
Dinner 晚膳
Set Menu 套餐 $ 2,500

■ **OPENING HOURS 營業時間**
Lunch 午膳 12:30-14:00
Dinner 晚膳 18:00-20:30

■ **ANNUAL AND WEEKLY CLOSING**
休息日期
Closed 4 days Lunar New Year and
Sunday 農曆新年4天及週日休息

🍽○

KAPPO RIN Ⓝ
割烹凜

Japanese • Classic Décor
日本菜 • 經典

A collaborative concept by Sushi Yoshitake in Tokyo and Sushi Shikon next door, Kappo Rin specialises in multi-course omakase menus with both cooked and raw dishes designed to bring out the natural flavours of the fresh, seasonal Japanese ingredients. Diners get to interact closely with the experienced chefs throughout the meal and can pair the food with some of the best sakes from Japan. With only 8 counter seats, reservations are a must.

由銀座名店吉武壽司與本地的志魂聯手創立，讓食客一嘗輕鬆而獨特的割烹料理。經驗豐富的日籍主廚採用各種日本時令食材，透過按季節變更的廚師發辦套餐，展示其對日本海陸產物的珍視，套餐中不論生或熟食菜式均旨在突顯材料的自然風味；不妨配搭優質日本清酒佐餐。唯座位有限，建議預訂。

KUNG TAK LAM (CAUSEWAY BAY)
功德林 (銅鑼灣)

Vegetarian • Cosy
素食 • 舒適

Don't be alarmed to find 'chicken', 'pork' and 'seafood' on the menu of this vegan restaurant – they are all made with soy. The food is based on Shanghainese cooking, minus the fattening sauces, and is easy on the salt and oil; the creations have punchy flavours and are exquisitely presented. Items such as dim sum and traditional stir-fries have been added to the menu recently. A set lunch is available in individual portions.

菜單上出現砂鍋獅子頭、無錫脆鱔等菜式，乍看猶如一般上海餐廳，但其實全是以大豆製品烹調的素菜。店家以傳統上海菜作藍本，配合少鹽少油的烹調方法，製作出健康與風味兼備的素食，且賣相精緻。菜單近年愈見多樣，加入多款點心和懷舊小菜，午市更設一人套餐。裝潢以翠綠配米白色系，清新自然；臨窗位置更可欣賞維港景致。

TEL. 2881 9966

10F, World Trade Centre,
280 Gloucester Road,
Causeway Bay

銅鑼灣告士打道280號世貿中心10樓

■ **PRICE** 價錢
Set Menu 套餐 $ 78-88
À la carte 點菜 $ 150-500

■ **OPENING HOURS** 營業時間
11:00-22:00

¶¶ ⌂ ⛲

TEL. 2455 2499

GF, 12-18 Wing Fung Street, Wan Chai

灣仔永豐街12-18號地下

www.legarconsaigon.com

■ **PRICE** 價錢
Lunch 午膳
Set Menu 套餐 $ 198
À la carte 點菜 $ 200-300
Dinner 晚膳
À la carte 點菜 $ 300-400

■ **OPENING HOURS** 營業時間
Lunch 午膳 12:00-14:30
Dinner 晚膳 18:00-22:45

¶|○

LE GARÇON SAIGON
Vietnamese • Chic
越南菜 • 新潮

At this brasserie-style Vietnamese grill house, the experience gets interactive with the must-try rice paper rolls – you wrap your own rolls with your choice of filling, such as Rangers Valley Wagyu bavette that melts in your mouth, alongside a caramelised fish sauce with intense smoky flavours. Crispy eggplant with mixed herbs and ginger glaze is also good and there's a selection of French wines, Vietnamese beers and coffee to complement the food.

牆上寫了食物名稱及價錢，甚有街頭特色。但有別於傳統越南餐廳，這裏的主角是糅合了奧地利元素的燒烤。此外，DIY米紙卷也是特色菜，當中以和牛口味最為出色：慢煮和牛配搭魚露，散發陣陣煙燻味，香濃可口。脆皮茄子配姜釉外脆內軟，同樣值得一試。飲品除了越南咖啡，也供應法國餐酒及越、法兩地的啤酒。

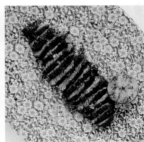

138

🍴⭘

LEI GARDEN (CENTRAL)
利苑酒家 (中環)

Cantonese • Contemporary Décor

粵菜 • 時尚

Forward planning is advisable here – not only when booking but also when selecting certain roast meat dishes and some of their famous double-boiled soups which require advance notice. The extensive menu features specialist seafood dishes and the lunchtime favourites include shrimp and flaky pastries filled with shredded turnip. All this is served up by an efficient team, in clean, contemporary surroundings.

這間利苑分店位於時尚的大型商場內，餐室採用了白色雲石作牆身，外觀潔淨明亮。菜單上可找到種類繁多的粵菜，其中以海鮮炮製的菜式最具特色，午市時段的巧製點心如銀蘿千層酥值得一試。燒味和燉湯尤其受食客歡迎，須提早預訂。一如其他分店，這裏常常座無虛席，建議訂座。

📞🍴♿⟷ **P**

TEL. 2295 0238

Shop 3008-3011, 3F, IFC Mall,
1 Harbour View Street, Central

中環港景街1號國際金融中心商場3樓
3008-3011號舖

www.leigarden.com.hk

■ **PRICE** 價錢
Lunch 午膳
À la carte 點菜 $ 150-300
Dinner 晚膳
À la carte 點菜 $ 200-600

■ **OPENING HOURS** 營業時間
Lunch 午膳 11:30-14:30
Dinner 晚膳 18:00-22:30

■ **ANNUAL AND WEEKLY CLOSING**
休息日期
Closed 3 days Lunar New Year
農曆新年休息3天

HONG KONG ISLAND 香港島

◎⫟ ⇦

TEL. 2806 0008

**1F, Block 9-10, City Garden,
10 City Garden Road, North Point**

北角城市花園道10號
城市花園9-10座1樓

www.leigarden.com.hk

■ **PRICE** 價錢
Lunch 午膳
À la carte 點菜 $ 150-300
Dinner 晚膳
À la carte 點菜 $ 200-600

■ **OPENING HOURS** 營業時間
Lunch 午膳 11:30-14:45
Dinner 晚膳 18:00-22:30

■ **ANNUAL AND WEEKLY CLOSING**
休息日期
Closed 3 days Lunar New Year
農曆新年休息3天

🍴◯

LEI GARDEN (NORTH POINT)
利苑酒家 (北角)

Cantonese • Classic Décor

粵菜 • 經典

Discreetly tucked away on the first floor of a
residential block and overlooking a pleasant
courtyard garden is this branch of the popular
chain. Things here can certainly get quite
frenetic as it accommodates up to 200 people.
The lengthy Cantonese menu mirrors what's
available at other branches, but particular
dishes worth noting here are the double-boiled
soups, the daily seafood specialities and roast
meats.

這家深受歡迎的連鎖酒家分店,隱藏在住宅大廈一
樓。從酒家外望是屋苑的翠綠庭園,寬敞的空間可容
納多達二百人,氣氛往往極為熱鬧。這裏的菜單與集
團內其他分店大致相同,提供的是味道正宗的傳統粵
菜,除了各式燉湯之外,亦可嘗試每日海鮮精選和各款
燒味,例如皮脆可口的冰燒三層肉。

LEI GARDEN (WAN CHAI)
利苑酒家 (灣仔)

Cantonese • Contemporary Décor

粵菜 • 時尚

An inventory of restaurants in Wan Chai wouldn't be complete without a Lei Garden. This branch is bigger than most and boasts a busy, bustling atmosphere, particularly at lunchtime. It follows the group's tried-and-tested formula of offering an extensive menu with luxurious dishes alongside less elaborate but classic Cantonese specialities. Seafood enthusiasts should consider pre-ordering the Alaskan king crab or Brittany blue lobster.

論灣仔區的出色粵菜食府，當然少不了利苑的份兒。餐廳面積不算小，但總是座無虛席，午市尤其人聲鼎沸。此店菜單與其他分店相若，包含珍饈百味與經典粵式小菜，加上巧手精製的點心，種類繁多，食客定能找到心頭好。喜愛海鮮的話，可於訂位時預訂特別海產如亞拉斯加蟹和法國藍龍蝦等。

TEL. 2892 0333

1F, CNT Tower, 338 Hennessy Road, Wan Chai
灣仔軒尼詩道338號北海中心1樓
www.leigarden.com.hk

■ **PRICE** 價錢
Lunch 午膳
À la carte 點菜 $ 200-400
Dinner 晚膳
À la carte 點菜 $ 200-800

■ **OPENING HOURS** 營業時間
Lunch 午膳 11:30-15:00
Dinner 晚膳 18:00-22:30

■ **ANNUAL AND WEEKLY CLOSING**
休息日期
Closed 3 days Lunar New Year
農曆新年休息3天

HONG KONG ISLAND 香港島

141

🍴

LOCANDA DELL' ANGELO

Italian • Contemporary Décor

意大利菜 • 時尚

TEL. 3709 2788

12 Yuen Yuen Street, Happy Valley

跑馬地源遠街12號

■ **PRICE** 價錢
Dinner 晚膳
Set Menu 套餐 $ 980-1,280
À la carte 點菜 $ 600-1,200

■ **OPENING HOURS** 營業時間
Dinner 晚膳 18:30-23:00

■ **ANNUAL AND WEEKLY CLOSING**
休息日期
Closed 4 days Lunar New Year
農曆新年休息4天

Tucked away on a quiet lane, this dining room boasts a clean modern look and a homely feel. The owner-chef has nearly 30 years of experience and grew up on the island of Sicily, hence the ocean-themed logo and seafood-biased menu. The 4- or 5-course set menu offers many options to choose from. Busiate trapanesi with Sicilian red prawn, and linguine 'Mancini' with Boston lobster are among the signatures. Booking is recommended.

生於西西里島的主廚曾於世界各地餐廳工作，最後選擇於跑馬地開設名下餐廳。他採用源自本地、西班牙及法國的海鮮及西西里島的乾貨製作正宗意大利菜。推介菜式包括西西里紅蝦意麵；以及用全隻波士頓龍蝦、限量供應的龍蝦濃湯扁意粉。四或五道菜的套餐讓食客從單點菜單中挑選菜式，選擇更具彈性。

🍴

LUCALE Ⓝ

Italian • Neighbourhood

意大利菜 • 親切

Doubling as a bar and a restaurant, this neighbourhood Italian joint was named after a portmanteau of the two chefs' first names. Fine artisanal ingredients from Italy are used to create Italian favourites, ranging from homemade pastas to seafood and meat dishes, best enjoyed with their choices of Italian wines. Black truffle chitarrino with Pienza pecorino is guaranteed to melt your heart with its al dente texture and tantalising aroma.

由兩位意大利大廚聯手經營，希望為客人帶來最地道的家鄉美食，因此店內的肉類、芝士、餐酒等，都由意大利空運到港。特別推介自家製的意大利粉，尤其是配搭羊奶芝士和核桃麵包碎的黑松露意粉，香氣四溢而且口感恰到好處。酒單豐富加上價錢合理，可以一邊享用美酒佳餚，一邊欣賞廚師在開放式廚房展示手藝。

🍸 ℗ 🏠 ⛲ 🚄

TEL. 3611 1842

Shop A, GF, 100 Third Street, Sai Ying Pun

西營盤第三街100號地下A舖

www.lucalehk.com

■ **PRICE** 價錢
Dinner 晚膳
À la carte 點菜 $ 400-800

■ **OPENING HOURS** 營業時間
Dinner 晚膳 18:00-22:30

■ **ANNUAL AND WEEKLY CLOSING**
休息日期
Closed Monday 週一休息

HONG KONG ISLAND 香港島

HONG KONG ISLAND 香港島

⊕🍴 ♿

TEL. 2523 5464

24-26 Stanley Street, Central

中環士丹利街24-26號

■ **PRICE** 價錢
À la carte 點菜 $ 200-600

■ **OPENING HOURS** 營業時間
07:00-21:30

■ **ANNUAL AND WEEKLY CLOSING**
休息日期
Closed 4 days Lunar New Year
農曆新年休息4天

🍴⃝

LUK YU TEA HOUSE
陸羽茶室

Cantonese • Vintage

粵菜 • 復古

Large numbers of both regulars and tourists come to Luk Yu Tea House for the traditionally prepared and flavoursome dim sum, and its three floors fill up quickly. The animated atmosphere and subtle colonial decoration are appealing but no one really stays too long; the serving team in white jackets have seen it all before and go about their work with alacrity. Popular dishes are crispy deep fried chicken and fried noodles with sliced beef.

樓高三層的陸羽茶室不但深受本地食客歡迎,更有不少外地遊客慕名而至,故經常門庭若市。店內環境典雅,以酸枝椅和字畫作裝飾,充滿懷舊味道之餘又帶點殖民地色彩,別具特色。穿着白色外套的侍應工作敏捷而專注;茶室以傳統方法製作美味點心,其他菜式如脆皮炸子雞及乾炒牛河也值得一試。

MONO Ⓝ

Latin American • Intimate

拉丁美洲菜 • 親密

The Venezuelan chef here has worked in some of the best kitchens in Spain, France and Hong Kong. His tasting menu reinterprets LatAm cuisine while respecting heritage, tradition and culinary roots. Specialities include 5-day-aged pigeon with mole, manioc and liver mousse bonbon. The chocolate mousse dessert Carupano 70% redefines the term 'from scratch' – beans are extracted from fresh cocoa fruits, fermented, roasted and ground in-house.

委內瑞拉主廚結合他在歐洲及本地的經驗,以優質食材和現代烹飪技巧,重新演繹拉丁美洲佳餚,菜單完整呈現其文化本源。招牌菜包括熟成五天的烤鴿以及甜品Carupano 70%,後者以新鮮可可自行發酵和研磨,味道香濃。於開放式廚房前觀看團隊的手藝,同時欣賞拉丁音樂,令人加倍陶醉。僅接受網上訂座。

TEL. 2510 8676

5F, 18 On Lan Street, Central
中環安蘭街18號5樓

mono.hk

■ **PRICE** 價錢
Lunch 午膳
Set Menu 套餐 $ 520-1,080
Dinner 晚膳
Set Menu 套餐 $ 1,280

■ **OPENING HOURS** 營業時間
Lunch 午膳 12:00-14:00
Dinner 晚膳 18:00-20:00

■ **ANNUAL AND WEEKLY CLOSING**
休息日期
Closed 3 days Lunar New Year, Sunday and Monday
農曆新年3天、週日及週一休息

HONG KONG ISLAND 香港島

NEIGHBORHOOD

European Contemporary • Intimate

時尚歐陸菜 • 親密

TEL. 2617 0891

61-63 Hollywood Road, Central

中環荷李活道61-63號

■ **PRICE 價錢**
Dinner 晚膳
À la carte 點菜 $ 400-1,000

■ **OPENING HOURS 營業時間**
Dinner 晚膳 18:00-22:00

■ **ANNUAL AND WEEKLY CLOSING**
休息日期
Closed 4 days Lunar New Year and
Tuesday
農曆新年4天及週二休息

Tucked away in an alley, this intimate spot is the brainchild of owner-chef Lai, a Hongkonger professionally trained in the U.S. The minimalistic and tasteful décor matches the short but sweet menu with 20 tapas-style items that rotate regularly. Don't miss the daily seafood specials as Lai shops for fresh wild-caught local fish himself. Other highlights include handmade pasta, and salt-baked chicken with rice, yellow wine and morels.

坐落在荷里活道旁的小巷，入口較隱蔽，低調的門面呼應着同樣簡約雅致的裝潢。老闆兼主廚曾於美國習廚，他會每天到漁市場採購本地海鮮，並以此創作家常歐陸菜式。菜單包括約二十種定期更換的小吃，及一些需預訂的菜餚，例如伴以黃酒和羊肚菌的鹽焗雞飯。甜品Chocolate Palette值得一試。

ONE HARBOUR ROAD
港灣壹號

Cantonese • Cosy

粵菜 • 舒適

The split-level room affords sweeping harbour views, while the high ceiling and sound of the fountain exude serenity. Exquisite Cantonese cooking is the name of the game here. Start with the crispy and appetising deep-fried shiitake in osmanthus honey glaze; for mains, opt for Wuxi-style Boston lobster that is spicy, tangy and sustainably sourced. Some dishes are available in smaller portions. Detailed and thoughtful service adds to the experience.

餐廳裝飾典雅，樓底高聳富空間感，落地大玻璃讓食客能飽覽維港景色，配上人工水池的潺潺流水聲感覺輕鬆舒適。各式粵菜由廚師團隊精心炮製，前菜桂花汁炸鮮冬菇甜而香脆，十分開胃；無錫燴波士頓龍蝦配上秘製酸辣醬汁，滿有特色。多款菜式設有輕怡份量，適合人數不多或欲多嘗不同菜品的客人。點心服務令用餐體驗倍添寫意。

TEL. 2584 7722

7-8F, Grand Hyatt Hotel,
1 Harbour Road, Wan Chai
灣仔港灣道1號君悅酒店7-8樓
**www.hongkong.grand.
hyatt restaurants.com**

■ **PRICE 價錢**
Lunch 午膳
À la carte 點菜 $ 350-800
Dinner 晚膳
À la carte 點菜 $ 550-1,000

■ **OPENING HOURS 營業時間**
Lunch 午膳 12:00-14:30
Dinner 晚膳 18:30-22:30

⊘🍴 ⇄

TEL. 2576 8886

GF, 23-25 Hysan Avenue, Causeway Bay

銅鑼灣希慎道23-25號

■ **PRICE** 價錢
À la carte 點菜 $ 200-500

■ **OPENING HOURS** 營業時間
11:00-22:30

🍴

PAK LOH CHIU CHOW (HYSAN AVENUE)
百樂潮州 (希慎道)

Chiu Chow • Family

潮州菜 • 溫馨

There are now four branches of this Chiu Chow restaurant in Hong Kong, but this is the original – which was founded in 1967. For lunch try the baby oyster congee or the fried noodle with sugar and vinegar; in the evening you can go for something a little heavier like soyed goose liver. It's also worth pre-ordering a speciality, like deep-fried king prawn with bread noodles, and finishing with the classic Chiu Chow dessert of fried taro with sugar.

在香港已是老字號的百樂潮州自1967年於銅鑼灣開業至今,已發展至多間分店,而這家位於希慎道的本店受歡迎程度始終如一。餐廳的各式滷水食物甚具水準,當中以鵝肝及鵝片等最受食客歡迎,還有凍蟹及凍魚。特別菜式如子母龍鬚蝦、薑米乳鴿及荷包豬肚雞湯等則需要預訂。

PIIN
品

*Chinese Contemporary •
Contemporary Décor*
時尚中國菜 • 時尚

A couple who own two vineyards in Burgundy opened this restaurant specialising in modern, refined Cantonese fare with big flavours, just like their wines. Along with an à la carte, 3 set menus showcase their greatest hits, most incorporating alcohol as seasoning, such as smoked abalone in sake plum sauce, and cigar duck rolls in red wine sesame sauce. Needless to say, the extensive wine list with some rare Burgundy vintages is also part of the appeal.

店主是勃艮第著名酒莊的莊主，首次於香港開設餐廳，便選擇以美酒配搭粵菜。主廚創作出多款以酒入饌的新派菜式，除了三種套餐，還有以一人分量為主的單點菜單，方便客人品嘗更多佳餚。招牌菜管鮑之友、草長鶯飛，分別配上以清酒和紅酒調製的醬汁，充滿特色。另可請侍酒師配對葡萄酒，提升滋味。

TEL. 2832 7123
2F, Low Block, H Code,
45 Pottinger Street, Central
中環砵典乍街45號H Code低座2樓
www.piin-hk.com

■ **PRICE 價錢**
Lunch 午膳
Set Menu 套餐 $ 368
À la carte 點菜 $ 400-800
Dinner 晚膳
Set Menu 套餐 $ 900-1,280
À la carte 點菜 $ 400-800

■ **OPENING HOURS 營業時間**
Lunch 午膳 12:00-14:30
Dinner 晚膳 17:30-23:00

■ **ANNUAL AND WEEKLY CLOSING**
休息日期
Closed Saturday lunch and Sunday
週六午膳及週日休息

HONG KONG ISLAND 香港島

🍴

POEM

Balinese • Trendy

峇里菜 • 前衛

Previously named TRi in Repulse Bay, this Balinese restaurant moved here in 2019 and was renamed. Regulars should be familiar with the décor – furniture and batik panels were brought in from the previous address and were supplemented by generous use of bamboo and lush plants for a tropical feel. The Balinese chef excels in dishes that pack a punch and reveal subtle layers of flavours. Try coconut smoked duck, satays and Wagyu short ribs.

前身是位於淺水灣的TRi，2019年遷址後改名為Poem。設計方面，沿用舊店的峇里風格和傢具，並以竹枝和茂盛的綠色植物，創造出悠閒的用餐環境。來自峇里的主廚堅持使用有機、時令、可持續發展的食材，並在菜式中添加一絲法國元素。招牌菜包括椰子燻鴨、家常沙嗲、和牛牛小排等。建議和親友分享菜餚。

☎ 🍴

TEL. 2810 6166

5F, LKF Tower, 33 Wyndham Street, Central

中環雲咸街33號LKF Tower 5樓

www.poem.hk

■ **PRICE** 價錢
Lunch 午膳
Set Menu 套餐 $ 188
À la carte 點菜 $ 250-800
Dinner 晚膳
À la carte 點菜 $ 250-800

■ **OPENING HOURS** 營業時間
Lunch 午膳 12:00-14:30
Dinner 晚膳 18:00-22:30

HONG KONG ISLAND 香港島

🍴⃝

SEVENTH SON
家全七福

Cantonese • Elegant

粵菜 • 典雅

With teak floors, gold accents and warm lighting, the dining room is smart and chic. The name refers to the owner – the seventh son who learned his culinary skills from his father from the age of 14. Cantonese barbecue meats are the must-try items, such as the roast suckling pig which is smoky and rich. Fish maw soup with shredded chicken boasts exquisite knife work and quality ingredients and delivers interesting textures and lingering aromas.

餐廳名稱包含了東主父親的名字及其在兄弟中的排序，也有傳承父親廚藝之意。餐室以柚木地板配上金色鏡牆，並綴以多幅畫作，甚顯富麗堂皇。東主自十四歲隨父習廚，以烹調高級功夫粵菜為長，其中花膠燴雞絲羹充分展演其細膩的刀工，用料豐富，令人齒頰留香。招牌菜大紅片皮乳豬以炭火烤製，油香四溢，每一啖都帶有淡淡炭火香氣，妙不可言。

⃝🍽 ⓰ ♿ 🈳

TEL. 2892 2888

**3F, The Wharney Guang Dong Hotel,
57-73 Lockhart Road, Wan Chai**

灣仔駱克道57-73號華美粵海酒店3樓

www.seventhson.hk

■ **PRICE** 價錢
Lunch 午膳
À la carte 點菜 $ 200-600
Dinner 晚膳
À la carte 點菜 $ 350-1,000

■ **OPENING HOURS** 營業時間
Lunch 午膳 11:30-14:30
Dinner 晚膳 18:00-22:30

HONG KONG ISLAND 香港島

⊘̶ ⛶ ⩻ ⌂

TEL. 2156 1688

26F, V Point, 18 Tang Lung Street, Causeway Bay

銅鑼灣登龍街18號 V Point 26樓

www.yu-yuan.hk

■ **PRICE** 價錢
Lunch 午膳
À la carte 點菜 $ 200-300
Dinner 晚膳
À la carte 點菜 $ 200-500

■ **OPENING HOURS** 營業時間
Lunch 午膳 12:00-15:00
Dinner 晚膳 18:00-22:00

🍴○

SHANGHAI YU YUAN
豫園

Shanghainese • Cosy

滬菜 • 舒適

Named after the famous garden in Shanghai, this restaurant uses a classic vase motif borrowed from the lattice windows there. A hand-painted mural depicting Yu Garden and Old Shanghai takes centre stage, and contrasts nicely with the gorgeous harbour views. Shanghainese classics such as steamed Reeves shad with distillers grains, fried pine nut fish, and braised whole pork ribs are recommended. Cantonese dim sum is also served.

一如其名，餐廳以上海豫園為主題，裝潢中也不難發現其蹤影：屏風上的花瓶圖案與上海豫園的窗花同出一轍，而大廳壁畫描繪的是豫園和老上海人物風貌。餐廳各個細節都別出心裁，碟具更是專程於景德鎮訂造。推薦菜式包括清蒸酒糟鰣魚、招牌松子鮮魚，以及較少見的豫園豬全骨；除了傳統滬菜，也供應粵式點心。

SUN FOOK KEE
新福記

Fujian • Traditional
閩菜 • 傳統

This restaurant prides itself on labour-intensive, traditional Fujian dishes that are hard to find elsewhere, such as a shredded vegetable pancake that uses 12 different ingredients, and deep-fried longans stuffed with minced shrimp and pork that are only available in summer. The chef shops for produce daily from the market to ensure freshness. Ask about the new dishes that are not on the menu and those that require pre-ordering when you book.

高級懷舊福建菜館不多，新福記是其中一員。菜單上有不少難得一見的傳統功夫菜，例如只在夏天供應的東壁龍珠，取新鮮龍眼肉去核後釀入蝦膠豬肉，再油炸而成。還有潤餅菜，將多種材料切絲炒香，以薄餅皮包裹享用，口感豐富五味紛陳，不容錯過。不少新創作並不列於菜單之上，建議訂座時查詢時令或推介菜式。

TEL. 2566 5898

1F, Circle Court, 3-5 Java Road, North Point

北角渣華道3-5號永光閣1樓

■ **PRICE** 價錢
Lunch 午膳
À la carte 點菜 $ 350-500
Dinner 晚膳
À la carte 點菜 $ 500-700

■ **OPENING HOURS** 營業時間
Lunch 午膳 11:00-14:30
Dinner 晚膳 18:00-22:00

HONG KONG ISLAND 香港島

SUSHI MASATAKA
Sushi • Minimalist
壽司 • 簡約

TEL. 2574 1333

GF, The Oakhill, 18 Wood Road, Wan Chai

灣仔活道18號萃峯地下

sushimasataka.com

■ **PRICE** 價錢
Dinner 晚膳
Set Menu 套餐 $ 2,980

■ **OPENING HOURS** 營業時間
Dinner 晚膳 18:00-20:30

■ **ANNUAL AND WEEKLY CLOSING**
休息日期
Closed 3 days Lunar New Year and Monday
農曆新年3天及週一休息

Named after its executive chef, the former Sushi Rozan reopened with a wood-clad interior that reflects the roots of its cuisine. The nine seats in front of an open counter allow diners to watch the chefs in action. Only fixed price omakase menus are available, featuring quality seafood flown straight from Japan daily, such as golden-eye snapper and white sea urchin. Lunch is by reservation only and requires a minimum of 4 people.

從原來的名字鮨魯山(Sushi Rozan)易名後，店子亦重新裝修過。淺啡色木板裝潢，極有日本風味。從十二個櫃枱座位減至九個座位，容納的人數少了，但廚師能更專注地服務每位客人。菜單仍是只供應廚師發辦套餐，食材和分量會按食客的需求調整。金目鯛和白海膽等高級食材每天從日本直送到店。

TORITAMA
酉玉

Yakitori • Contemporary Décor

雞肉串燒 • 時尚

There appears to be no end to the number of Tokyo restaurants opening branches in Hong Kong and this time here in LKF it's all about yakitori. Seating is limited so it's worth booking ahead and asking for the bar counter to watch the expert preparation in the semi-open kitchen. 40-day-old chickens are used and 28 different parts of the chicken are offered – all you have to do is decide how many skewers you want.

室內座位數量不多，建議預先訂座。餐廳選用的雞隻只有四十天大，確保肉質鮮嫩，供應超過二十八種由不同部位製作的雞串。由日籍大廚主理的串燒，每一件都烤得恰到好處。廚師會因應食客的進食速度預備每一道食物，並會親自送到食客面前。

TEL. 2388 7717

GF, Greenville, 2 Glenealy, Central

中環己連拿利2號翠怡閣地舖

www.toritama.hk

■ **PRICE** 價錢

Dinner 晚膳

Set Menu 套餐 $ 298-598

À la carte 點菜 $ 200-600

■ **OPENING HOURS** 營業時間

Dinner 晚膳 18:00-23:00

■ **ANNUAL AND WEEKLY CLOSING** 休息日期

Closed 10 days Lunar New Year and Sunday

農曆新年10天及週日休息

◎🍴 ⟷

TEL. 2506 1018

**Shop B, 17F, Lee Theatre Plaza,
99 Percival Street, Causeway Bay**

銅鑼灣波斯富街99號
利舞臺廣場17樓B舖

www.wukong.com.hk

■ **PRICE** 價錢
Lunch 午膳
Set Menu 套餐 $ 98
À la carte 點菜 $ 200-400
Dinner 晚膳
À la carte 點菜 $ 200-400

■ **OPENING HOURS** 營業時間
Lunch 午膳 11:45-14:30
Dinner 晚膳 17:45-21:45

■ **ANNUAL AND WEEKLY CLOSING**
休息日期
Closed 3 days Lunar New Year
農曆新年休息3天

🍴◎

WU KONG (CAUSEWAY BAY)
滬江 (銅鑼灣)

Shanghainese • Traditional

滬菜 • 傳統

The many customers of this Shanghainese restaurant on the upper level of Lee Theatre Plaza come for the nice views and spacious environment in which to eat. An experienced kitchen shows its practised hand in specialities such as braised pig's knuckle with brown sauce and smoked free-range chicken, while the latter needs pre-ordering. Do not miss the hairy crab menu in the autumn season.

除了空間寬敞，環境舒適，滬江飯店更佔盡位處商場高層的優勢，為顧客帶來開揚景觀，享用美食的同時還可以欣賞鬧市的繁華美景。廚藝精湛的團隊為顧客炮製多款巧手小菜，如紅燒元蹄和煙燻走地雞，後者需提前預訂。於秋季期間更會有肥美的大閘蟹供應，是不容錯過的時令佳餚。

YAKINIKU JUMBO

Barbecue • Cosy

燒烤 • 舒適

This outpost of the famous barbecue chain serves the same beef as its flagship in Japan. Try the signature A5 Wagyu set menu to sample different cuts with rice, salad, soup and pickles. The velvety noharayaki is a thin slice of seared sirloin dipped into raw egg. You then grill the ichibo, zabuton, misuji and premium kalbi to medium-rare doneness according to the instructions. Dip them in the tart kombu sauce to cut through the richness.

必試極上A5黑毛和牛套餐,可品嘗五款不同部位的牛肉,包括野原燒、腰脊蓋肉、特上肩肉、牛板腱和上牛小排。其中野原燒是店內的招牌,採用薄切A5和牛西冷,由服務生代燒,食用前沾上日本生雞蛋,入口即融。其他四款則由食客自行燒烤,配搭前菜、湯和日本飯,非常飽足。同時提供不少韓式食品,口味多元。

TEL. 2151 3887

Shop 302, 3F, Man Yee Building, 68 Des Voeux Road Central, Central

中環德輔道中68號
萬宜大廈3樓302號舖

www.globallink.com.hk

■ **PRICE** 價錢
Lunch 午膳
Set Menu 套餐 $ 150-598
À la carte 點菜 $ 500-1,300
Dinner 晚膳
Set Menu 套餐 $ 690-980
À la carte 點菜 $ 500-1,300

■ **OPENING HOURS** 營業時間
Lunch 午膳 12:00-14:00
Dinner 晚膳 18:00-22:00

■ **ANNUAL AND WEEKLY CLOSING**
休息日期
Closed Sunday 週日休息

HONG KONG ISLAND 香港島

🍴○

YONG FU

甬府

Ningbo · Elegant

寧波菜 · 典雅

📞🍴 ⟷

TEL. 2881 7899

**Shop 2 at GF & 1F,
Golden Star Building,
20-24 Lockhart Road, Wan Chai**

灣仔駱克道20-24號
金星大廈地下2號舖及1樓

■ **PRICE** 價錢
Lunch 午膳
Set Menu 套餐 $ 358
À la carte 點菜 $ 350-2,500
Dinner 晚膳
À la carte 點菜 $ 700-2,500

■ **OPENING HOURS** 營業時間
Lunch 午膳 11:30-15:00
Dinner 晚膳 18:00-23:00

The upmarket Shanghai-based brand opened its first outpost in Hong Kong. The high ceiling is adorned with crystal-pavé wave-like chandeliers and dangling colour glass fish, hinting at its fish-heavy menu. Most signatures from the parent branch are available here, including the must-try raw mud crab marinated with wine, ginger and coriander, yellow croaker jelly, and sautéed greens. Sesame glutinous rice balls are the perfect end to the meal.

高聳的樓底，配上水晶燈和玻璃魚形裝飾，如海洋般閃耀。主打從東海進口的海鮮，招牌菜十八斬以秘製醬汁醃製膏蟹，肉質鮮甜，蟹膏豐腴。琥珀黃魚凍以魚籽和魚蛋白所做，手工精美，充滿鹹香。甬府捨得則從十斤小棠菜中挑出最鮮嫩部分清炒，同樣出色。設最低消費，宜於訂座時查詢並預訂菜式。

ola_p/iStock

STREET FOOD
街頭小吃

FOOK YUEN
福元湯圓

Tasty glutinous rice balls with a filling of black sesame or peanut. The rice balls go well with traditional sweet soups, such as black sesame or walnut.

此中式糖水店主打每天手工製作的湯圓,可選黑芝麻或花生餡,皮薄餡靚。湯圓亦可配搭其他中式糖水,如芝麻糊、杏仁茶、合桃露等。

**Shop I-1, GF, Lei Do Building,
7 Fuk Yuen Street, North Point**
北角福元街7號利都樓地下I-1舖

PRICE 價錢: $ 20-40

OPENING HOURS 營業時間: 16:00-00:00

KELLY'S CAPE BOP

As well as its famous kimbop in various flavours, it's well worth waiting for the à la minute egg rolls. You can also find spicy rice cakes, fried seaweed dumplings and other Korean dishes.

供應多款韓式美食,如辣炒年糕和炸紫菜卷等,推介不同口味的紫菜飯卷,即叫即做的煎蛋卷也值得等待。

**C1, GF, Southorn Mansion,
55-61 Johnston Road, Wan Chai**
灣仔莊士敦道55-61號修頓大廈C1舖

PRICE 價錢: $ 70-170

OPENING HOURS 營業時間: 11:00-19:00

KEUNG KEE
強記美食

The glutinous rice with preserved meat is available all year. Chinese sausages can be added on request. Hong Kong-style dishes like fried rice rolls and pork bone congee are also available.

供應臘味糯米飯、煎蝦米腸粉及花生旺菜豬骨粥等港式美食。糯米飯全年有售，更可加配臘腸或膶腸。

382 Lockhart Road, Wan Chai
灣仔駱克道382號

PRICE 價錢: $ 25-50
OPENING HOURS 營業時間: 12:00-00:00
Closed Sunday 週日休息

MAK KEE (NORTH POINT)
麥記美食（北角）

Offers daily made Shanghainese buns and cakes. Scallion pancakes are sold from 3pm until they run out.

每天鮮製的上海包點，其中葱油餅只在下午三時開售，售完即止。

Shop 1, 21 Fort Street, North Point
北角堡壘街21號1號舖

PRICE 價錢: $ 30-50
OPENING HOURS 營業時間: 11:00-22:00
Closed Monday 週一休息

THE BUTCHERS CLUB (WAN CHAI)

Burgers made with Australian grain-fed beef and their duck fat fries are a perfect match. Vegan burger is also available.

供應多款特色漢堡,其中澳洲穀飼牛肉漢堡和鴨油薯條是絕配!另有素食漢堡可供選擇。

GF, 2 Landale Street, Wan Chai
灣仔蘭杜街2號

PRICE 價錢: $ 100-150
OPENING HOURS 營業時間: 12:00-22:30

HOTELS
酒店

FOUR SEASONS
四季

Grand Luxury • Contemporary

奢華•時尚

Four Seasons hotel not only offers some of the most spacious accommodation in Hong Kong but the bedrooms, which have wall-to-wall windows, also feature an impressive array of extras. It also boasts two swimming pools and three world class restaurants. The hotel has been undergoing an extensive renovation of its guest rooms and lobby since late 2020, and will introduce a lobby café, cocktail bar, and transformed lobby in spring 2021.

四季酒店與維港毗鄰，景色壯麗，提供香港最寬敞時尚的客房，且設有大型豪華浴室。水療設施令人印象難忘，更設有兩個溫度不同的泳池。舒適的環境與高質素服務兩者俱備。酒店於2020年下旬為客房及大堂展開大型翻新，並將於2021年春季迎來嶄新的大堂、大堂咖啡室及雞尾酒吧。

HONG KONG ISLAND 香港島

TEL. 3196 8888
www.fourseasons.com/hongkong

8 Finance Street, Central
中環金融街8號

345 Rooms/客房 $ 3,800-7,000
54 Suites/套房 $ 6,500-12,800

Recommended restaurants/推薦餐廳:
Caprice ❀❀❀
Lung King Heen 龍景軒 ❀❀❀
Sushi Saito 鮨‧齋藤 ❀❀

165

TEL. 2522 0111
www.mandarinoriental.com/
hongkong

5 Connaught Road Central, Central
中環干諾道中5號

432 Rooms/客房 $ 4,200-8,000
67 Suites/套房 $ 6,000-20,500

Recommended restaurants/推薦餐廳:
Man Wah 文華廳 ❀
Mandarin Grill + Bar 文華扒房+酒吧 ❀

MANDARIN ORIENTAL
文華東方

Grand Luxury • Classic

奢華 • 經典

One of Hong Kong's most iconic hotels continues to update itself whilst remaining true to its heritage. The last renovation gave the rooms a fresher, more contemporary feel. Suites range from traditional Asian to those that are more eye-catching – like the one dedicated to the late photographer Lord Lichfield. The spa is an oasis of tranquillity and dining options are varied.

開業逾半世紀,這家標誌性的酒店在保留優良傳統之餘,還致力提升其質素。客房感覺新鮮時尚,無論是典雅的大班風格或陽台房間的裝潢均非常精緻。套房主題多元,除了傳統亞洲風格,甚至有以攝影師里奇菲德爵士為靈感的設計。附設的水療設施令你猶如置身樂園;更不乏飽餐一頓的餐飲選擇。

THE ST. REGIS
瑞吉

Grand Luxury • Elegant

奢華 • 典雅

TEL. 2138 6888
www.stregishongkong.com

1 Harbour Drive, Wan Chai
灣仔港灣徑1號

112 Rooms/客房 $ 3,450-8,000
17 Suites/套房 $ 5,100-120,000

Recommended restaurants/推薦餐廳:
L'Envol ❀❀
Rùn 潤 ❀

The lavish interior of this sophisticated hotel – which opened to much fanfare in 2019 – was designed by André Fu who used luxury materials to great effect in creating a stylish East-meets-West motif. The public spaces are impressive and guestrooms spacious. Dining options include a bar and French and Cantonese restaurants. The outdoor pool, the gym and the spa are great for unwinding.

酒店於2019年開幕，風格奢華而不失細緻，是本港著名室內設計師傅厚民的作品。優質的建材、令人過目不忘的公共空間，再加上法式及粵式食府、出色的酒吧和下午茶，令住客能夠放鬆心情，好好享受。運動愛好者也會對這裏的運動俱樂部、室外泳池和水療中心感到滿意。客房極為寬敞，並提供管家服務。

HONG KONG ISLAND 香港島

TEL. 2521 3838
www.conradhongkong.com

Pacific Place, 88 Queensway, Admiralty
金鐘金鐘道88號太古廣場

467 Rooms/客房 $ 2,600-5,300
45 Suites/套房 $ 5,000-8,300

CONRAD
港麗

Luxury • Elegant
豪華 • 典雅

It's been a feature in Admiralty for almost 30 years now and while this hotel still looks modern from the outside, the interior has more of an understated feel. Choose a Harbour or Peak view room – or a corner suite which offers both. The outdoor pool comes complete with cabanas, and dining options include Italian cuisine in Nicholini's and Cantonese in Golden Leaf.

酒店位處集購物娛樂於一身的太古廣場之上，即使坐落金鐘近三十年，外觀仍歷久常新；大堂設計簡樸古典，配上中式花瓶及銅像擺設，優雅而壯麗。寢室設在40至61樓，套房能讓你盡享海景和山景，而且空間寬敞。室外游泳池坐擁香港全景，池畔設有帷幔。酒店設意大利及粵菜餐館。

HONG KONG ISLAND 香港島

ISLAND SHANGRI-LA
港島香格里拉

Grand Luxury • Elegant
奢華 • 典雅

In contrast to its modern exterior, the décor inside is a more classic style, with a little glamour thrown in thanks to an array of chandeliers and gilt-framed pictures. A vast Chinese silk painting of mountains and rivers adorns the vast atrium rising up 16 floors. Choose Harbour or Peak views; those on floors 52-55 have exclusive use of the executive lounge.

摩登的外觀內是樸素典雅的裝潢,金光閃爍的吊燈及掛畫更添韻味。大堂掛上延伸至16樓、世上最大幅的中國山水絲綢畫,筆工細膩、構圖錯綜複雜,散發着攝人魅力。住客可在海景及山景房間中任選其一,海景房空間寬敞,更顯時尚。52至55樓豪華閣樓層的住客可享用專屬會客廳和美不勝收的天台庭園。

TEL. 2877 3838
www.shangri-la.com/island

Pacific Place, Supreme Court Road, Admiralty
金鐘法院道太古廣場

531 Rooms/客房 $ 3,200-6,500
34 Suites/套房 $ 5,400-8,700

Recommended restaurants/推薦餐廳:
Petrus 珀翠 ✤
Summer Palace 夏宮 ✤

169

TEL. 2132 0188
www.mandarinoriental.com/
landmark

15 Queen's Road, Central
中環皇后大道中15號

98 Rooms/客房 $ 4,100-4,700
13 Suites/套房 $ 7,800-11,800

Recommended restaurants/推薦餐廳:
Amber ✿✿
Kappo Rin 割烹凜 ⑩
Sushi Shikon 志魂 ✿✿✿

THE LANDMARK
MANDARIN ORIENTAL
置地文華東方

Luxury • Elegant
豪華 • 典雅

From the personal airport pick-up to the endless spa choices, this is the hotel for those after a little pampering. Not only are the comfortable, smartly designed bedrooms big on luxury and size but they also come with stylish bathrooms attached; these feature either sunken or circular baths. MO is the cool ground floor bar for all-day dining or night time cocktails.

從專人機場接送服務到設備完善的水療中心,置地文華東方讓你盡享尊貴服務。令人讚歎的不光是設計型格獨特、面積達450至600呎的寬敞客房,還有房內豪華時尚的浴室設備,包括巨型下沉式或圓形浴缸。位於地下的MO Bar是解決一日三餐和品嘗雞尾酒的好去處。葡萄酒愛好者將在SOMM流連忘返。

THE MURRAY
美利

Luxury · Design
豪華·型格

Built in 1969, this former government office got a new lease of life when it was re-designed and re-opened as a stylish, luxury hotel. Popinjays is a relaxed rooftop bar and restaurant with stunning views; Tai Pan offers sophisticated Asian-influenced food. Bedrooms radiate style, with Italian marble, leather and wood. Ask for one with views over Hong Kong Park or the western city districts.

前身為政府辦公室，建於1969年，現改建為集奢華時尚於一身的酒店。室內設計由著名建築師包辦，客房採用意大利大理石、皮革及木材等特製傢具，色調樸實卻不失貴氣，建議選擇面向香港公園或西區的房間。餐飲選擇亦別具特色：天台酒吧Popinjays坐擁迷人景緻；Tai Pan則提供帶亞洲風情的菜餚。

TEL. 3141 8888
www.niccolohotels.com/hotels/hongkong/central/the_murray

22 Cotton Tree Drive, Central
中環紅棉道22號

298 Rooms/客房 $ 3,500-6,000
38 Suites/套房 $ 5,600-8,100

Recommended restaurants/推薦餐廳:
Guo Fu Lou 國福樓 ❀

HONG KONG ISLAND 香港島

171

TEL. 2588 1234
www.grandhyatthongkong.com

1 Harbour Road, Wan Chai
灣仔港灣道1號

495 Rooms/客房 $ 3,200-4,800
47 Suites/套房 $ 6,200-7,800

Recommended restaurants/推薦餐廳:
One Harbour Road 港灣壹號 |◯

GRAND HYATT
君悅

Luxury • Contemporary
豪華 • 時尚

Towering above its neighbour, the Convention and Exhibition centre, this hotel was refurbished by an Australian design studio and now comes with a smart and contemporary look. The best rooms are between floors 31-36. The pool is long enough for decent lengths and there's an array of restaurants, including Tiffin which brings the lobby alive day and night.

毗鄰香港會議展覽中心，盡享維港兩岸遼闊景色。富麗堂皇的大堂早於1989年酒店開業時便已落成，由澳洲設計師操刀修葺後更見時尚；31-36樓的客房能讓你有更佳享受，並設豪華雲石浴室。大型室外泳池是盡情舒展的好去處。餐廳選擇良多，其中茶園更可欣賞悠揚的即場音樂演奏。

EAST
東隅

Business • Modern

商務 • 現代

East is a modern business hotel designed for those who, like the hotel staff, can wear a pair of Converse with their suit. It has an uncluttered lobby, a bright, open plan restaurant serving international cuisine, and a great rooftop terrace bar named 'Sugar', as this was once a sugar factory. Bedrooms are minimalist but well-kept; corner rooms are especially light.

標榜為品味商務酒店。整潔的大堂、時尚的酒吧、提供國際美食的餐廳,加上可觀看迷人維港景色的天台酒吧Sugar——名字靈感源自酒店前身的糖廠,絕對切合你的需要。客房佈置簡約優雅,以大量玻璃與木材塑造出溫暖感覺與品味。位處轉角的客房景觀尤佳。

TEL. 3968 3968
www.easthotels.com/hongkong

**29 Taikoo Shing Road,
Tai Koo Shing**
太古城太古城道29號

336 Rooms/客房 $ 2,800-3,800
6 Suites/套房 $ 4,500-6,800

HONG KONG ISLAND 香港島

TEL. 3477 6888
hongkong.lansonplace.com

133 Leighton Road, Causeway Bay
銅鑼灣禮頓道133號

164 Rooms/客房 $ 1,600-2,400
30 Suites/套房 $ 2,800-3,600

LANSON PLACE
逸蘭

Boutique Hotel • Cosy
精品酒店•舒適

Despite being ideally located for the shopping malls and restaurants of Causeway Bay, this hotel with its elegant façade is a calming oasis. Its lounge is the perfect place for an evening cocktail before setting out for dinner. Each of the bedrooms is classically furnished and comes with a kitchenette; choose a Premier room on an upper floor for its space and relative quiet.

位於購物及美食集中地的銅鑼灣，逸蘭擁有歐洲風格的典雅外觀，猶如鬧市中一片寧靜的綠洲。休息室設計優雅，裝潢交織古典與現代風格，晚餐前坐下呷杯雞尾酒更添愜意。客房舒適雅致，且都附設小廚房供簡單煮食之用。想要更寧靜舒適的體驗可選擇較高層的房間。

ONE96

壹96

Boutique Hotel • Central
精品酒店•便捷

With only one suite on each floor and private elevator access, One96 caters to those who value privacy. Each suite is divided into distinct sleeping, living and kitchenette areas, with floor-to-ceiling windows to bring in sweeping city vistas. A complimentary smartphone with unlimited data could come in handy and staying guests have access to a gym in the hotel next door.

位置優越，距離地鐵站僅三分鐘路程，並鄰近餐廳、酒吧林立的蘇豪區。全酒店只有29間套房，各房佔用整個樓層，間格分明分為睡房和大廳，落地玻璃窗令設計毫不侷促。浴室則採用白色雲石，感覺雅致舒適。提供咖啡機及手提電話，住客可以免費享用本地數據並致電多個國家，亦可以到集團其餘三家酒店享用健身設備。

TEL. 3519 6196
www.one96.com

196 Queen's Road Central,
Sheung Wan
上環皇后大道中196號

29 Suites/套房 $ 2,050-4,000

TEL. 2918 1838
www.upperhouse.com

Pacific Place, 88 Queensway, Admiralty
金鐘金鐘道88號太古廣場

96 Rooms/客房 $ 3,900-7,000
21 Suites/套房 $ 18,000-30,000

THE UPPER HOUSE
奕居

Luxury • Minimalist
豪華・簡約

This hotel has one clear focus: the wellbeing of its guests. There are subtle Japanese influences to its decoration thanks to designer André Fu, who also sourced the various pieces of art and sculpture seen in the rooms and around the hotel. The garden, whilst small, is still a great feature in the heart of the city; try one of the weekend yoga sessions held there.

奕居由建築師傅厚民精心設計，在客房及酒店四周都放置了不少藝術品，格調時尚且隱隱透出和式風格。酒店希望營造私人居所感覺，住客入住時會給直接帶到房間，由服務員送上飲品，並以平板電腦作簡單登記。六樓的小花園陽台是洗滌繁囂的好去處；住客更可參與逢週末舉行的瑜伽活動。

INDIGO
英迪格

Business • Design
商務 • 型格

Bordering Tai Yuen Street and its market, so ideally placed for discovering old Hong Kong, Indigo is also a good choice for those who've come to shop – there's even a shopping bag placed in every room! For others, there's always the rooftop bar and infinity pool. The bedrooms come with floor-to-ceiling windows and boast some cute design touches.

這幢外觀獨特的建築物坐落於灣仔商業區及住宅區交界，不光擁有完善的交通網絡，更毗鄰地區色彩濃厚的市集，讓你深入了解本區生活脈搏。全部房間設有落地玻璃窗，傢具擺設均經過精心設計，設施亦十分齊全，文具、購物袋一應俱全。天台玻璃底泳池，前臨山巒，感覺開揚，是放鬆身心的好地方。

TEL. 3926 3888
www.hotelindigo.com/hongkong
246 Queen's Road East, Wan Chai
灣仔皇后大道東246號

132 Rooms/客房 $ 1,650-2,650
6 Suites/套房 $ 4,000-5,500

🏠

MIRA MOON

問月

Boutique Hotel • Design

精品酒店 • 型格

Only 5 minutes' walk from Causeway Bay or Wan Chai Ferry Pier is this conveniently located hotel. It sports a modern take on the fable of the Moon Festival, alongside stylised Chinese details. Rooms furnished in a white and rich wood palette are dotted with bright red and mod cons include a tablet and a Bluetooth sound system. Those with a bigger budget should splurge on the Moonshine Suite.

地理位置優越，距離銅鑼灣鬧市或灣仔碼頭只有數分鐘路程，方便乘坐小輪前往對岸或欣賞維港景致。酒店名字和設計概念源自民間故事嫦娥奔月，傢具、裝飾等都巧妙地以現代手法演繹中國傳統文化。所有房間各有不同主題，但都配備小型平板電腦和藍牙音樂系統。餐廳亦設有香檳吧，讓住客於忙碌的一天後淺酌放鬆。

♿ 🚭 📶 **P**

TEL. 2643 8888

www.miramoonhotel.com

388 Jaffe Road, Causeway Bay

銅鑼灣謝斐道388號

90 Rooms/客房 $1,500-2,800
1 Suite/套房 $4,800-8,800

THE POTTINGER
中環・石板街

Boutique Hotel · Contemporary
精品酒店・時尚

Standing in the middle of Central, and on one of Hong Kong's oldest 'stone slab streets', is this elegant and stylish hotel. Its location is celebrated through its collection of iconic and historic photographs taken by award-winning artist Fan Ho. The 68 bedrooms are contemporary and graceful and boast all the amenities the modern traveller expects.

位於有過百年歷史的砵甸乍街（又名石板街）旁邊，故以此命名。斜斜的石板路見證了中環百多年來的故事，也為酒店增添了一分魅力。接待廳雖小卻流露着歐陸優雅格調，共有68間客房，面積適中、設備齊全。位處中環心臟地帶，無論往辦公、飲食、娛樂或乘搭交通工具都非常便利，是商務住宿的理想選擇。

TEL. 2308 3188
www.thepottinger.com

21 Stanley Street, Central
中環士丹利街21號

61 Rooms/客房 $ 1,950-6,800
7 Suites/套房 $ 4,350-10,000
Recommended restaurants/推薦餐廳:
Ta Vie 旅 ✿✿

HONG KONG ISLAND 香港島

179

99 BONHAM
99號寶恒

Boutique Hotel • Design
精品酒店•型格

TEL. 3940 1111
www.99bonham.com

99 Bonham Strand, Sheung Wan
上環文咸東街99號

84 Suites/套房 $ 1,500-3,450

Rooms at this conveniently located hotel don't feel claustrophobic in the least, thanks to full-length windows that drench the space in natural light and let in the electric nightscape. The rooms also boast all the mod-cons that business travellers would appreciate and some of them even include a kitchenette. On top of regular laundry service, a self-service option is also offered.

坐落於繁華鬧市,不僅鄰近港鐵站,附近亦有大量酒吧和餐廳,十分便利。室內環境相當講究,設計師採用多面落地玻璃,令房間充滿自然光,大大提升空間感,晚上更可欣賞城市璀璨景色。另外,酒店提供完善配套,除了一般的洗衣服務,也備有自助洗衣設施,部分房間更設置煮食爐具,方便商務旅客。

OVOLO CENTRAL

Boutique Hotel • Art Déco

精品酒店•藝術

Perched between Lan Kwai Fong and SoHo, this boutique hotel appeals to both nightlife lovers and business travellers alike. Each room is uniquely decorated and you'll also find a bar and a vegetarian restaurant in the building. With a free minibar, coffee machine, DVD player, a 24-hour gym, and even video game consoles upon request, every guest can find their perfect way to unwind.

這所充滿藝術元素的精品酒店，位於蘭桂坊和蘇豪區交界，適合喜愛夜生活的旅客。除了酒吧、素食餐廳、24小時開放的健身室和自助洗衣房，酒店更提供遊戲機借用服務、DVD機、免費迷你吧、咖啡機，部分房間甚至有製作雞尾酒的用具，即使足不出戶也充滿樂趣。經官網訂房會獲贈早餐，為一天做好準備。

TEL. 3755 3000
www.ovolohotels.com

2 Arbuthnot Road, Central
中環亞畢諾道2號

40 Rooms/客房 $ 2,500-5,000
1 Suite/套房 $ 5,000-10,000

HONG KONG ISLAND 香港島

TEL. 3460 8100
www.ovolohotels.com

**64 Wong Chuk Hang Road,
Wong Chuk Hang**
黃竹坑黃竹坑道64號

160 Rooms/客房 $ 1,500-3,000
2 Suites/套房 $ 3,000-6,000

OVOLO SOUTHSIDE Ⓝ
南岸奧華

Boutique Hotel • Industrial
精品酒店・工業風

Minutes away from Ocean Park by MTR, this warehouse-turned hotel melds industrial chic and modern aesthetics. There are many room types to choose from, but the two Rockstar suites stand out with their fun-filled décor, generous space and private bar. Unwind in the rooftop bar or book a table in the Mexican restaurant. The gym and laundry room are open 24-7.

酒店由倉庫改建而成,結合了工業風和時尚設計元素,簡潔舒適。特別設有兩間特色套房,空間寬敞而且附私人酒吧。此外,露天酒吧餐廳景觀開揚,墨西哥餐廳則提供各式美食和雞尾酒,不妨一試。由於毗鄰主題公園和港鐵站,並備有活動場地、廿四小時開放的健身房和自助洗衣房,同時適合商務和觀光旅客。

THE FLEMING Ⓝ
芬名

Boutique Hotel • Vintage
精品酒店•復古

Besides the unmistakable retro chic a la yesteryear Hong Kong, the subtle smell of sandalwood and amber in public spaces also leaves a lasting impression, echoing with Chinese herbs. Rooms are categorised according to sizes, which vary from small to extra-large, some with his and her sinks or trundle beds. The restaurant on the ground floor serves coastal Italian food.

酒店全面翻新後，雅緻中帶有濃厚的老香江情懷。房間分為四種大小，可以按需要，選擇配有雙人盥洗台或子母床的房型，並享用漢方研製的沐浴用品。除了酒店內的意大利餐廳，附近亦有不少著名食店、酒吧。可步行前往灣仔碼頭、地鐵站和電車站，交通便利。加上鄰近香港會議展覽中心，特別適合商務旅客。

TEL. 3607 2288
www.thefleming.com
41 Fleming Road, Wan Chai
灣仔菲林明道41號

66 Rooms/客房 $ 1,588

HONG KONG ISLAND 香港島

THE JERVOIS
哲維斯

Boutique Hotel • Central
精品酒店 • 便捷

TEL. 3994 9000
www.thejervois.com

89 Jervois Street, Sheung Wan
上環蘇杭街89號

49 Suites/套房 $ 1,900-3,900

Design aesthetics here emphasise minimalism and serenity – dark wood, leather, rich upholstery and white marble render the space lavish but understated. Suites are bright and airy, with the two-bedroom penthouse units commanding panoramic harbour views. All suites come with an induction cooktop and cooking utensils available upon request. Macau Ferry Pier is 10 minutes away.

鄰近港鐵站及上環港澳碼頭,方便市內觀光和同時前往澳門的旅客。採用全套房式設計,提供一個或兩個睡房的選項,其中,兩臥室套房可欣賞維多利亞港的美景。以優質木材、皮革和豪華大理石作裝飾,簡約舒適但又不失時尚。每間房均配備電磁爐,也可以向職員索取煮食用具。另外設有健身室和自助洗衣房。

LAN KWAI FONG
蘭桂坊

Boutique Hotel • Contemporary
精品酒店•時尚

A hotel which feels part of the local area and mixes Chinese and contemporary furniture, neutral tones and dark wood veneers to create a relaxing environment. Try to secure one of the deluxe corner bedrooms or a suite with a balcony if you want more space; those higher than the 21st floor have the harbour views. Celebrity Cuisine offers accomplished Cantonese food.

融合了中國傳統與現代品味的傢具，中性色調及深色木間隔，環境舒適。如果你需要更寬敞的空間，建議預訂轉角位置的豪華客房或附設露台的套房。21樓以上的房間可飽覽維港景色。客人可借用房間內的流動電話，方便於外與朋友聯絡。

TEL. 3650 0000
www.lankwaifonghotel.com.hk

3 Kau U Fong, Central
中環九如坊3號

157 Rooms/客房 $ 1,080-3,080
5 Suites/套房 $ 2,280-6,800

Recommended restaurants/推薦餐廳:
Celebrity Cuisine 名人坊 ✿

♿

TEL. 3423 3286
www.ovolohotels.com

**286 Queen's Road Central,
Sheung Wan**
上環皇后大道中286號

50 Rooms/客房 $ 700-1,100
6 Suites/套房 $ 2,500-4,500

🏠

THE SHEUNG WAN

Inn • Functional
旅館・實用

Perfect for culture-vultures, backpackers and business travellers, this utilitarian hotel is just a stone's throw away from a MTR, a historical temple and PMQ, an art and design hub. Rooms are simply furnished to give serenity amid the bustling city, while luxury bedding ensures a good night's sleep. Its Mexican restaurant comes with a tequila bar, great for after-dinner drinks.

位於上環市中心，距離港鐵站和電車站僅需數分鐘路程。同時毗鄰文武廟和元創方，不僅可以了解本土歷史，亦可體驗文創氣息、購買特色紀念品，對商務和觀光旅客都是不錯的選擇。房間採用簡約設計及名貴床上用品，讓客人在舒適的環境下，一洗整天的疲勞。酒吧提供各類雞尾酒，是淺酌放鬆的好地方。

Redphotographer/iStock

Westend 61/hemis.fr

KOWLOON
九龍

KOWLOON 九龍

RESTAURANTS
餐廳

✿✿✿

T'ANG COURT
唐閣

Cantonese • Traditional

粵菜 • 傳統

It's easy to see why this restaurant remains so popular and celebrated its 30th birthday in 2019. Comfort and luxury are factors, thanks to the plush fabrics, beautifully dressed tables and Chinese art. But it is the ability and experience of the head chef and his kitchen that plays the greatest part. Their classic and accomplished Cantonese cuisine includes dishes like Peking duck, lobster with onions and shallot, and baked stuffed crab shell with onion.

這家常客眾多的食府開業逾三十年，其超凡水準不言而喻。高雅的布藝裝飾、一絲不苟的餐桌佈置和一系列藝術品均引人入勝，然而最教人叫好的要數其由經驗豐富廚房團隊所呈獻的傳統粵式珍饈佳餚。北京片皮鴨、三葱爆龍蝦和釀焗鮮蟹蓋等，巧奪天工的擺盤、無可挑剔的精細處理，叫人再三回味。

☎ TEL. 2132 7898

1-2F, The Langham Hotel,
8 Peking Road, Tsim Sha Tsui

尖沙咀北京道8號朗廷酒店1-2樓

www.langhamhotels.com/hongkong

KOWLOON 九龍

■ **PRICE 價錢**

Lunch 午膳
Set Menu 套餐 $ 400-550
À la carte 點菜 $ 400-1,700
Dinner 晚膳
Set Menu 套餐 $ 1,280-1,680
À la carte 點菜 $ 400-1,700

■ **OPENING HOURS 營業時間**

Lunch 午膳 12:00-14:30
Dinner 晚膳 18:00-22:30

◎♨ & ⇄ **P**

TEL. 2152 1417

**Shop 401, L4, FoodLoft,
Mira Place One, 132 Nathan Road,
Tsim Sha Tsui**

尖沙咀彌敦道132號
美麗華廣場一期食四方4樓401號舖
www.suntunglok.com.hk

■ **PRICE** 價錢
Lunch 午膳
Set Menu 套餐 $ 298-438
À la carte 點菜 $ 300-500
Dinner 晚膳
À la carte 點菜 $ 800-1,200

■ **OPENING HOURS** 營業時間
Lunch 午膳 11:30-15:00
Dinner 晚膳 18:00-21:45

SUN TUNG LOK
新同樂

Cantonese • Elegant
粵菜 • 典雅

Synonymous with top-quality Cantonese cooking, Sun Tung Lok spares no effort in ensuring every item on the menu, from dim sum and barbecue meats to gourmet dried seafood, is as good as it could be. Must-tries include the abalone, braised beef ribs in house gravy, stuffed crab shell, and roast suckling pig. Certain à la carte items are available in smaller portions, while the lone diner can order set menus for one.

素以高品質見稱的新同樂，無論是點心、燒味還是海味，皆處理得盡善盡美。當中不乏選用本地新鮮雞隻的佳餚，用於烹調的雞湯更是每日新鮮熬煮。推薦菜式包括燒汁乾焗牛肋骨、鮮蘑菇焗釀蟹蓋、燒乳豬件及鮑魚。點心每隔三個月更換款式。為了方便不同人數的食客，部分單點項目可調整分量，也提供個人套餐。

TIN LUNG HEEN
天龍軒

Cantonese • Luxury

粵菜 • 豪華

Aptly named 'sky dragon pavilion' in Chinese, this grand restaurant perched on the 102nd floor of a skyscraper is furnished generously in red wood veneer. The vast windows flood the room with natural light and make it a good spot to see the sunset or the city's nightscape. Among the signature dishes are honey-glazed Iberian pork char siu (pre-ordering needed), and double-boiled chicken soup with fish maw in coconut. Private rooms are also charming.

高踞全港最高大樓的102樓，這間粵菜餐館以天龍為名，不論位置與佈局都極具氣派。裝潢以紅木為主，樓高兩層的落地玻璃窗不但令餐廳光線充沛，更把維港的醉人景色盡收眼底；殷勤的服務人員讓你倍感親切。菜單着重傳統菜式，值得一試的有原個椰皇花膠燉雞，以及需提前預訂的蜜燒西班牙黑豚肉叉燒。

TEL. 2263 2270

102F, The Ritz-Carlton, International Commerce Centre, 1 Austin Road West, Tsim Sha Tsui

尖沙咀柯士甸道西1號環球貿易廣場麗思卡爾頓酒店102樓

www.ritzcarlton.com/hongkong

■ **PRICE** 價錢
Lunch 午膳
Set Menu 套餐 $ 568-1,788
À la carte 點菜 $ 500-1,800
Dinner 晚膳
Set Menu 套餐 $ 988-1,788
À la carte 點菜 $ 500-1,800

■ **OPENING HOURS** 營業時間
Lunch 午膳 12:00-14:30
Dinner 晚膳 18:00-22:30

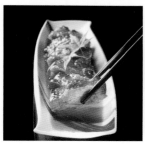

KOWLOON 九龍

AH YAT HARBOUR VIEW
阿一海景飯店

Cantonese • Classic Décor

粵菜 • 經典

⊙¶ 🚻 ⋖ ⇔ 🎁 **P**

TEL. 2328 0983

29F, iSquare, 63 Nathan Road, Tsim Sha Tsui

尖沙咀彌敦道63號iSquare29樓

■ **PRICE** 價錢
Lunch 午膳
Set Menu 套餐 $ 300-500
À la carte 點菜 $ 400-2,200
Dinner 晚膳
Set Menu 套餐 $ 800-1,500
À la carte 點菜 $ 400-2,200

■ **OPENING HOURS** 營業時間
Lunch 午膳 11:30-14:30
Dinner 晚膳 18:00-22:00

There are two components to the name of this much-loved establishment: 'Ah Yat' the owner-chef famous for his flavourful braised abalones, and 'harbour view' which is another key draw. Order the prized molluscs with other Cantonese favourites such as goose web or sea cucumber. Try also his signature fried rice served in a claypot, and crispy chicken. The wine list features selections from Bordeaux, Australia and New Zealand.

置身於商場高層的阿一海景，不但可飽覽窗外的醉人維港美景，更可一嘗一系列經典粵菜，包括馳名脆皮雞、招牌砂鍋炒飯，還有老闆楊貫一的名菜──阿一鮑魚，客人更可配搭鵝掌、海參等一同享用。其酒單亦選擇良多，除了法國波爾多的佳釀，亦包羅澳洲及新西蘭等地酒莊的出品。餐廳設有四間私人廂房，照顧重視私隱的客人。

ÉPURE

French Contemporary • Intimate

時尚法國菜 • 親密

Have a drink on the terrace of this professionally run Harbour City restaurant before enjoying French dishes that are classically based in their makeup but enhanced by clever modern touches. You can expect perfectly matched combinations of flavours of textures – and don't miss their Paris mushroom soup! The two tasting menus are paired with carefully considered wine choices. There's also a café which is a great spot for afternoon tea.

由法國廚師及侍酒師帶領，菜式毋庸置疑是正宗法國口味，午、晚市分別設有不同的精選套餐，菜式選材經典，卻是以現代手法演繹，味道配搭恰到好處，更佐以經過精心配搭的餐酒。其中，巴黎白蘑菇湯不容錯過。位處購物熱點，逛累了不妨到附設的咖啡廳享用下午茶。

TEL. 3185 8338

Shop 403, 4F, Ocean Centre,
Harbour City, 3-27 Canton Road,
Tsim Sha Tsui

尖沙咀廣東道3-27號
海港城海洋中心4樓403號鋪

www.epure.hk

■ **PRICE** 價錢
Lunch 午膳
Set Menu 套餐 $ 498-568
Dinner 晚膳
Set Menu 套餐 $ 1,488-1,888

■ **OPENING HOURS** 營業時間
Lunch 午膳 12:00-14:30
Dinner 晚膳 18:30-21:30

■ **ANNUAL AND WEEKLY CLOSING**
休息日期
Closed first day of Lunar New Year
年初一休息

KOWLOON 九龍

⊘⑪ ⇦ 🅿

TEL. 2736 2228

**Shop 402, 4F, FoodLoft,
Mira Place One, 132 Nathan Road,
Tsim Sha Tsui**

尖沙咀彌敦道132號
美麗華廣場一期食四方4樓402號舖
www.fuho.com.hk

■ **PRICE** 價錢
Lunch 午膳
À la carte 點菜 $ 300-1,500
Dinner 晚膳
À la carte 點菜 $ 600-1,500

■ **OPENING HOURS** 營業時間
Lunch 午膳 11:00-15:00
Dinner 晚膳 18:00-22:00

FU HO
富豪

Cantonese • Classic Décor

粵菜 • 經典

Thanks to his considerable experience, the head chef has been enticing diners back here for over a decade with his skilfully executed dishes, such as pan-fried Longgang chicken with ginger and scallion, and fried Chinese kale with dried plaice. Named after the owner, the signature Ah Yung abalone is slow-braised in a secret sauce for up to 20 hours. The dining room now has a contemporary, elegant and relaxing feel.

位於商場內不甚起眼的位置，這家酒家十多年來依然屹立不倒，足證正宗而不花巧的粵菜自有引人入勝之處。掌勺二十多年的廚師一直堅持用心烹煮傳統菜式，招牌菜阿翁鮑魚採用自家調製的鮑汁燜煮近二十小時，製作需時且考功夫；以龍崗雞製作的薑蔥煎鹽香雞和方魚炒芥蘭亦值得一試。

GADDI'S
吉地士

French • Classic Décor

法國菜 • 經典

This grand restaurant opened in 1953 and now occupies what was once The Peninsula's ballroom – it even has its own dedicated entrance on Nathan Road. The well-versed team looks after the guests so well here you may find yourself loathed to leave. Top quality European and Japanese produce are well prepared in a modern French style. Classics such as dover sole meunière are not to be missed. For those wanting something a little different book the Chef's Table in the kitchen.

穿過專用入口到達這家於1953年開業的傳奇食店。這裏原是酒店宴會廳,原來的典雅格調依舊保存,餐室內盡是酒店的珍藏品。主廚把來自歐洲及日本的優質食材以現代法式手法烹調,經典菜式如香草牛油煮法國龍脷魚不容錯過。想要一趟與眾不同的體驗,可預訂位於廚房內的「廚師之桌」,在用餐同時欣賞大廚風采。

TEL. 2696 6763

**1F, The Peninsula Hotel,
Salisbury Road, Tsim Sha Tsui**

尖沙咀梳士巴利道半島酒店1樓

www.peninsula.com/hongkong

■ **PRICE** 價錢
Lunch 午膳
Set Menu 套餐 $ 508-708
À la carte 點菜 $ 1,400-1,700
Dinner 晚膳
Set Menu 套餐 $ 2,088
À la carte 點菜 $ 1,400-1,700

■ **OPENING HOURS** 營業時間
Lunch 午膳 12:00-14:30
Dinner 晚膳 19:00-22:30

KOWLOON 九龍

IMPERIAL TREASURE FINE CHINESE CUISINE (TSIM SHA TSUI)
御寶軒 (尖沙咀)

Cantonese • Contemporary Décor
粵菜 • 時尚

Finding success in Singapore and Shanghai, Imperial Treasure opened its first Hong Kong branch in this sky-scrapping landmark, with panoramic views of the harbour. The stylish dining room is embellished with subtle Chinese touches, such as the ceramic Koi carps and calligraphy. A fish tank in the kitchen ensures live seafood is available every day. Poached garoupa in fish soup with crispy rice and stir fried crab in pepper are worth a try.

御寶軒在香港的首家分店選址在九龍半島地標北京道一號，坐擁無敵維港兩岸景色，加上時尚中帶點中國風的設計——水泥牆上的立體陶瓷鯉魚和樑柱上的書法——令人悠然神往！廚房內附設魚缸，每天都有鮮活的海鮮供應。脆米海鮮浸東星、糯米釀脆皮乳豬及胡椒炒蟹是招牌菜。

TEL. 2613 9800

10F, One Peking, 1 Peking Road, Tsim Sha Tsui
尖沙咀北京道1號10樓
www.imperialtreasure.com

■ **PRICE** 價錢
Lunch 午膳
À la carte 點菜 $ 200-400
Dinner 晚膳
À la carte 點菜 $ 500-1,000

■ **OPENING HOURS** 營業時間
Lunch 午膳 11:30-14:30
Dinner 晚膳 18:00-22:30

LEI GARDEN (KWUN TONG)
利苑酒家（觀塘）

Cantonese • Family

粵菜 • 溫馨

Conveniently located in a shopping mall, this branch of the famous chain is perfect for hungry shoppers after a spree and is always jam-packed with regulars during lunch. It essentially serves the same classic Cantonese menu as other branches – dim sum and stir-fries never disappoint. Live seafood such as Alaskan king crab and giant lobster can sometimes be ordered in smaller portions. Check out the daily-changing specials.

這家利苑位於連接鐵路的大型商場內，位置非常便利。簡潔的屏風將餐廳分隔成不同區域。一如其他分店，食客同樣可在這裏找到傳統的粵式美饌，諸如點心和各式小炒。餐廳設有每天不同的特色菜單，選用大型生猛海鮮分拆饗客，適合與三兩知己共享。中午時段經常擠滿集團忠實顧客，故最好先行訂座。

TEL. 2365 3238

L5-8, 5F, apm, Millennium City 5, 418 Kwun Tong Road, Kwun Tong
觀塘觀塘道418號創紀之城第5期 apm 5樓L5-8
www.leigarden.com.hk

■ **PRICE** 價錢
Lunch 午膳
À la carte 點菜 $ 150-500
Dinner 晚膳
À la carte 點菜 $ 250-800

■ **OPENING HOURS** 營業時間
Lunch 午膳 11:30-15:00
Dinner 晚膳 18:00-21:30

■ **ANNUAL AND WEEKLY CLOSING**
休息日期
Closed 3 days Lunar New Year
農曆新年休息3天

KOWLOON 九龍

∞ ⊙ ⅃ ⏥ ⑃ **P**

TEL. 3552 3028

**6F, Cordis Hotel,
555 Shanghai Street, Mong Kok**

旺角上海街555號康得思酒店6樓

www.cordishotels.com/en/hong-
kong

■ **PRICE** 價錢
Lunch 午膳
Set Menu 套餐 $ 468-538
À la carte 點菜 $ 350-1,400
Dinner 晚膳
Set Menu 套餐 $ 988-1,188
À la carte 點菜 $ 350-1,400

■ **OPENING HOURS** 營業時間
Lunch 午膳 11:00-14:30
Dinner 晚膳 18:00-22:00

MING COURT (MONG KOK)
明閣 (旺角)

Cantonese • Elegant
粵菜 • 典雅

Diners are greeted at the door by the dazzling collection in the glass wine cellar. Chef Li has over 20 years of experience, having worked at Ming Court since it opened its doors. Quality ingredients are shipped from all over the world to make remarkable dishes such as drunken sea prawns with Shaoxing wine, roasted crispy chicken, and shrimp dumplings made with blue angel prawns. It's busy any time of the day, so it's wise to book ahead.

餐室裝潢典雅,以青銅器作擺設,但最引人注目還是門外的玻璃酒窖,其庫存豐富毋庸置疑。嗜酒之人可請服務員協助挑選佳釀,配合菜餚佐吃。具二十多年入廚經驗的主廚由開業效力至今,其招牌菜太白醉翁蝦及明閣炸子雞不容錯過。點心選用由世界各地進口的食材,例如以藍天使蝦製作的蝦餃,叫人耳目一新。

SHANG PALACE
香宮

Cantonese • Luxury

粵菜 • 豪華

Chandeliers and Sung-style paintings create an impressive backdrop for some sophisticated cooking that has changed little over the years. Signature dishes include steamed garoupa with egg white sauce and sautéed giant green crab with peppercorns in clay pot. This elegant restaurant in the Kowloon Shangri-La has been a reliable favourite for classic Cantonese cooking for over 35 years.

位處九龍香格里拉酒店、開業逾三十五年的香宮，一直是老饕心目中享用傳統粵菜的可靠選擇。用餐區裝潢華麗古雅，水晶吊燈與宋代風格油畫多年來一直點綴餐室，用餐環境更添韻味。食物維持一定水準，招牌菜有錦繡星斑件及胡椒焗大肉蟹。

TEL. 2733 8754

Lower Level 1, Kowloon Shangri-La Hotel, 64 Mody Road, Tsim Sha Tsui

尖東麼地道64號
九龍香格里拉酒店地庫1樓
www.shangri-la.com/kowloon

■ **PRICE** 價錢
Lunch 午膳
À la carte 點菜 $ 400-1,000
Dinner 晚膳
Set Menu 套餐 $ 1,388
À la carte 點菜 $ 400-1,000

■ **OPENING HOURS** 營業時間
Lunch 午膳 12:00-14:00
Dinner 晚膳 18:30-22:00

KOWLOON 九龍

SPRING MOON
嘉麟樓

Cantonese • Vintage

粵菜 • 復古

🕸 ◎⧉ ⛱ 👜 📗 **P**

TEL. 2696 6760

**1F, The Peninsula Hotel,
Salisbury Road, Tsim Sha Tsui**

尖沙咀梳士巴利道半島酒店1樓

www.peninsula.com/hongkong

■ **PRICE** 價錢
Lunch 午膳
Set Menu 套餐 $ 598-800
À la carte 點菜 $ 400-800
Dinner 晚膳
Set Menu 套餐 $ 2,188
À la carte 點菜 $ 800-1,200

■ **OPENING HOURS** 營業時間
Lunch 午膳 11:30-14:30
Dinner 晚膳 18:00-22:00

The room, spread over two levels, evokes old-Shanghai circa 1920s – stained glass windows, teak floors and rugs all speak of the golden era. On the menu, however, classics are showcased side by side with novel creations such as scrambled egg white with lobster and crabmeat, and dishes garnished with edible flowers that taste of spring. Dim sum lunch is also recommended, to be enjoyed with your choice of tea from 30 varieties.

古典風格的柚木地板，配襯東方地氈和彩色玻璃，以至一道道遵照傳統烹調而成的廣東菜，反映這家餐廳對傳統的重視。但另一方面，主廚亦為經典美食注入新思維，如加入蟹肉、蛋白同炒的乳香龍蝦球，或是以花入饌的時令菜式。午市供應的點心不容錯過。茗茶選項近三十種，更展出古董茶壺收藏品。

THE ARAKI N

Sushi • Classic Décor

壽司 • 經典

Helmed by Mitsuhiro Araki himself, The Araki is the second overseas venture of this highly acclaimed chef, following his five years in London. The minimalistic dining room in a heritage building boasts a 200-year-old cypress counter with just 12 seats. There is only one 20-course omakase menu, with fish mostly flown in from Japan. But the chef's considerable skills in melding local culinary culture and sushi tradition are evident in creative courses using bird's nest and fish maw.

倫敦壽司名店的姊妹店，並由大廚荒木水都弘監督。舊水警總部的悠久歷史，加上以二百年柏樹製成的吧檯，構成沉靜而優雅的氛圍。除了大量來自日本的海產，大廚更善用燕窩、花膠、本地海鮮等材料，配合以赤醋混和的壽司飯，帶來令人驚喜的二十道菜廚師發辦套餐。團隊甚至會手把手教授享用壽司的方法。

TEL. 3988 0168

GF, Stable Block, FWD House 1881,
2A Canton Road, Tsim Sha Tsui

尖沙咀廣東道2A號
富衛1881公館前馬廄地下

www.house1881.com

■ **PRICE** 價錢
Dinner 晚膳
Set Menu 套餐 $ 4,000

■ **OPENING HOURS** 營業時間
Dinner 晚膳 18:00-20:30

■ **ANNUAL AND WEEKLY CLOSING**
休息日期
Closed Monday 週一休息

KOWLOON 九龍

🛵 🍴 🖘

TEL. 2788 1226

9-11 Fuk Wing Street, Sham Shui Po
深水埗福榮街9-11號

■ **PRICE** 價錢
À la carte 點菜 $ 50-100

■ **OPENING HOURS** 營業時間
10:00-21:30

■ **ANNUAL AND WEEKLY CLOSING**
休息日期
Closed 3 days Lunar New Year
農曆新年休息3天

TIM HO WAN (SHAM SHUI PO)
添好運 (深水埗)

Dim Sum • Simple
點心 • 簡樸

The second branch of this famous dim sum chain is roomier than the original, but don't be surprised to still find a queue of expectant diners at the entrance. Over 20 different dim sum are on offer, all skilfully made and reasonably priced. Some items rotate every two to three months to keep the menu fresh. Don't miss their shrimp dumplings, baked buns with barbecue pork filling and steamed beef balls. Two rooms on the first floor offer more privacy.

一如添好運其他分店，這家店子的二十多款精美點心全由廚師巧手製作，且價錢相宜，加上選址於人口稠密的住宅區內，受食客歡迎乃屬意料之中。由於不設訂座，要有排隊輪候和拼桌的準備。不可不試的點心包括蝦餃、酥皮焗叉燒包和陳皮牛肉球。店家每隔兩至三個月會轉換部分點心款式。一樓設兩間小型貴賓房。

TOSCA DI ANGELO

Italian • Elegant

意大利菜 • 典雅

The Sicilian chef champions dishes that may look deceptively unfussy on the plate but their obvious refinement and sophistication makes them especially delicious. His spaghetti Mancini is a must-try, while his modern take on rum babà is quite something. The wine list sees mostly Italian labels with a top-notch by-the-glass selection. This airy dining room on the 102nd floor with its high ceiling and open kitchen provides diners with commanding views.

遼闊的天花、店中央的開放式廚房、巨型穆拉諾吊燈、以及置身102樓的迷人海景，令餐廳閃耀華麗光芒。行政主廚來自意大利西西里，菜單上的菜式簡潔但充滿風味，盡顯意式烹飪傳統的韻味。必試菜式包括藍龍蝦沙律、西西里扭紋粉等，加上美酒和服務員營造的悠閒氣氛，令客人加倍享受。

TEL. 2263 2270

102F, The Ritz-Carlton, International Commerce Centre, 1 Austin Road West, Tsim Sha Tsui

尖沙咀柯士甸道西1號
環球貿易廣場麗思卡爾頓酒店102樓

www.ritzcarlton.com/hongkong

■ **PRICE** 價錢
Lunch 午膳
Set Menu 套餐 $ 448-698
Dinner 晚膳
Set Menu 套餐 $ 1,288-1,680
À la carte 點菜 $ 900-1,200

■ **OPENING HOURS** 營業時間
Lunch 午膳 12:00-14:30
Dinner 晚膳 18:30-21:30

KOWLOON 九龍

YAN TOH HEEN
欣圖軒

Cantonese • Luxury

粵菜 • 豪華

🍴 ⓘ & ⩣ ⎕ 🅿

TEL. 2313 2243

(accessible via K11 Musea, ground floor), 18 Salisbury Road, Tsim Sha Tsui

尖沙咀梳士巴利道18號
（可經K11 Musea商場進入）

hongkong-ic.intercontinental.com

■ **PRICE** 價錢
Lunch 午膳
Set Menu 套餐 $ 488-888
À la carte 點菜 $ 400-2,000
Dinner 晚膳
Set Menu 套餐 $ 1,688-2,688
À la carte 點菜 $ 400-2,000

■ **OPENING HOURS** 營業時間
Lunch 午膳 12:00-14:30
Dinner 晚膳 18:00-22:00

The location may be somewhat concealed but it's well worth seeking out this elegant Cantonese restaurant and that's not just because of the lovely views of Hong Kong Island. The authentic, carefully prepared specialities include stuffed crab shell with crabmeat; Wagyu beef with green peppers, mushrooms and garlic; double-boiled fish maw and sea whelk; and wok-fried lobster with crab roe and milk. It is now accessible via K11 Musea.

食客現可透過毗鄰的K11 Musea商場進入這家優雅的粵菜餐廳。室內裝潢設計仍保留了原有的玉石主題，精緻華美，遠眺窗外更能細賞維港及香港島的美景。廚師團隊經驗豐富，繼續帶來傳統粵式佳餚，精心之作包括脆釀鮮蟹蓋、蒜片青尖椒爆和牛、花膠響螺燉湯及龍皇炒鮮奶等。

KOWLOON 九龍

YAT TUNG HEEN
逸東軒

Cantonese • Design

粵菜 • 型格

The dining room boasts dark wood panels and moody lighting, which is refreshingly different from its formerly conventional décor. Since 1990, the kitchen team has been creating traditional but refined Cantonese fare that highlights the ingredients' natural tastes. Dim sum, barbecued meats, stir-fries and slow-cooked soups are hugely popular. Regulars also order the abalone and bird's nest set menu for their banquet dinners in the private rooms.

裝潢設計簡約，深色木材配上富情調的燈光，異於傳統中菜廳格調。反展現年輕型格。自1990年開業至今，廚師團隊一直為食客烹調傳統而精緻的粵菜，沒花巧噱頭卻以扎實的烹調功夫盡顯四時食材真鮮味。點心、燒味、小菜和老火湯均深得食客歡迎，不少人更愛於廂房以鮑魚燕窩套餐設宴款客。

TEL. 2710 1093

B2F, Eaton Hotel, 380 Nathan Road, Jordan

佐敦彌敦道380號逸東酒店地庫2樓

www.yattungheen.com

■ PRICE 價錢
Lunch 午膳
À la carte 點菜 $ 400-1,200
Dinner 晚膳
À la carte 點菜 $ 400-1,200

■ OPENING HOURS 營業時間
Lunch 午膳 11:00-14:30
Dinner 晚膳 18:00-22:30

KOWLOON 九龍

KOWLOON 九龍

◎🍴 ⚅ ♿ **P**

TEL. 2376 3322

702, 7F, K11 Musea,
18 Salisbury Road, Tsim Sha Tsui

尖沙咀梳士巴利道18號
K11 Musea 7樓702號舖

www.elite-concepts.com

■ **PRICE 價錢**
Lunch 午膳
À la carte 點菜 $ 200-400
Dinner 晚膳
À la carte 點菜 $ 400-800

■ **OPENING HOURS 營業時間**
Lunch 午膳 11:30-14:30
Dinner 晚膳 18:00-22:30

❀

YÈ SHANGHAI (TSIM SHA TSUI) ᴺ
夜上海 (尖沙咀)

Shanghainese · Elegant
滬菜 · 典雅

It may have moved to a swanky mall in 2020, but this household name in Shanghainese food has been on the radar of gastronomes for over two decades. The room is spread across two floors with a modern take on 1930s Shanghai charm. As well as Shanghainese, the menu includes Jiangsu and Zhejiang dishes, all exhibiting remarkable skill and technique. Specialities include drunken chicken, stir-fried river shrimps and crab shell stuffed with crabmeat and roe.

開業超過二十年，於2020年搬到現址，佔地兩層，用餐環境舒適。昏暗的燈光配上深色木材，散發着三十年代老上海的味道。廚師手藝精湛，選用中國各地的新鮮食材，重新演繹一系列極具風味的上海及江浙名菜。花雕醉雞酒香濃郁，雞肉嫩滑；清炒河蝦仁爽口美味；蟹粉釀蟹蓋鮮美滑溜，都是這裏的必吃菜式。

AH CHUN SHANDONG DUMPLING
阿純山東餃子

Dumplings • Friendly

餃子 • 友善

The shop has a traditional feel to it. Green wooden window frames on the wall are reminiscent of old-time Hong Kong. Dumplings are handmade daily and only the freshest ingredients are used in the fillings. Try their most-ordered item lamb and Peking scallion dumplings. Or surprise yourself with the specialty, such as mackerel dumplings and cuttlefish dumplings. Shandong roast lamb and meat pie are also recommended.

綠色木窗框和木製傢具帶傳統味道，很有老香港感覺。這裏供應不同味道的傳統餃子，每天在店內以人手包製，並以新鮮食材作餡，其中最受歡迎的要數京蔥羊肉餃、薺菜鮮肉餃也值得一試。此外，店家秘製數款青島海鮮餃，如墨魚餃和馬鮫魚餃，也給顧客帶來驚喜。餃子以外，山東手撕雞和家鄉餡餅也是招牌菜。

TEL. 2789 9611

60 Lai Chi Kok Road, Prince Edward

太子荔枝角道60號

■ **PRICE** 價錢
À la carte 點菜 $ 50-100

■ **OPENING HOURS** 營業時間
11:00-22:30

■ **ANNUAL AND WEEKLY CLOSING**
休息日期
Closed 6 days Lunar New Year and Wednesday
農曆新年6天及週三休息

KOWLOON 九龍

CHUEN CHEUNG KUI (MONG KOK)
泉章居 (旺角)

Hakkanese • Family
客家菜 • 溫馨

⏱🍴
TEL. 2396 0672

Shop E, Lisa House,
33 Nelson Street, Mong Kok
旺角奶路臣街33號依利大廈E舖

■ **PRICE** 價錢
À la carte 點菜 $ 100-300

■ **OPENING HOURS** 營業時間
11:00-22:15

■ **ANNUAL AND WEEKLY CLOSING**
休息日期
Closed 4 days Lunar New Year
農曆新年休息4天

This two-storey restaurant has been owned by the same family since the 1960s. It moved to this location in 2004 and has been jam-packed at night ever since. Diners line up to enjoy its traditional Hakkanese fare, including the unmissable salt-baked chicken and braised pork belly with dried mustard greens. The ground floor is smaller in size and rice plates that are less complicated to prepare are served there during lunch hours.

菜館自六十年代起一直由同一家族經營，直至2004年才遷至現址。雖然餐廳樓高兩層，但晚上經常座無虛席，門外排隊等候的客人，為的都是這裏的傳統客家菜，不能錯過的有鹽焗雞和梅菜扣肉。下層地舖面積較小，中午時分主要供應烹調工序較簡單的碟頭飯。

TEL. 2730 6928

Shop 306, 3F, Silvercord,
30 Canton Road, Tsim Sha Tsui

尖沙咀廣東道30號
新港中心3樓306號舖
www.dintaifung.com.hk

■ **PRICE** 價錢
À la carte 點菜 $ 200-400

■ **OPENING HOURS** 營業時間
11:30-21:30

■ **ANNUAL AND WEEKLY CLOSING**
休息日期
Closed 4 days Lunar New Year
農曆新年休息4天

DIN TAI FUNG (SILVERCORD)
鼎泰豐 (新港中心)

Shanghainese • Friendly

滬菜 • 友善

From Mr Yang's first shop in Taiwan in 1958 grew a multinational chain with branches in all major Asian cities. It's famous for good service, competitive prices and listening to its customer's feedback, but mostly for its xiao long bao made on the spot. Taiwanese chefs visit regularly to ensure the quality is maintained. Even the vinegar, free of artificial colours and preservatives, is shipped from Taiwan. Expect long queues at peak hours.

楊先生在1958年於台灣開辦首家小籠包店,至今分店遍佈各個主要亞洲城市。主打的上海小籠包以人手製作,材料新鮮,餡料充足,並選用無色素及防腐劑的台灣米醋佐吃,令人食指大動。創辦人特別注重品質、服務及價格,除了定期監控品質,也重視客人反饋,台灣師傅亦會定期來港交流,確保食物水準。

KOWLOON 九龍

211

KOWLOON 九龍

◎🍴

TEL. 2381 5261

1-2F, European Asian Bank Building, 749 Nathan Road, Mong Kok

旺角彌敦道749號歐亞銀行大廈
1及2樓

■ **PRICE** 價錢
Lunch 午膳
À la carte 點菜 $ 100-200
Dinner 晚膳
À la carte 點菜 $ 200-400

■ **OPENING HOURS** 營業時間
Lunch 午膳 09:00-15:00
Dinner 晚膳 18:00-22:30

■ **ANNUAL AND WEEKLY CLOSING**
休息日期
Closed 4 days Lunar New Year
農曆新年休息4天

😃

ETON N
頤東

Shun Tak • Traditional

順德菜・傳統

In 2019, the long-standing household name Fung Shing closed its doors as the owner-chef retired. A regular customer and the staff then got together to re-open it as Eton in 2020. The room was renovated and about 80% of the kitchen and service teams returned. The menu is largely the same; dim sum, crispy fried chicken, deep-fried shrimp toast, scrambled egg white with milk in Daliang style, and Shun Tak fish tripe thick soup are still recommended.

前旺角鳳城酒家於2019年結業後由新老闆接手,並在內部翻新後重新營業,改名為「頤東」。沿用大部分舊有班底,將順德菜手藝延續,其招牌龍鳳大禮堂和食物都保留原來風貌。招牌菜鴻運乳豬、炸子雞和蝦多士等依舊美味。大良炒鮮奶口感順滑、充滿奶香;順德魚肚羹則用料十足,充滿傳統風味。

GLORIOUS CUISINE
增煇藝廚

Cantonese • Neighbourhood

粵菜 • 親切

The owner shops for seafood daily to ensure freshness and quality. Picking out your favourite live critters from the tank is part of the fun – Hokkaido scallops, Thai marble goby, and even Hanasaki crab if you're lucky. Apart from the signature braised chicken stuffed with abalone and sea cucumber, try also their salt-baked sea whelks or virgin crabs. Double-boiled chicken soup with conpoy and Yunnan ham is available in limited quantities every night.

北海道帶子、泰國筍殼魚……門外的魚缸內是來自各地的海鮮，幸運的話，或能吃到日本花咲蟹。曾經營雞隻生意的老闆乘貨源之便，每天親自選購當造的新鮮食材。自創的金瑤雲腿樂湯雞，選用清遠雞加上瑤柱及雲腿等，清燉約一小時而成，每晚限量供應；同樣大受歡迎的頭抽雞需提前預訂。

🍽️ ⬍

TEL. 2778 8103
31-33 Shek Kip Mei Street, Sham Shui Po
深水埗石硤尾街31-33號

■ **PRICE** 價錢
Dinner 晚膳
À la carte 點菜 $ 200-400

■ **OPENING HOURS** 營業時間
Dinner 晚膳 17:30-01:30

■ **ANNUAL AND WEEKLY CLOSING**
休息日期
Closed 2 days Lunar New Year
農曆新年休息2天

KOWLOON 九龍

GOOD HOPE NOODLE
好旺角粥麵專家

Noodles and Congee • Neighbourhood

粥麵 • 親切

Founded in 1971, this noodle shop once had several branches in Mong Kok, but this is the only one left. Regulars flock here for the duck-egg noodles – made fresh daily with dough kneaded with a bamboo pole for extra bouncy texture, to be topped with prawn-and-pork wontons, zhajiang sauce or braised pork trotter. Congee and snacks are also recommended. You can also witness how the noodles are made in the show kitchen by the entrance.

品牌創立於1971年，雖然曾經搬遷，但頗得街坊支持。進入餐廳時，可以看到開放式廚房和打麵過程。其麵條、雲吞和炸醬均自家製作，尤其是竹昇麵，選用新鮮鴨蛋手打而成，充滿蛋香且帶韌性。配搭皮薄餡鮮的雲吞，或是辣中帶甜的炸醬，都十分美味。除了麵食，這裏也提供多款生滾粥和小吃。

TEL. 2393 9036

123 Sai Yee Street, Mong Kok
旺角洗衣街123號

■ **PRICE** 價錢
À la carte 點菜 $ 50-100

■ **OPENING HOURS** 營業時間
11:00-23:30

■ **ANNUAL AND WEEKLY CLOSING**
休息日期
Closed 3 days Lunar New Year
農曆新年休息3天

KOWLOON 九龍

JU XING HOME
聚興家

Cantonese · Friendly

粵菜 · 友善

This hole-in-the-wall is always jam-packed and that's down to chef-owner Ng's cooking, not the décor or service. Cantonese stir-fries prevail, alongside a few spicy options. The must-try salt-baked Wenchang chicken is succulent, flavourful and tends to run out early. Live seafood is also big on the menu, like lobster with pan-fried rice vermicelli. Reservations are recommended and it's worth pre-ordering the chicken to avoid missing out.

作為許多影視名人和酒店大廚的飯堂，即使店舖經過擴充，仍然經常客滿，請務必訂座。翻開餐牌，可以看到各式各樣的廣東小炒，為了照顧嗜辣的客人，更加入一些精選川菜。用新鮮文昌雞炮製的鹽焗雞不容錯過，為免撲空，建議於訂座時預留。店內同時供應多款時令生猛海鮮，包括招牌菜上湯澳洲龍蝦煎米粉底。

TEL. 2392 9283

GF, 416 and 418 Portland Street, Prince Edward

太子砵蘭街416及418號地下

KOWLOON 九龍

■ **PRICE** 價錢
Dinner 晚膳
À la carte 點菜 $ 250-400

■ **OPENING HOURS** 營業時間
Dinner 晚膳 17:30-00:30

■ **ANNUAL AND WEEKLY CLOSING**
休息日期
Closed 4 days Lunar New Year
農曆新年休息4天

215

KOWLOON 九龍

🍴 ⊠

TEL. 3484 9126

Shop E, 1 Wing Lung Street, Cheung Sha Wan

長沙灣永隆街1號E舖

■ **PRICE 價錢**
Set Menu 套餐 $ 48-80
À la carte 點菜 $ 35-85

■ **OPENING HOURS 營業時間**
11:00-20:45

KWAN KEE BAMBOO NOODLES
坤記竹昇麵

Noodles • Friendly

麵食・友善

It's inside a local market but easy to spot, thanks to the big yellow sign. Watch the kitchen at work through the glass wall as egg noodles are made the traditional way – with the chef seesawing on a bamboo pole to painstakingly knead the dough for that stringy texture. Don't miss the signature noodles tossed in shrimp roe and oyster sauce. Try replicating it all at home by buying their pre-packaged noodles, dried shrimp roe and ground dried plaice.

秉承店東在廣州的家族麵店做法，麵條全在工房經人手以傳統竹竿壓法每日新鮮打製，配方含大量雞蛋和少量鹼水，製成的麵條彈牙爽口，啖啖蛋香全無鹼水味，配以自製的大地魚湯和蝦籽更是滋味；推介鮮蝦雲吞麵和蝦籽蠔油撈麵。店家另有出售樽裝蝦籽、大地魚粉、秘製XO醬及盒裝竹昇蛋麵。

LAU SUM KEE (FUK WING STREET)
劉森記麵家 (福榮街)

Noodles · Simple

麵食 • 簡樸

Since 1956, this branch (and the original shop around the corner) has been packed with customers buzzing in and out. The third-generation family business still kneads noodle dough with a bamboo pole like it used to be done. Wontons are made on the spot with whole prawns and pork and even the crunchy radish pickles on the table are homemade. Recommendations include wonton noodles, and tossed noodles with dry shrimp roe or pork knuckle.

始創於1956年，此家族經營的麵店已傳至第三代。這分店與轉角位的總店位於麵店林立的街道上，店內依然人頭湧湧，質素自是不言而喻。店家所有竹昇麵及雲吞均在店內新鮮人手製造，雲吞包入原隻鮮蝦及豬肉，飽滿爽口。推薦雲吞麵、蝦籽撈麵及豬手撈麵。餐桌上的自製醃蘿蔔爽脆美味，亦不可不試。

TEL. 2386 3583
82 Fuk Wing Street, Sham Shui Po
深水埗福榮街82號

■ **PRICE** 價錢
À la carte 點菜 $ 35-55

■ **OPENING HOURS** 營業時間
12:00-22:00

■ **ANNUAL AND WEEKLY CLOSING**
休息日期
Closed 3 days Lunar New Year
農曆新年休息3天

KOWLOON 九龍

LUCKY INDONESIA
好運印尼餐廳

Indonesian • Friendly

印尼菜 • 友善

Ⓢ

TEL. 2389 3545

46 Tung Ming Street, Kwun Tong
觀塘通明街46號

■ **PRICE** 價錢
À la carte 點菜 $ 60-100

■ **OPENING HOURS** 營業時間
11:00-20:30

■ **ANNUAL AND WEEKLY CLOSING**
休息日期
Closed 5 days Lunar New Year and
Monday
農曆新年5天及週一休息

One's first impression of this small dining room, with its wooden furniture and traditional wall hangings, is that it's a little dated, but you'll soon feel as though you have been transported to the Indonesian countryside. The Middle Java cuisine is not unlike the décor – there's no fancy presentation, just authentic and tasty flavours. Satay is charcoal roasted which creates a lovely aroma; also try the Nasi Kuming and Mee Goreng.

細小的用膳區、木製的傢具及傳統的掛牆吊飾,室內裝潢予人點點懷舊感覺,令食客感到身處印尼郊區。一如其裝潢,此店的食物不賣弄花巧,只用真材實料炮製出正宗美味的爪哇中部菜式。炭燒沙嗲烤肉風味特別,而印尼黃薑飯和印尼炒麵更不容錯過。

MAK MAN KEE
麥文記

Noodles • Neighbourhood

麵食 • 親切

No one is here for the no-frills interior, typical of any noodle shop in Hong Kong. This 60-year-old establishment is all about Cantonese wonton soup noodles – firm and bouncy prawns, visible through the paper-thin translucent skin, with springy duck egg noodles swimming in a flavourful broth. The serving size isn't the most filling so you may want to order their pork knuckles braised in red taro curd on the side.

麵店已有六十年歷史，裝潢簡單樸素，是典型港式麵食店的陳設。鮮蝦雲吞是這兒最具人氣的食物，薄薄的雲吞皮內包着的就只有滿滿的蝦肉，用料十足，吃起來很爽口。南乳豬手同樣是必吃之選。店家用的生麵並非用雞蛋而是鴨蛋製作，蛋味香而麵質爽彈。

TEL. 2736 5561
51 Parkes Street, Jordan
佐敦白加士街51號
www.mmk.hk

■ **PRICE** 價錢
À la carte 點菜 $ 50-100

■ **OPENING HOURS** 營業時間
12:00-00:00

■ **ANNUAL AND WEEKLY CLOSING**
休息日期
Closed Tuen Ng Festival, Mid-autumn Festival and 3 days Lunar New Year
農曆新年3天、端午節及中秋節休息

KOWLOON 九龍

◎🍴 🚻

TEL. 2723 8660

**Shop 103, 1F, Regal Kowloon Hotel,
71 Mody Road, Tsim Sha Tsui**

尖沙咀麼地道71號
富豪九龍酒店1樓103室

■ **PRICE 價錢**
Lunch 午膳
Set Menu 套餐 $ 100-120
À la carte 點菜 $ 200-400
Dinner 晚膳
Set Menu 套餐 $ 400
À la carte 點菜 $ 200-400

■ **OPENING HOURS 營業時間**
Lunch 午膳 12:00-14:00
Dinner 晚膳 18:00-22:00

NISHIKI
錦

Japanese · Friendly
日本菜 • 友善

Despite opening over 20 years ago, the bustling atmosphere and tasty grill dishes of this izakaya-style place still shine. The Japanese owner-chef teaches his kitchen team the tricks for perfect barbecue – his famous tsukune, for example, is made with boneless chicken thigh from Japan and Brazil in a specific ratio. Grilled chicken liver from local farms is another speciality. Reservations are recommended; ask for counter seats to get close to the action.

典型居酒屋格局多年來始終如一，熱鬧非常；開放式廚房旁邊的座位能觀賞烹調過程，氣氛更佳。一向大受歡迎的燒烤由師承日籍老闆的年輕主廚負責，其中免治雞肉棒用上日本及巴西的雞扒肉，按特定比例搓成，深得食客熱愛；生燒本地雞肝亦為鎮店之寶，此外雞肉丸豆腐鍋也不容錯過。建議訂座。

TAKEYA
竹家

Japanese • Friendly
日本菜 • 友善

This intimate 15-seater yakitori shop is the brainchild of a Japanese engineer, now the chef, and his wife, now the maître d'. For over a decade, they've been feeding hungry diners in the neighbourhood with quality grilled food, with some ingredients flown in from Japan. Rare cuts such as chicken heart and hatsumoto (artery) are definitely worth a try. Pair them with their selection of sake or home-brewed umeshu. Reservations are recommended.

雖然隱藏在巷子裏，但鄰近港鐵站，交通便利。由居港多年的日籍主廚和妻子共同經營，以竹子為主題，提供種類繁多的串燒。從挑選食材到製作皆一絲不苟，所用的豬肉和雞隻均來自日本。幸運的話，更可嘗到雞血管、雞心臟等特別部位。備有多款日本酒，特別推介自家浸製的梅酒。但座位有限，建議訂座。

◎🍴

TEL. 2365 8878

Shop 1, On Wah Building, 31C1 Tak Man Street, Whampoa Estate, Hung Hom

紅磡黃埔新村德民街31C1
安華樓1號舖

■ **PRICE** 價錢
Dinner 晚膳
À la carte 點菜 $ 250-400

■ **OPENING HOURS** 營業時間
Dinner 晚膳 18:00-22:30

■ **ANNUAL AND WEEKLY CLOSING**
休息日期
Closed 2 weeks Lunar New Year and Monday
農曆新年兩週及週一休息

KOWLOON 九龍

TIM HO WAN (TAI KOK TSUI)
添好運 (大角咀)

Dim Sum • Friendly
點心 • 友善

The first and original shop of the chain moved into this shopping mall from Mong Kok. Crowds still flock in like before, but this place is much more spacious and airy, thanks to the high ceiling and a light colour scheme. Most of the regulars care more about the food – over 20 handmade dim sum are on the menu, along with a few exclusive items not available at other branches. The ingredients are fresh and the prices are more than reasonable.

添好運的旺角總店遷至大角咀現址後更見寬敞舒適，高聳的樓底配搭白色主調的裝潢感覺明淨清新。二十多款廣式點心不賣弄外形或配搭，而是以傳統手藝配上新鮮食材取勝。這裏更設有本店限定的點心，每隔數月轉換，食客每次到訪都有驚喜。滋味十足且價錢相宜，說明了何以總是座無虛席。

TEL. 2332 2896

Shop 72A-C, GF, Olympian City 2, 18 Hoi Ting Road, Tai Kok Tsui
大角咀海庭道18號
奧海城2期地下72A-C舖

■ **PRICE** 價錢
À la carte 點菜 $ 50-100

■ **OPENING HOURS** 營業時間
10:00-21:30

■ **ANNUAL AND WEEKLY CLOSING** 休息日期
Closed 3 days Lunar New Year
農曆新年休息3天

KOWLOON 九龍

WING LAI YUEN
詠藜園

Shanghainese and Sichuan •
Traditional

滬菜及川菜 • 傳統

Originally a run-down shop in a squatter village, it moved to this location in 2000 and had a major facelift. But one thing never changed – the food is as delicious and affordably priced as always. The signature Dan Dan noodles come in two versions: a meat one with ground pork and a traditional one without, plus a spicy or mild broth to choose from. Shuizhu mandarin fish, a secret menu item that packs numbing heat, is great to share with others.

原店位於新蒲崗，楊氏家族於早年遷至現址，繼續提供價廉物美的川滬美食。招牌菜四川擔擔麵，除了保留傳統口味，還有加入肉碎的改良版本，兩者均有辣或不辣的湯底選擇。同時供應多款小菜，例如並未列入菜單的水煮桂花魚，選用原條鮮魚製作，適合多人共享。室內設計採用傳統中式風格，並附有私人廂房。

TEL. 2320 6430

Shop 102-105, 1F, Gourmet Place, Whampoa Plaza, Site 8, Whampoa Garden, 7 Tak On Street, Hung Hom

紅磡德安街7號黃埔花園第8期
黃埔美食坊1樓102-105號舖

■ PRICE 價錢
Lunch 午膳
À la carte 點菜 $ 100-300
Dinner 晚膳
À la carte 點菜 $ 100-300

■ OPENING HOURS 營業時間
Lunch 午膳 11:00-15:20
Dinner 晚膳 18:00-22:20

223

TEL. 5300 2682
GF, 36 Man Yuen Street, Jordan
佐敦文苑街36號地下

■ **PRICE** 價錢
Lunch 午膳
À la carte 點菜 $ 50-100
Dinner 晚膳
À la carte 點菜 $ 50-100

■ **OPENING HOURS** 營業時間
Lunch 午膳 12:00-17:00
Dinner 晚膳 18:00-22:00

YAU YUEN SIU TSUI (JORDAN)
有緣小敍 (佐敦)

Shaanxi • Simple
陝西菜 • 簡樸

This hole-in-the-wall eatery is a bit out of the way but is frequented by regulars who come mostly for its signature Biang Biang noodles – long, flat, handmade strands dressed in a spicy chilli sauce bursting with flavour. Other Shaanxi specialities include vegetable and pork noodles in spicy sour soup, stewed pork sandwich and stewed chicken with Sichuan pepper. Braised duck with young ginger, and steamed egg custard with clams need pre-ordering.

這間位於佐敦的小店，儘管位置不太起眼，仍然吸引不少食客。來自陝西的店東太太以人手製作獨特的Biang Biang麵，麵身寬長配上特製醬料，香辣味濃，令人回味無窮。店內還提供哨子麵、肉夾饃和麻辣大盤雞等多款家鄉美食。子薑燜鴨和花甲蒸水蛋則須提前預訂。

ABOVE & BEYOND
天外天

Cantonese • Elegant

粵菜 • 典雅

The stylish décor, sweeping harbour views and extensive menu make the restaurant a popular choice for Cantonese fine dining. The chef puts a new spin on the dim sum tradition with European techniques and tastes. Signatures such as deep-fried scallop puff with lily bulb in lobster broth, and steamed crabmeat and egg white dumplings with aged vinegar are nothing short of ingenious. The set lunch can be ordered individually with a vegan option.

天外天位於唯港薈頂層，出自名師手筆的室內裝潢時尚典雅；臨窗座位把維港醉人景致盡收眼底，更是叫人讚歎不已。餐單上的廣東菜式琳瑯滿目，午市點心富創意特色，部分結合了歐陸烹調技巧和食材，如龍蝦湯鮮百合帶子酥盒，教人耳目一新。單人套餐設有素食選擇，充分照顧不同食客需要。

TEL. 3400 1318

28F, Hotel Icon, 17 Science Museum Road, Tsim Sha Tsui

尖東科學館道17號唯港薈28樓

www.hotel-icon.com/dining/above-beyond

■ **PRICE** 價錢
Lunch 午膳
Set Menu 套餐 $ 288-398
À la carte 點菜 $ 250-1,000
Dinner 晚膳
Set Menu 套餐 $ 1,528
À la carte 點菜 $ 250-1,000

■ **OPENING HOURS** 營業時間
Lunch 午膳 11:30-14:30
Dinner 晚膳 18:00-21:30

KOWLOON 九龍

BOSTONIAN SEAFOOD & GRILL

Steakhouse • Rustic

扒房 • 樸實

TEL. 2132 7898

**Lower Lobby Level,
The Langham Hotel, 8 Peking Road,
Tsim Sha Tsui**

尖沙咀北京道8號朗廷酒店低層大堂

www.langhamhotels.com/hongkong

■ **PRICE** 價錢
Lunch 午膳
Set Menu 套餐 $ 268
À la carte 點菜 $ 600-2,000
Dinner 晚膳
À la carte 點菜 $ 600-2,000

■ **OPENING HOURS** 營業時間
Lunch 午膳 12:00-14:30
Dinner 晚膳 18:00-22:00

The self-assured Bostonian is a handsome and sophisticated restaurant offering all the things you'd expect from an American restaurant: plenty of hearty salads, lots of lobster, oysters, assorted seafood and, of course, a huge choice of prime beef from the grill. The set lunch with the seafood buffet is particularly popular, as is brunch on a weekend. It's unlikely anyone has ever left here still feeling hungry.

深色系和木製傢具為餐廳添上型格感覺，牆上的藝術畫令環境生色不少，生蠔吧變成了小型酒吧，供客人餐前或飯後淺酌。任職多年的大廚繼續提供具水準的美食，波士頓龍蝦等各類海鮮仍然是餐牌的焦點所在，當然亦少不了種類多樣而且處理得恰到好處的特級烤牛扒，完全符合你對美式餐廳的期望。

CELESTIAL COURT
天寶閣

Cantonese • Classic Décor

粵菜 • 經典

The astute chef has over 25 years of experience and was brought up in a family who owned a dried seafood business. His shrewd insights on sourcing and preparing those gourmet ingredients are reflected in the menu. The speciality roast whole suckling pig with pearl barley and black truffles needs pre-ordering. Scrambled egg with lobster and caviar is another highlight. The windowless dining room is nicely furnished with rich wood accents.

位於喜來登酒店內，餐室的裝潢典雅堂皇，菜餚亦甚具水準。主廚擁有超過二十五年傳統粵菜經驗，功夫扎實。生於經營海味生意的家族使他對挑選和運用名貴海味食材別有一番心得，且擅於烹調以海味為題的菜式。除此之外，需預訂的黑松露薏米燒釀乳豬和魚子芙蓉蛋白龍蝦球均值得一試。

TEL. 2732 6991

2F, Sheraton Hotel,
20 Nathan Road, Tsim Sha Tsui
尖沙咀彌敦道20號喜來登酒店2樓
www.sheratonhongkonghotel.com

KOWLOON 九龍

■ PRICE 價錢
Lunch 午膳
À la carte 點菜 $ 300-1,000
Dinner 晚膳
Set Menu 套餐 $ 1,088
À la carte 點菜 $ 600-1,500

■ OPENING HOURS 營業時間
Lunch 午膳 11:30-14:45
Dinner 晚膳 18:00-22:45

KOWLOON 九龍

◎📶 ⏴ Ⓟ

TEL. 5239 9220

5F, Rosewood, 18 Salisbury Road,
Tsim Sha Tsui

尖沙咀梳士巴利道18號瑰麗酒店5樓

chaat.hk

■ **PRICE** 價錢
Lunch 午膳
À la carte 點菜 $ 400-800
Dinner 晚膳
À la carte 點菜 $ 400-800

■ **OPENING HOURS** 營業時間
Lunch 午膳 12:00-14:30
Dinner 晚膳 18:00-22:30

■ **ANNUAL AND WEEKLY CLOSING**
休息日期
Closed Tuesday to Friday lunch and
Monday
週二至週五午膳及週一休息

🍴○

CHAAT

Indian • Chic

印度菜 • 新潮

'Chaat' means 'to lick' in Hindi, as the food here is so good that you'd have the urge to lick the plate. The menu covers classics from all over India, re-imagined with finesse and acumen. The must-try black pepper chicken tikka from the tandoor oven is best enjoyed with its signature cocktails. The food, the fragrant spices in the glass-clad Masala room, and a terrace affording nice harbour views work together to render a feast for all the senses.

名字在印地語中解作「舔」，寓意客人把桌上的食物一掃而空。包羅來自印度各地的經典菜式，特別推介以土窯爐炮製的黑胡椒烤雞。配上一系列特色雞尾酒和招牌飲品，全面體驗印度風情。設有擺滿香料、名為Masala Room的玻璃房，令人眼界大開。坐擁無敵海景及戶外陽台，由印度藝術家創作的壁畫也充滿巧思。

CHESA
瑞樵閣

Swiss • Friendly

瑞士菜 • 友善

Even since opening as a 'pop-up' restaurant created by the Swiss-born manager back in 1965, Chesa has been the go-to place in town for those wanting authentic Swiss cuisine. The Alpine chalet-style décor more than compensates for the room's lack of windows, while the menu covers all bases, offering fondue, raclette and the famous Chemin de Fer wines. You can even specify how strong you want the brandy taste to be in your fondue.

推開餐廳的木門,四周的木製裝飾讓人彷彿踏進了瑞士農舍。自1965年起瑞士美食的魅力在此得以展現,店內的傳統瑞士菜式與特選芝士系列,包括瓦萊州烤芝士(熱熔的芝士配馬鈴薯、醃洋蔥及青瓜)或瑞士芝士火鍋均惹人垂涎,芝士火鍋更設有不同酒精濃度可供選擇。現任主廚生於瑞士,保證所有出品均是正宗風味。

TEL. 2696 6769

1F, The Peninsula Hotel,
22 Salisbury Road, Tsim Sha Tsui
尖沙咀梳士巴利道半島酒店1樓
www.peninsula.com/hongkong

■ **PRICE** 價錢
Lunch 午膳
Set Menu 套餐 $ 338-438
À la carte 點菜 $ 600-1,200
Dinner 晚膳
À la carte 點菜 $ 600-1,200

■ **OPENING HOURS** 營業時間
Lunch 午膳 12:00-14:30
Dinner 晚膳 18:30-22:30

KOWLOON 九龍

CHINA TANG (TSIM SHA TSUI)
唐人館 (尖沙咀)

Cantonese • Design
粵菜 • 型格

TEL. 2157 3148

Shop 4101, 4F, Gateway Arcade, Harbour City, 17 Canton Road, Tsim Sha Tsui

尖沙咀廣東道17號海港城
港威商場4樓4101號舖

www.chinatang.hk

■ **PRICE** 價錢
Lunch 午膳
À la carte 點菜 $ 300-800
Dinner 晚膳
À la carte 點菜 $ 400-1,000

■ **OPENING HOURS** 營業時間
Lunch 午膳 12:00-15:00
Dinner 晚膳 18:00-22:30

The second China Tang to open in Hong Kong was another ingenious work by the late Sir David Tang. Traditional Chinese embroidery is set against bold-coloured chinoiserie fabrics for a dynamic yet graceful look. The menu is dominated by Cantonese cuisine, but chefs are hired from their respective provinces to take care of other regional dishes. Recommendations include marinated shrimps in plum-scented Huadiao wine.

唐人館在香港的第二家店子設計同樣出自已故鄧永鏘爵士手筆,他巧妙地將歐陸式裝潢和中式元素融合,色彩繽紛的布料配搭優雅的花卉圖案,雅致舒適。粵菜是餐單的主角,也不乏南北點心、佐酒小食和大笪地爐端燒菜式;廚師團隊來自中國不同地區,各負責不同菜系。陳年花雕話梅蝦值得一試,也不乏別具特色的小菜供選擇。

KOWLOON 九龍

CUISINE CUISINE AT THE MIRA
國金軒 (尖沙咀)
Cantonese • Luxury
粵菜 • 豪華

You'll be greeted by a striking feature of crystal glass spheres hanging from the ceiling and calming blue and green colours, which help bring the feel of the outside gardens into the room at the Mira hotel. They like to add the odd modern slant to the Cantonese cooking too and regularly create special dim sum, such as crispy frogs' legs with spicy salt. The wine pairings are thoughtfully matched.

這家型格餐廳充滿現代感，圓球狀的水晶吊燈引人注目，在此享受融入精巧現代元素的廣東美食，可謂相得益彰。午市供應多達三十款精美點心，目不暇給。欲體驗廚房的功力則可自選菜式，侍酒師能為你提供餐酒配搭的建議。宜先作預訂，以免撲空。

TEL. 2315 5222

3F, The Mira Hotel, 118 Nathan Road, Tsim Sha Tsui

尖沙咀彌敦道118號The Mira 3樓

www.themirahotel.com

■ PRICE 價錢
Lunch 午膳
Set Menu 套餐 $ 438-568
À la carte 點菜 $ 450-1,200
Dinner 晚膳
Set Menu 套餐 $ 1,288-1,888
À la carte 點菜 $ 450-1,200

■ OPENING HOURS 營業時間
Lunch 午膳 11:30-14:30
Dinner 晚膳 18:00-22:30

KOWLOON 九龍

⊘🍴 ♿ ⎚ 🚭 🅿

TEL. 2733 2020

**B2F, The Royal Garden Hotel,
69 Mody Road, Tsim Sha Tsui**

尖東麼地道69號帝苑酒店地庫2樓

www.rghk.com.hk

■ **PRICE** 價錢
Lunch 午膳
Set Menu 套餐 $ 178
À la carte 點菜 $ 200-700
Dinner 晚膳
À la carte 點菜 $ 200-700

■ **OPENING HOURS** 營業時間
Lunch 午膳 11:30-14:30
Dinner 晚膳 18:00-22:30

🍴○

DONG LAI SHUN
東來順

*Beijing Cuisine & Huai Yang •
Elegant*

京菜及淮揚菜 • 典雅

The original may have opened in Beijing in 1903 but the room here shows more of a contemporary style of décor and also includes a relaxing water feature and a bridge. The cooking blends recipes from Beijing and Huaiyang. Paper thin slices of Mongolian black-headed mutton remains a speciality, along with the drunken chicken.

東來順將北京與淮揚菜共冶一爐，火鍋、北京填鴨及涮羊肉等菜式自然齊備；當中涮羊肉採用蒙古黑頭白羊的上乘部分，肉質極為細軟；而醉雞也值得一試。餐室裝潢混搭現代和傳統格調，牆板和壁畫展現出鮮明的亞洲特色；坐在人工噴泉旁用餐，更是別有一番閒情逸致。

HING KEE
避風塘興記

Seafood • Traditional

海鮮 • 傳統

It started two generations ago in Causeway Bay but the family's reputation for Boat People style cuisine was made in Tsim Sha Tsui; further testimony comes from the celebrity signatures lining the walls. Elder sister heads the serving team; younger brother runs the kitchen. They are famous for their stir-fried crabs with black beans and chilli, roast duck and rice noodles in soup and congee. Guests aren't seated until everyone in the party has arrived.

歷經三代，原址在銅鑼灣，其後才遷到尖沙咀現址，這家由祖父輩創辦的餐廳主打仍是避風塘特色小菜。廚房由弟弟掌舵，大家姐則負責領導服務團隊。海鮮每天新鮮進貨，供應有限，不妨於訂座時預留，招牌菜包括避風塘炒蟹、燒鴨湯河及艇仔粥。座位不多，食客須到齊方能入座。

TEL. 2722 0022

1F, Bowa House, 180 Nathan Road, Tsim Sha Tsui

尖沙咀彌敦道180號寶華商業大廈1樓

■ **PRICE** 價錢
Dinner 晚膳
À la carte 點菜 $ 300-700

■ **OPENING HOURS** 營業時間
Dinner 晚膳 18:00-02:00

■ **ANNUAL AND WEEKLY CLOSING** 休息日期
Closed 2 days Lunar New Year
農曆新年休息2天

KOWLOON 九龍

KOWLOON 九龍

HYDE PARK GARDEN
海德花園
Seafood • Rustic
海鮮 • 樸實

TEL. 2717 6381

**44 Hoi Pong Road Central,
Lei Yue Mun**

鯉魚門海傍道中44號

www.hydeparkdeli.com

■ **PRICE** 價錢
Lunch 午膳
À la carte 點菜 $ 500-1,000
Dinner 晚膳
À la carte 點菜 $ 500-1,000

■ **OPENING HOURS** 營業時間
Lunch 午膳 11:30-15:00
Dinner 晚膳 16:30-22:30

■ **ANNUAL AND WEEKLY CLOSING**
休息日期
Closed 4 days Lunar New Year
農曆新年休息4天

The owner also sells seafood from a nearby stall so diners can pick from the selection that is flown in daily and have it cooked in the restaurant for a fee. Also try their razor clams in chilli black bean sauce, or the signature fish soup which is simmered for hours with freshwater fish and tofu. Other recommendations include ginger and scallion abalone in a claypot, and tofu skin sweet soup with pearl barley.

店東同時經營對面的明月海鮮檔，客人可先到此挑選空運到港的生猛海鮮，再交給廚房處理。師傅烹調海鮮的時間拿捏精準，如鮮甜爽脆豉椒炒鱆子就火候十足；推介淡水鮮魚湯，以大量淡水魚加入豆腐熬煮至少兩小時，每天新鮮製作。此外，腐竹洋薏米糖水、炸茄子皇和無添加人造色素的咕嚕肉也是招牌菜。

🍴◯

KAM FAI
金輝

Seafood • Simple

海鮮 • 簡樸

It has over 50 years of history and is managed by a head chef with over 40 years of kitchen experience. Cooking is customised so you can specify how you want your seafood prepared – oysters can be lightly floured, tempura-battered, or breadcrumbed before being deep-fried. Try their salt-baked virgin crabs, and deep-fried mantis shrimps in peppered salt. Pre-order the braised abalone in peppercorn soup to avoid missing out.

開業逾五十年，歷史悠久之餘更向以信譽和品質見稱。有四十年入廚經驗的羅先生既是店舖掌舵，亦是廚房主帥，其烹調海鮮的技術毋庸置疑。靈活的經營模式，服務以客為本，如酥炸生蠔可應客人要求以不同作法烹調。招牌菜包括油鹽焗奄仔蟹、火候十足的椒鹽瀨尿蝦，及建議預訂的胡椒扣鮑魚。

◯🍴 🛏 🚗

TEL. 2347 7434

10 Hoi Pong Road Central, Lei Yue Mun

鯉魚門海傍道中10號

■ **PRICE** 價錢
À la carte 點菜 $ 600-1,100

■ **OPENING HOURS** 營業時間
12:00-21:00

■ **ANNUAL AND WEEKLY CLOSING** 休息日期
Closed 4 days Lunar New Year
農曆新年休息4天

KOWLOON 九龍

◎🍴 ⇦➡ **P**

TEL. 2331 3306

Shop F2, Telford Plaza 1,
33 Wai Yip Street, Kowloon Bay

九龍灣偉業街33號
德福廣場一期F2號舖

www.leigarden.com.hk

■ **PRICE 價錢**
Lunch 午膳
À la carte 點菜 $ 200-400
Dinner 晚膳
À la carte 點菜 $ 300-600

■ **OPENING HOURS 營業時間**
Lunch 午膳 11:30-15:00
Dinner 晚膳 18:00-22:30

■ **ANNUAL AND WEEKLY CLOSING**
休息日期
Closed 3 days Lunar New Year
農曆新年休息3天

🍴○

LEI GARDEN (KOWLOON BAY)
利苑酒家 (九龍灣)

Cantonese • Neighbourhood
粵菜 • 親切

This conveniently-located branch of the chain is famous for authentic Cantonese dishes such as barbecue meats and seafood specialities. Crispy roast pork is too good to miss and you can pre-order it to avoid missing out. The health conscious can also pre-order any of the double-boiled tonic soups in advance. Ask about the combos that offer good value. Reservations are recommended at lunch; if you vacate your table by 12:45pm you get a discount.

這家分店鄰近港鐵站，地理位置佔優，服務也相當周到。食物方面，提供多款經濟實惠的組合菜式，其中尤以精選明爐燒味、海鮮佳餚值得推薦。而真材實料的燉湯，和大受歡迎的冰燒三層肉，均建議預訂。餐廳為中午12:45前離席的顧客提供折扣優惠，然而午膳時段人流眾多，沒有訂座的話可能會掃興。

LEI GARDEN (MONG KOK)
利苑酒家 (旺角)

Cantonese • Classic Décor

粵菜 • 經典

The multinational group began life here in the 1970s with this, their original shop; it's still as busy as ever and worth booking ahead. The restaurant is spread over two floors with the upper floor boasting a large live fish tank and views of the busy street below. The long and varied menu certainly represents good value. Tonic soups like double-boiled teal with cordyceps and fish maw are hugely popular and need pre-ordering.

開業於七十年代，這家利苑總店大受歡迎，食客必須預先訂座。餐廳共分兩層，二樓可俯瞰旺角繁華的街景，更設有一個特大魚缸，供應各式生猛海鮮。以廣東菜為主的菜單花樣多變令人目不暇給，絕對物有所值。特別推薦各式燉湯如蟲草鷚燉花膠水鴨。湯品供應有限，建議訂位時先查詢預留。

TEL. 2392 5184
121 Sai Yee Street, Mong Kok
旺角洗衣街121號
www.leigarden.com.hk

■ **PRICE** 價錢
Lunch 午膳
À la carte 點菜 $ 200-500
Dinner 晚膳
À la carte 點菜 $ 300-850

■ **OPENING HOURS** 營業時間
Lunch 午膳 11:30-15:00
Dinner 晚膳 18:00-22:30

■ **ANNUAL AND WEEKLY CLOSING**
休息日期
Closed 3 days Lunar New Year
農曆新年休息3天

KOWLOON 九龍

KOWLOON 九龍

🍴⏐

ODYSSÉE

French Contemporary • Romantic
時尚法國菜 • 浪漫

TEL. 2977 5266

**Shop A, 101F,
International Commerce Centre,
1 Austin Road West, Tsim Sha Tsui**

尖沙咀柯士甸道西1號
環球貿易廣場101樓A號舖

**www.jcgroup.hk/restaurants/
odyssee**

■ **PRICE** 價錢
Lunch 午膳
Set Menu 套餐 $ 360-480
Dinner 晚膳
Set Menu 套餐 $ 980-1,580

■ **OPENING HOURS** 營業時間
Lunch 午膳 12:00-14:30
Dinner 晚膳 18:00-22:00

Having honed her skills in Europe and the U.S. for two decades, the chef here pairs classic French cooking with creative sides and sauces for visually stunning dishes that look ethereal. Her ingenious creations are complemented by sweeping harbour views from the privileged vantage point. Set menus offer exceptional value with the freedom to mix and match any item listed, whereas the tasting menu lets the chef's vision unravel in full glory.

坐擁101樓的無敵海景，氣氛宜人，加上開放式廚房，客人在美景相伴下觀看廚師獻技，可謂目不暇給。來自倫敦的主廚經驗豐富，為經典法國菜注入無窮創意。她亦擅於擺盤，每道菜都設計得精緻奪目。提供套餐和品嘗菜單，前者可以自行選擇三或四款菜式，後者則包括八至九道菜，並每月變更，以保持新鮮感。

🍴○

QI (TSIM SHA TSUI)
呇 (尖沙咀)

Sichuan • Trendy

川菜 • 前衛

Before you taste the creative Sichuanese fare, feast your eyes on the dining room itself – a dragon mural, carved wood panels and red accents are juxtaposed with Hong Kong's electric skyline. Guests can also opt to dine al fresco on the rooftop terrace. Must-try dishes include sugar-glazed ginger beef, and crispy mala beef. Creative items such as spicy seafood and egg fried rice in stone bowl is worth to try.

裝潢以深啡色刻花木飾板和飛龍壁畫，配上仿辣椒燈飾，外觀已顯四川風味；食客可坐在玻璃窗旁飽覽維港景致，或登上天台露天區用膳。這裏的新派川菜賣相吸引，蘊含甜、酸、麻、辣、苦、香、鹹等多種滋味。除了必試菜式薑牛及麻牛外，團隊亦不時研發創意菜式，其中四川風味的海鮮石鍋飯就是一例。

⊙🍴🏠 ⚹ ⌂

TEL. 2799 8899

20F, Prince Tower, 12A Peking Road, Tsim Sha Tsui

尖沙咀北京道12號A
太子集團中心20樓

www.qi-ninedragons.hk

KOWLOON 九龍

■ **PRICE** 價錢
Lunch 午膳
Set Menu 套餐 $ 120-165
À la carte 點菜 $ 250-800
Dinner 晚膳
À la carte 點菜 $ 250-800

■ **OPENING HOURS** 營業時間
Lunch 午膳 12:00-14:00
Dinner 晚膳 18:00-22:00

■ **ANNUAL AND WEEKLY CLOSING**
休息日期
Closed first day of Lunar New Year
年初一休息

TEL. 3891 8732

5F, Rosewood Hotel,
18 Salisbury Road, Tsim Sha Tsui
尖沙咀梳士巴利道18號瑰麗酒店5樓

www.rosewoodhotels.com/tc/
hong-kong

■ **PRICE 價錢**
Lunch 午膳
Set Menu 套餐 $ 480-880
À la carte 點菜 $ 500-1,000
Dinner 晚膳
Set Menu 套餐 $ 1,280-2,180
À la carte 點菜 $ 500-1,000

■ **OPENING HOURS 營業時間**
Lunch 午膳 12:00-14:15
Dinner 晚膳 18:00-22:15

THE LEGACY HOUSE
彤福軒
Shun Tak • Design
順德菜 • 型格

This restaurant pays homage to the hotel's founding patriarch. A variety of Shun Tak dishes – such as minced fish soup and wok-fried milk Daliang style – are served, to a backdrop of breathtaking harbour views and modern Chinese décor. It also supports the local economy by ordering ingredients and cookware from local fishermen, artisans and farms directly. A dress code applies for dinner.

以現代順德菜為主，如順德拆魚羹、大良鮮奶炒燕窩。餐廳對食材非常講究，嚴選本地優質材料，包括海釣船的海鮮、本地農場的蔬菜和香料，就連竹蒸籠，也是本地老店的出品。不妨一邊享用美食，一邊欣賞維多利亞港景色。但要注意晚餐時段設有服裝要求，最好預先查詢。

THE SWISS CHALET
瑞士餐廳

Swiss • Exotic Décor

瑞士菜 • 異國風情

It was relocated next door, but you may not have noticed, because with its wood furniture and beams set against whitewashed walls, it has retained the same quaint Alpine chalet ambiance. The menu is classic Swiss with a variety of cured meats and sausages, over 20 different cheeses, and of course the unmissable fondue made with five cheeses and kirsch, to be paired with their extensive selection of Swiss wines.

遷到隔鄰舖位後，裝潢仍然保留原店的樣子：木傢具、小窗戶，像極了瑞士高山上的小木屋。店東兼主廚與全店職員共事二十年，食物和服務水準一直維持不變。選用的瑞士香腸、芝士、醃肉和小牛肉等質素都很好。牛面沙律、炸牛仔肉和五種芝士混合櫻桃酒而成的芝士火鍋不可錯過。多款瑞士美酒任你挑選。

TEL. 2191 9197

GF, 8 Hart Avenue, Tsim Sha Tsui

尖沙咀赫德道8號地下

■ **PRICE** 價錢
Lunch 午膳
Set Menu 套餐 $ 123-173
À la carte 點菜 $ 250-650
Dinner 晚膳
Set Menu 套餐 $ 368-468
À la carte 點菜 $ 250-650

■ **OPENING HOURS** 營業時間
Lunch 午膳 12:00-14:30
Dinner 晚膳 18:00-22:30

KOWLOON 九龍

241

TOMINOKOJI YAMAGISHI
富小路山岸
Japanese • Minimalist
日本菜・簡約

Chef Yamagishi's intimate kaiseki spot on Tominokoji alley, Kyoto attracts much attention from bon vivants. Its first overseas outpost arrived in Hong Kong in 2019 with just 10 counter seats and a private room for four. The omakase dinner includes 10-plus courses that change according to the season. The uni hand roll made generously with layers of sea urchin roe wrapped in rice and seaweed is among the specialities most sought-after.

京都富小路的首家海外分店，由當地副總廚擔任料理長。設有吧檯和可容納四人的包廂，前者讓食客近距離欣賞廚師手藝，對方更會用日語講解每道菜式，並由服務員翻譯。晚市提供超過十道菜的懷石料理套餐，食材每天由日本送到，菜式按月變更。其中招牌菜海膽壽司運用大量海膽，豐腴鮮美。吧檯僅容十人，須提早訂座。

TEL. 2686 1866

Shop 506, 5F, K11 Musea,
18 Salisbury Road, Tsim Sha Tsui

尖沙咀梳士巴利道18號
K11 MUSEA 5樓506號舖

www.tominokojiyamagishi.hk

■ **PRICE** 價錢
Lunch 午膳
Set Menu 套餐 $ 1,280
Dinner 晚膳
Set Menu 套餐 $ 2,500

■ **OPENING HOURS** 營業時間
Lunch 午膳 12:00-13:30
Dinner 晚膳 18:00-20:45

🍽️○

TSUI HANG VILLAGE (TSIM SHA TSUI)
翠亨邨 (尖沙咀)

Cantonese • Cosy

粵菜 • 舒適

A staple of the Tsim Sha Tsui restaurant scene since 1970s, this place is famous for its authentic Cantonese and Shun Tak fare, namely its bestselling honey-glazed char siu pork, braised beef ribs and shredded chicken, alongside some original creations by the head chef, such as fried king prawns in mango sauce topped with caviar. The dim sum is also good. Watching the chefs work their magic through the large window is all part of the experience.

翠亨邨早於1970年代在尖沙咀開業，菜式以傳統粵菜為主，如醬燒牛肋排、翠亨邨靚一雞及最暢銷的蜜汁叉燒；此外亦不乏順德菜式，以及注入現代元素的新創作，如黑魚子醬芒貴妃蝦球。在這裏，你可以透過大玻璃窗，欣賞廚師烹調各式佳餚，同時滿足視覺和味覺享受。

○🎍 ♿ ⇔ 🅿️

TEL. 2376 2882

Shop 507, 5F, FoodLoft,
Mira Place One, 132 Nathan Road,
Tsim Sha Tsui

尖沙咀彌敦道132號美麗華廣場一期
食四方5樓507號舖

www.miradining.com

■ **PRICE** 價錢
Lunch 午膳
À la carte 點菜 $ 200-500
Dinner 晚膳
À la carte 點菜 $ 300-500

■ **OPENING HOURS** 營業時間
Lunch 午膳 11:30-14:30
Dinner 晚膳 18:00-22:30

TEL. 2315 5999

**5F, The Mira Hotel,
118 Nathan Road, Tsim Sha Tsui**

尖沙咀彌敦道118號The Mira 5樓

www.themirahotel.com

■ **PRICE** 價錢

Lunch 午膳
Set Menu 套餐 $ 368-428
Dinner 晚膳
Set Menu 套餐 $ 890-1,288
À la carte 點菜 $ 600-1,300

■ **OPENING HOURS** 營業時間

Lunch 午膳 12:00-14:00
Dinner 晚膳 18:30-22:00

■ **ANNUAL AND WEEKLY CLOSING**
休息日期

Closed 3 days Lunar New Year and
Sunday dinner

農曆新年3天及週日晚膳休息

WHISK

*European Contemporary •
Contemporary Décor*

時尚歐陸菜 • 時尚

The chef's new-found love of all things Japanese means his cooking now falls into two distinct halves. On the one side you have sharing dishes, like dry aged in-house Kagoshima A4 Wagyu beef served 4 ways, which blend modern European dishes with subtle Asian tones. On the other side you'll find the newer, "infused" Japanese-style dishes where, for example, your grouper comes with galangal and wasabi apple sorbet. Some may be a work in progress but they certainly show innovation.

熟悉當代歐洲烹調技巧的廚師在歐陸菜基礎上糅合日本元素,令菜式出現了有趣迴異的兩種風格,一方面有適合大伙兒分享的歐陸菜式,如法國洛林區Genisse頂級熟成有骨肉眼扒;另一方面也有濃濃的日本風佳餚,如尾崎和牛配鮑魚竹筍,細嫩的和牛味道濃郁。酒單羅列超過二百款全球佳釀,在露台享用另有一番風情!

R. Taylor/4Corners/Sime/Photononstop

STREET FOOD
街頭小吃

KOWLOON 九龍

KAI KAI
佳佳甜品

Offers traditional Chinese sweet soups. Ginkgo and job's tears sweet soup and black sesame soup are worth trying.

售賣傳統中式糖水，白果薏米腐竹糖水和芝麻糊值得一試。

29 Ning Po Street, Jordan
佐敦寧波街29號

PRICE 價錢: $ 25-35
OPENING HOURS 營業時間: 12:00-03:30

BLOCK 18 DOGGIE'S NOODLE (JORDAN)
十八座狗仔粉（佐敦）

Fried pork fat noodles, pork skin and radish, and roast duck leg.

狗仔粉（豬油渣麵）、豬皮蘿蔔、火鴨翅，還有火鴨髀。

GF, 27A Ning Po Street, Jordan
佐敦寧波街27A地下

PRICE 價錢: $ 30-40
OPENING HOURS 營業時間: 24 hours 24小時

🍴○

🍴○

COCONUT-SOUP
(PRINCE EDWARD)
椰小盅（太子）

Tonic soup made with fresh coconut and its water. No MSG or additional water added.

以新鮮椰子及椰子水製成的燉湯，無加水或味精，味道清甜。甜品金脆鮮奶椰小凍也不容錯過。

2A Poplar Street, Prince Edward
太子白楊街2A號舖

PRICE 價錢: $ 65-95
OPENING HOURS 營業時間: 12:00-22:30

DURIAN LAND
(TSIM SHA TSUI)
榴槤樂園（尖沙咀）

Offers different types of durian from their own farm, as well as durian desserts.

供應產自自置果園的不同品種原個榴槤，及各種榴槤甜品。

92 Kimberly Road, Tsim Sha Tsui
尖沙咀金巴利道92號

PRICE 價錢: $ 25-110
OPENING HOURS 營業時間: 15:00-23:00

KOWLOON 九龍

FAT BOY
第三代肥仔

Hong Kong-style snacks including octopus, pork liver & turkey gizzard marinated in soy sauce. Sweet sauce and mustard add to the flavour.

售賣墨魚、生腸、火雞腎及豬膶等港式小食，味道濃淡適中，加入甜醬和芥末更為惹味。

3 Hau Fook Street, Tsim Sha Tsui
尖沙咀厚福街3號

PRICE 價錢: $ 25-40
OPENING HOURS 營業時間: 13:30-00:00

HOP YIK TAI
合益泰小食

Rice rolls; fish balls and radish.

供應豬腸粉、魚蛋、豬皮及蘿蔔等港式小食，每天也人頭湧湧。

121 Kweilin Street, Sham Shui Po
深水埗桂林街121號

PRICE 價錢: $ 10-40
OPENING HOURS 營業時間: 06:30-20:00

KOWLOON 九龍

JOYFUL DESSERT HOUSE

Western desserts like mango Napoleon, pineapple sherbet and green tea lava cake.

西式甜品如芒果拿破崙、燒菠蘿雪葩及綠茶心太軟伴雪糕。

Shop 2-3, GF, Ngai Hing Mansion, 74 Hak Po Street, Mong Kok
旺角黑布街74號藝興大廈地下2-3號舖

PRICE 價錢: $ 55-65
OPENING HOURS 營業時間: 15:00-01:00

KI TSUI
奇趣餅家

Cantonese traditional puddings and pastries like Xiaofeng cake and walnut cookies.

中式餅食如雞仔餅、老婆餅、光酥餅、合桃酥及香蕉糕等。

135 Fa Yuen Street, Mong Kok
旺角花園街135號

PRICE 價錢: $ 10-60
OPENING HOURS 營業時間: 08:00-20:00

KING OF SOYABEANS (SAN PO KONG)
豆漿大王（新蒲崗）

Provides freshly made Shanghainese sticky rice rolls, along with soy milk and other bean curd snacks.

粢飯即場製作，口感尤佳；鹹甜豆漿及其他豆製品亦不容錯過。

**Shop 9, GF, New Tech Plaza,
34 Tai Yau Street, San Po Kong**
新蒲崗大有街34號新科技廣場地下9號舖

PRICE 價錢: $ 15-50

OPENING HOURS 營業時間: 08:00-21:00

KUNG WO BEANCURD FACTORY
公和荳品廠

Besides the renowned tofu pudding, this shop also offers soy milk and soy products such as deep-fried tofu, tofu puff, and golden fish and soya cake.

除了馳名豆腐花外，還有豆漿和各類豆製品，如煎釀豆腐、豆卜和黃金魚腐等。

118 Pei Ho Street, Sham Shui Po
深水埗北河街118號

PRICE 價錢: $ 10-30

OPENING HOURS 營業時間: 07:00-21:00

KOWLOON 九龍

KWAN KEE STORE
坤記糕品

Traditional Chinese desserts, such as red bean pudding, white sugar cake and black sesame rolls.

售賣多種懷舊糕點，例如砵仔糕、芝麻糕、白糖糕、馬蹄糕等。

115-117 Fuk Wa Street, Sham Shui Po
深水埗福華街115–117號

PRICE 價錢: $ 20-40
OPENING HOURS 營業時間: 08:00-20:00

MAMMY PANCAKE
(CARNARVON ROAD)
媽咪雞蛋仔（加拿分道）

Egg puffs made to order, in over 10 classic or innovative flavours. Prepare to queue.

雞蛋仔口味多達十多款，不時推出新款式，且即叫即製，人多時或需要輪候。

8-12 Carnarvon Road, Tsim Sha Tsui
尖沙咀加拿分道8–12號

PRICE 價錢: $ 30-40
OPENING HOURS 營業時間: 11:00-22:00

KOWLOON 九龍

🍴○

🍴○

MAN KEE CART NOODLE
文記車仔麵

Cart noodles with a large selection of toppings. Chinese chive dumpling and Swiss chicken wings are recommended.

配料多樣的車仔麵，推介自製韭菜餃及瑞士雞中翼，另有蘿蔔、牛肚、豬手等任君選擇。

121 Fuk Wing Street, Sham Shui Po
深水埗福榮街121號

PRICE 價錢: $ 40-60
OPENING HOURS 營業時間: 11:00-01:00

OWL'S

Homemade choux and gelato with different condiments. Choose from the menu or just go for your favourite flavour.

以泡芙夾着手工意大利雪糕，外脆內軟。除了餐牌上的選擇外，也可自行配搭不同口味。

GF, 32 Mody Road, Tsim Sha Tsui
尖沙咀麼地道32號地下

PRICE 價錢: $ 30-60
OPENING HOURS 營業時間: 15:00-20:00
Closed Monday 週一休息

HOTELS
酒店

ROSEWOOD
瑰麗

Grand Luxury • Contemporary

奢華 • 時尚

Artwork and sculptures feature here at this hotel set within a skyscraper by the harbour. Rooms are spacious and most have harbour views. There are impressive staff numbers and suites come with butler service. The marble bathrooms, with their freestanding bathtubs and double showers, are the epitome of luxury. There are several dining options, including the Legacy House serving Cantonese and Shun Tak cooking.

坐落尖沙咀海傍的黃金地段，八成房間都擁有無敵海景。從庭園到大堂，沿路氣派不凡，擺放着許多頂級藝術品，並有大量職員隨時提供服務。由著名美國設計師Tony Chi負責室內佈置，無論是豪華的浴室還是巨大的衣櫥和電視，都充滿品味。除了管家服務，更設有室外泳池、健身中心、多個休息室，以及多家餐廳。

TEL. 3891 8888
www.rosewoodhotels.com

18 Salisbury Road, Tsim Sha Tsui
尖沙咀梳士巴利道18號

322 Rooms/客房 $ 3,900-12,800
91 Suites/套房 $ 6,900-37,800

Recommended restaurants/推薦餐廳:
Chaat ⑪○
The Legacy House 彤福軒 ⑪○

255

TEL. 2920 2888
www.peninsula.com/hongkong

Salisbury Road, Tsim Sha Tsui
尖沙咀梳士巴利道

244 Rooms/客房 $ 3,880-8,800
53 Suites/套房 $ 6,880-45,800

Recommended restaurants/推薦餐廳:
Chesa 瑞樵閣 ⭑○
Gaddi's 吉地士 ⭑
Spring Moon 嘉麟樓 ⭑

THE PENINSULA
半島

Grand Luxury · Elegant
奢華·典雅

This grand dame of Hong Kong hotels has been welcoming guests since 1928 and does a fine job of blending age old traditions with modern day comforts. Whilst there is not a bad room in the house it's worth taking one higher up for the views across to Hong Kong Island. The host of facilities include a helipad on the roof and a serene spa. The lobby remains the place for afternoon tea.

於1928年開幕的半島，一直把現代舒適標準融入傳統建築之中，於2013年修葺過後，客房更時尚雅致，房內設備全部透過高科技觸控屏操作，高層房間能遠眺香港島景色。作為酒店標誌的大堂保留原來樣式，供顧客享用下午茶。羅馬式泳池及水療服務一應俱全，天台更設直升機場。

THE RITZ-CARLTON
麗思卡爾頓

Palace • Grand Luxury
宮殿 • 奢華

Occupying the top 16 floors of the International Commerce Centre, this hotel remains, for now, the highest in the world. The spacious, elegant bedrooms have subtle Asian influences in their decoration and most of the suites have harbour and mountain views. The indoor swimming pool is on the 116th floor; the cool Ozone bar is on the 118th!

位於香港最高建築物最頂的16層樓，至今仍是全球最高的酒店。空間偌大的客房裝潢高雅，展現亞洲韻味；套房窗外是宜人的海景或山景，更設有望遠鏡，讓住客居高臨下俯瞰香港景色。時尚酒吧Ozone位於118層，設有戶外露台；室內泳池亦設於海拔490米高處的116層。

TEL. 2263 2263
www.ritzcarlton.com/hongkong

**International Commerce Centre,
1 Austin Road West, Tsim Sha Tsui**
尖沙咀柯士甸道西1號環球貿易廣場

262 Rooms/客房 $ 2,800-19,800
50 Suites/套房 $ 3,600-15,900

Recommended restaurants/推薦餐廳:
Tin Lung Heen 天龍軒 ✿✿
Tosca di Angelo ✿

TEL. 3400 1000
www.hotel-icon.com

**17 Science Museum Road,
Tsim Sha Tsui**
尖東科學館道17號

236 Rooms/客房 $ 960-5,000
26 Suites/套房 $ 2,200-15,000

Recommended restaurants/推薦餐廳:
Above & Beyond 天外天 ⏱○

ICON
唯港薈

Luxury • Elegant
豪華 • 典雅

Several of the world's leading designers helped create this rather cool hotel which returns all profits to its owner, the Hong Kong Polytechnic University, to reinvest in the building. Students are actively involved as part of their studies. Rooms have an uncluttered look and features include a living wall garden in the foyer and over 100 pieces from local artists.

這間香港理工大學名下的酒店由著名設計師嚴迅奇、泰倫斯·康藍爵士和林偉而等攜手設計，該院校學生亦著手參與酒店發展，實踐酒店管理知識。房間整潔有序，精美之餘兼具功能性。整所酒店設計風格鮮明，陳設了超過一百件本地藝術家的作品，亦有令人驚歎的現代化樓梯和垂直花園。

CORDIS
康得思

Business • Modern
商務・現代

The modern, luminous lobby of this 42-storey glass tower features contemporary Chinese paintings and sculptures – part of the collection of 1,500 pieces that you'll find dotted around the hotel. Good-sized rooms with picture windows come with smart marble bathrooms and nice views. There's a pool on the top floor and an all-day buffet restaurant on the lobby floor.

康得思坐落於行人如鯽的旺角心臟地帶，連接地鐵站和購物商場。琉璃塔般的大樓高42層，不僅有科技發燒友夢寐以求的電子產品，還有超過1,500幅畫作、雕塑與裝置藝術品，是一個中國現代美術展覽館。客房的設計含蓄而時髦，窗外是五光十色的繁華市景；天台設有室外恒溫游泳池，並有多間餐廳供客人選擇。

TEL. 3552 3388
cordishotels.com/hongkong
555 Shanghai Street, Mong Kok
旺角上海街555號

640 Rooms/客房 $ 1,400-2,200
29 Suites/套房 $ 2,400-4,200
Recommended restaurants/推薦餐廳:
Ming Court (Mong Kok) 明閣（旺角）✿

KOWLOON 九龍

🏠 KOWLOON SHANGRI-LA
九龍香格里拉

Business · Elegant

商務·典雅

This is one of Kowloon's most respected hotels, both for its longevity and for the quality of the service. Harbour view bedrooms are the most sought after; choose a Horizon Club room for its luxury. Pick from Japanese cuisine in Nadaman, Italian in Angelini or Cantonese in Shang Palace. Afternoon tea in the lounge, with its fountains and chandeliers, is a special experience.

別具氣派的雲石大堂與三層噴泉水池,都令人對這歷史悠久的酒店留下深刻印象。坐擁維多利亞港迷人景觀,海景客房自然最受歡迎,若入住豪華閣的客房更可享受最奢華的體驗。酒店不乏環球美饌,包括日本餐廳灘萬、提供粵菜的香宮等,在大堂的吊燈下享用下午茶亦是不錯的選擇。

TEL. 2721 2111
www.shangri-la.com/kowloon
64 Mody Road, Tsim Sha Tsui
尖東麼地道64號

646 Rooms/客房 $ 2,000-6,000
42 Suites/套房 $ 3,150-7,250

Recommended restaurants/推薦餐廳:
Shang Palace 香宮 ✿

THE LANGHAM
朗廷

Luxury • Elegant
豪華 • 典雅

The clamour of Peking Road will seem but a distant memory once you're in the hushed surroundings of this elegant hotel. Its striking lobby, furnished in a classical European style, features some impressive modern art and sculptures, and bedrooms are furnished in a smart, contemporary style. The charm of the hotel is underpinned by modern facilities and attentive service.

進入這幢優雅建築物，讓你立刻忘卻北京道熙來攘往的煩囂。大堂以傳統歐洲風格裝潢，配上當代藝術品及雕塑作點綴，奢華奪目。客房設計典雅時尚，極具吸引力。迷人之處，盡見於其現代設施及細心周到的服務。

TEL. 2132 7898
www.langhamhotels.com/hongkong

8 Peking Road, Tsim Sha Tsui
尖沙咀北京道8號

471 Rooms/客房 $ 1,500-2,950
27 Suites/套房 $ 3,300-4,750

Recommended restaurants/推薦餐廳:
Bostonian Seafood & Grill ⅈ○
T'ang Court 唐閣 ✿✿✿

KOWLOON 九龍

TEL. 2368 1111
www.themirahotel.com

118 Nathan Road, Tsim Sha Tsui
尖沙咀彌敦道118號

436 Rooms/客房 ＄1,400-3,000
56 Suites/套房 ＄2,200-4,500

Recommended restaurants/推薦餐廳:
Cuisine Cuisine at The Mira
國金軒（尖沙咀）⑩
Whisk ⑩

THE MIRA

Luxury • Design
豪華•型格

It's all about design at this hotel in the heart of Kowloon's main shopping district. The bedrooms may not be the largest but they feature plenty of modern gadgets, including your own transportable wi-fi link. The penthouse is the space for an event, with views overlooking Kowloon Park, and the heated water beds in MiraSpa are perfect for de-stressing.

位於九龍心臟地帶的購物區，客房面積相對不大，但出色的設計彌補了不足，房間設施非常現代化，提供流動無線上網連接；套房裝潢豪華。宴會廳擁有最時尚的音訊設備和巨型入牆顯示屏，適合各種宴會，頂樓更能俯瞰九龍公園園景。水療設施舒適豪華，熱療水床讓您能肆意放鬆。

KOWLOON 九龍

HYATT REGENCY TSIM SHA TSUI
尖沙咀凱悅

Chain • Modern

連鎖式•現代

Occupying floors 10-24 of the impressive K11 skyscraper means that bedrooms here at the Hyatt Regency benefit from impressive views of the city or harbour. The rooms are decorated in a crisp, modern style; anyone choosing the Regency Club level has access to a private lounge. There are dining options galore and an impressive selection of whiskies in the Chin Chin Bar.

TEL. 2311 1234
hyattregencyhongkongtsimshatsui. com

18 Hanoi Road, Tsim Sha Tsui
尖沙咀河內道18號

348 Rooms/客房 $ 1,800-3,000
33 Suites/套房 $ 3,300-4,500

尖沙咀凱悅佔據K11摩天大樓的10至24層，並與K11購物藝術館相連，酒店房間能看到城市的繁華景色，或是醉人的維港景致。房間風格清新時尚，選擇嘉賓軒樓層的住客更可享受專用酒廊服務。酒店提供多種餐飲選擇，請請吧內的威士忌種類之多更是令人歎為觀止。

263

TEL. 2721 5215
www.rghk.com.hk

69 Mody Road, Tsim Sha Tsui
尖東麼地道69號

396 Rooms/客房 $ 1,000-4,200
54 Suites/套房 $ 1,600-7,800

Recommended restaurants/推薦餐廳:
Dong Lai Shun 東來順

THE ROYAL GARDEN
帝苑

Luxury • Contemporary
豪華•時尚

This hotel continues to evolve thanks to its newer, more spacious and contemporary bedrooms in the Sky Tower, along with a smart gym and spa. J's Bar is for cocktails and live music and the numerous dining options include Chinese, Vietnamese, Italian and Japanese; there's even a mini food store selling some irresistible cakes and biscuits.

帝苑酒店不斷革新,客房時尚舒適,附有現代化設備, 位於16-19樓的天際套房更坐擁維港兩岸景色。餐廳 種類繁多,有中菜、越南菜、意大利菜及日本菜任君選 擇。J´s酒吧提供雞尾酒及現場音樂表演;想在正餐以 外來點小吃的話,大堂餅店還有使人無法抗拒的蛋糕 和餅乾。水療和健身設施足夠你享受一整天。

MADERA (JORDAN)
木的地（佐敦）

Family • Contemporary

溫馨 • 時尚

The hotel, designed by a Spanish team with a nature theme, is aptly named with the Spanish word for lumber. Though it is close to a bustling night market overflowing with street food and vendors, the rooftop bar comes with a surprisingly relaxed vibe. Besides the duplex penthouse suites on the top floors, those prone to allergies can also consider the hypoallergenic rooms on the 21st floor.

Madera是西班牙文的「木頭」，和酒店的中文名一樣，透露出大自然氣息。由西班牙團隊設計，設有特選複式套房，更有坊間少見的防敏感樓層，為體質敏感的客人提供安全舒適的住宿。除了頂樓的露天酒吧、全天候開放的健身室和瑜伽中心，旅客更可以到訪毗鄰的廟街夜市，體驗充滿香港情懷的街邊小販和大牌檔。

TEL. 2121 9888
www.maderagroup.com

1 Cheong Lok Street, Jordan
佐敦長樂街1號

80 Rooms/客房 $ 700-1,200
7 Suites/套房 $ 2,000-8,000

KOWLOON 九龍

RESIDENCE G

Boutique Hotel • Functional

精品酒店・實用

&. ⇥

TEL. 2355 8888
www.hotels-g.com/hong-kong

2 Austin Avenue, Tsim Sha Tsui
尖沙咀柯士甸路2號

32 Rooms/客房 $ 700-1,800
6 Suites/套房 $ 1,500-3,500

Within walking distance from Hunghom station and the Science Museum, this hotel is nestled in an area with a vibrant dining and bar scene. Rooms range from 220 to 800 ft2 in size and come with an industrial chic look, with wood and black metal tubing furniture. Alongside a complimentary smartphone, guests have access to the lounge and communal work station. The café bar opens till 1am.

位於香港歷史博物館對面，能步行前往火車站，交通便利。除了設有西餐廳和營業至凌晨一時的酒吧，毗鄰的餐廳及大型商場林立，定能滿足餐飲和消費需求。備有多種大小的房間，包括附設完整廚房的大型套房，適合一家大小入住。免費提供歐陸早餐和手提電話，住客更可使用共享休息室及工作間。

KOWLOON 九龍

STAGE  N

登臺

Business · Central

商務·便捷

Location, location, location! It's hard to beat the position of this boutique hotel as it's just minutes away from a MTR station, a night market and tons of dining options. But with all-day dining, a wine bar and a gallery, guests don't have to even leave the building if they don't want to. Rooms are minimalistic but well appointed, with remote controlled lighting and duo-head massage shower.

立於九龍心臟地段，毗鄰廟街，吃喝購物不愁選擇，與鐵路站站更只有數分鐘路程。房間設計簡約舒適、設備齊全，浴室特設雙頭式按摩花灑，讓人疲勞盡消。酒店除設有餐廳和地下酒窖，更不時舉辦藝術文化活動、展覽和演出。不妨到訪藝術精品店，選購世界各地的書籍和手工藝製品，作為富特色的紀念品。

KOWLOON 九龍

TEL. 3953 2222

www.hotelstage.com

1 Chi Wo Street, Jordan

佐敦志和街1號

86 Rooms/客房 $ 950-1,600
11 Suites/套房 $ 2,150-2,800

J. Arnold Images/hemis.fr

NEW TERRITORIES

新界

RESTAURANTS
餐廳

LOAF ON
六福菜館

Seafood • Cosy

海鮮 • 舒適

It may not have the large displays of seafood that its promenade rivals boast but this restaurant stands out because of its cooking. Wonderfully fresh seafood is prepared using traditional home recipes that let the quality of the ingredients speak for themselves. Must-try dishes include minced fish in pumpkin soup, mantis shrimp with chilli and garlic and their steamed fish with sea salt. Traditional Cantonese dishes are also done well, like deep-fried tofu.

這家小菜館佔地三層，藏身於西貢海鮮餐廳一帶後街，門口並未見一般海鮮餐館常設的大魚缸，僅以出色的烹調技巧便吸引了不少食客。以生猛海鮮炮製的小菜選料高質，每一口都散發着鮮味。金湯魚蓉羹、椒鹽瀨尿蝦和鹽水蒸西貢魚仔是必吃菜式，傳統粵式小菜如椒鹽奇脆豆腐也值得一試。

☺¶ 📠

TEL. 2792 9966

49 See Cheung Street, Sai Kung

西貢市場街49號

■ **PRICE** 價錢
À la carte 點菜 $ 200-500

■ **OPENING HOURS** 營業時間
11:00-22:30

■ **ANNUAL AND WEEKLY CLOSING**
休息日期
Closed 2 days Lunar New Year
農曆新年休息2天

NEW TERRITORIES 新界

⊘¶ ⚕ ⇔ **P**

TEL. 2450 6366

Miles 19, Castle Peak Road, Tuen Mun

屯門青山公路19咪

www.dragoninn1939.com

■ **PRICE 價錢**
À la carte 點菜 $ 300-400

■ **OPENING HOURS 營業時間**
10:00-23:00

■ **ANNUAL AND WEEKLY CLOSING**
休息日期
Closed 2 days Lunar New Year
農曆新年休息2天

😀

DRAGON INN
容龍

Seafood • Classic Décor

海鮮 • 經典

This restaurant is known by almost everyone in the neighbourhood and was revamped in 2017 to include more private rooms alongside the main dining hall. Most guests pick their seafood from the nearby wet market for the chefs here to cook up; others choose from the catch of the day without looking at the menu. Baked baby lobster with cheese and baked oysters with port are not to be missed. It also serves dim sum during the day.

容龍在本區可謂赫赫有名，裝修後換上更時尚的佈置，新增更多私人廂房，滿足注重私人空間的食客，其中兩間更坐擁海畔美景。為數不少的客人會自攜海鮮加工，個別更不看主菜牌，直接從海鮮單上挑選食物。招牌菜包括芝士焗開邊龍蝦與砵酒焗生蠔；日間則有點心供應。

HAO TANG HAO MIAN
好湯好麵

Noodles · Simple

麵食 • 簡樸

An owner-chef with over 20 years of experience in French cooking opened this 20-seater specialising in just 12 noodle soup items, each with a specific soup base and toppings. The signature flat noodles in beef soup with Sichuan beef cheek and French braised oxtail takes two days to make, involving eclectic techniques. The flavourful seafood potage with crab, prawns and scallops works surprisingly well with thin Chinese noodles.

店主擁有逾廿年法國菜經驗，他融合法菜、西菜和中菜烹調方法，設計十二款湯麵，各有湯底和配料，且均以優質食材新鮮熬煮，香濃鮮甜且不含味精。推介以多款海鮮和蔬菜炮製的海龍皇湯，口感順滑海鮮味濃。限量的「好頭好尾」加入了牛骨湯和牛尾濃汁，配搭川式燜牛臉肉和法式燜牛尾，製作需時兩天，值得一試。

TEL. 2813 5077

GF, 20 Chik Chuen Street, Tai Wai
大圍積存街20號地舖

■ **PRICE** 價錢
À la carte 點菜 $ 100-200

■ **OPENING HOURS** 營業時間
12:00-20:30

■ **ANNUAL AND WEEKLY CLOSING**
休息日期
Closed 4 days Lunar New Year
農曆新年休息4天

NEW TERRITORIES 新界

HO TO TAI (YUEN LONG)
好到底 (元朗)

Noodles • Neighbourhood

麵食 • 親切

Traditional shops that make their own noodles from scratch are hard to come by. Founded in 1946, this household name is among the remaining few. The nostalgic two-storey shop has quintessential Cantonese dumplings on the menu, the must-try wonton soup and fish skin dumplings. Those craving more carbs can order the hugely popular tossed noodles with shrimp roe. The owner also runs a dried noodle factory with retail outlets all over town.

自家製麵的傳統店舖愈來愈少,這家於1946年開業、位處元朗的老字號麵家是其中之一。樓高兩層的店舖內是濃濃的懷舊氣氛。蝦籽撈麵和特製魚皮水餃向來是最受歡迎的食物,而雲吞更是非試不可!麵店附近設有製麵工場,店主同時在市區設立多個麵食銷售店,出售自製乾麵及蝦籽。

🖵 ⓢ ✗🍴

TEL. 2476 2495

67 Fau Tsoi Street, Yuen Long
元朗阜財街67號

■ **PRICE** 價錢
À la carte 點菜 $ 30-70

■ **OPENING HOURS** 營業時間
10:00-19:30

■ **ANNUAL AND WEEKLY CLOSING**
休息日期
Closed 10 days Lunar New Year
農曆新年休息10天

NEW TERRITORIES 新界

TAI WING WAH
大榮華

Cantonese • Traditional

粵菜 • 傳統

A refit in 2016 resulted in this Cantonese restaurant, located in the north of New Territories, looking a little brighter and feeling a little fresher. It serves dim sum and 'Walled Village' cuisine, alongside assorted classic Cantonese dishes. Try the roast duck with bean paste and coriander; claypot rice with lard and premium soy sauce; and, above all, the steamed sponge cake. A seasonal menu is available and changes every month.

光顧大榮華是很多人長途跋涉來到元朗的主要原因。此酒家除了供應點心外，還提供近百款圍村小菜及經典粵式名菜，如香茜燒米鴨、缽仔豬油頭抽撈飯及鹹水檸蒸烏頭等，更少不了奶黃馬拉糕。大廚亦每月更新時令菜式。餐廳用上五彩繽紛的地氈和明亮的燈光，配上傳統裝飾，感覺煥然一新。

♿ ♻

TEL. 2476 9888

2F, 2-6 On Ning Road, Yuen Long

元朗安寧路2-6號2樓

■ **PRICE** 價錢
À la carte 點菜 $ 100-300

■ **OPENING HOURS** 營業時間
07:00-21:15

⊙🖥 ⇦ 🛏 **P**

TEL. 2491 0105

9 Sham Hong Road, Sham Tseng

深井深康路9號

www.yuekee.com.hk

■ **PRICE** 價錢
À la carte 點菜 $ 150-550

■ **OPENING HOURS** 營業時間
11:00-22:15

■ **ANNUAL AND WEEKLY CLOSING**
休息日期
Closed 3 days Lunar New Year
農曆新年休息3天

YUE KEE
裕記
Cantonese • Friendly
粵菜 • 友善

From humble beginnings as a tiny countryside joint in 1958, this second-generation family business has gone big, but without losing its flair. Geese are sourced from eight farms in China to ensure quality and a steady supply. The owner insists on chargrilling them according to his family recipe, to give them their distinctive smokiness, crispy skin and juicy meat. They're served after 11:45am and the menu also includes seafood and stir-fries.

裕記於1958年開業，現由第二代打理。從鄉村小店到現在的規模，仍保留着傳統食店風味。其招牌燒鵝是店東按家傳秘方以炭火烤製，味道獨特且酥香肉嫩，採用的鵝從內地八個農場合作伙伴中挑選，確保貨源和質素。每天第一爐鵝於11:45出爐，早到埗的食客需稍候。燒鵝以外，亦供應海鮮及特色小菜。

CHUEN KEE SEAFOOD (HOI PONG STREET)
全記海鮮 (海傍街)

Seafood • Rural

海鮮 • 田園

Two family-run restaurants overlook a pleasant harbour to distant islands; choose the one with the rooftop terrace and the quayside plastic seats. An extraordinary range of seafood is available from adjacent fishmongers: cuttlefish, bivalve, crab and lobster, mollusc, shrimps, prawns... Go to the tank, select your meal, and minutes later it appears in front of you: steamed, poached, or wok-fried. Try the abalone or mantis shrimp in peppered salt.

兩家相連的餐廳是家族生意,可選擇有陽台的那一家,坐在碼頭邊的膠座椅上觀賞宜人海灣及離島景致。魚缸內的海鮮種類繁多,墨魚、貝類、蟹、龍蝦、瀨尿蝦等任你隨意挑選,蒸、灼、炒也好,不一會就奉到餐桌上,然後你便可輕鬆地邊品嘗海鮮邊細覽海上景色。推介菜式有古法椒鹽鮑魚和椒鹽瀨尿蝦。

◎⑪ 斋 ≼ ⇔

TEL. 2791 1195

53 Hoi Pong Street, Sai Kung

西貢海傍街53號

■ **PRICE** 價錢
À la carte 點菜 $ 400-600

■ **OPENING HOURS** 營業時間
11:00-22:30

NEW TERRITORIES 新界

LEI GARDEN (SHA TIN)
利苑酒家（沙田）

Cantonese • Family
粵菜 • 溫馨

TEL. 2698 9111

Shop 628, 6F, Phase I,
New Town Plaza,
18-19 Shatin Centre Street, Sha Tin

沙田沙田正街18-19號
新城市廣場第1期6樓628號舖
www.leigarden.com.hk

■ PRICE 價錢
Lunch 午膳
À la carte 點菜 $ 200-500
Dinner 晚膳
À la carte 點菜 $ 250-800

■ OPENING HOURS 營業時間
Lunch 午膳 11:30-14:30
Dinner 晚膳 18:00-22:00

■ ANNUAL AND WEEKLY CLOSING
休息日期
Closed 3 days Lunar New Year
農曆新年休息3天

Regular refurbishment has kept this 20-year-old branch feeling fresh. It's set in a shopping mall connected to an MTR station and gets busy at weekends when everyone needs refuelling after a day of shopping. The menu is basically the same as other branches; always ask for the catch of the day. Peking duck, char siu, and rice in seafood soup made with lobster, prawns and crabs are also great options. Reservations are recommended at lunch time.

屹立沙田逾二十年，這家利苑分店憑着精心烹調的正宗粵菜及舒適的室內環境，成為區內居民的熱門聚腳點，午市建議訂座。大受歡迎的海鮮湯泡飯選用龍蝦、蝦及蟹等多款海鮮做湯底，每啖都充溢濃郁海鮮味道。其他熱門菜式包括當日推介海鮮、片皮鴨、叉燒及老火湯，建議於訂座時一併預訂。

🍴○

SAI KUNG SING KEE
勝記

Seafood • Family

海鮮 • 溫馨

Diners are spoiled for choice when it comes to seafood restaurants in Sai Kung, but this one stands out from the competition with its varied ways to cook live abalone – try them stewed in oyster sauce or deep-fried with peppered salt. There are 12 rooms spread across three floors, each one decorated differently; those on the 1st and 2nd floors are more modern. Al fresco dining on the patio overlooking the waterfront is a plus in balmy weather.

在西貢比比皆是的三層建築中，勝記的紅色外牆尤其引人注目。餐廳內備有十二個大小不一、裝飾各異的房間，其中一樓和二樓的餐室裝潢較時尚；若天公造美選擇戶外臨海位置更是一大享受。這家海鮮菜館的特別之處，在於其選擇多樣的鮑魚菜式，由酥炸到蒸煮式式俱備，當中以蠔皇扣鮮鮑魚和椒鹽鮮鮑魚特別出色。

📶🛗 ↔

TEL. 2791 9887

39 Sai Kung Tai Street, Sai Kung

西貢西貢大街39號

www.singkee.hk

■ **PRICE** 價錢
À la carte 點菜 $ 300-1,000

■ **OPENING HOURS** 營業時間
11:30-22:00

■ **ANNUAL AND WEEKLY CLOSING**
休息日期
Closed 2 days Lunar New Year
農曆新年休息2天

NEW TERRITORIES 新界

TEL. 2474 8849

Shop D, GF, Yan Yee Building,
88 Kin Yip Street, Yuen Long

元朗建業街88號仁義大廈地下D舖

■ PRICE 價錢
Lunch 午膳
À la carte 點菜 $ 60-200
Dinner 晚膳
À la carte 點菜 $ 60-200

■ OPENING HOURS 營業時間
Lunch 午膳 11:00-14:30
Dinner 晚膳 17:00-22:30

TIN HUNG
天鴻燒鵝

Cantonese Roast Meats • Simple

燒味 • 簡樸

Popular with locals since 2001, this shop sells its signature roast geese in specific cuts, halves or whole. Geese are slaughtered daily in a farm in Foshan, China before being shipped here. They are then marinated and roasted to perfection, and served piping hot. Other standouts include honey-glazed char siu pork, roast duck and drunken chicken. Those looking to pair the meats with a local drink should try their homemade herbal tea.

天鴻燒鵝2001年開業，尤為區內居民熟悉。來自佛山養殖場的黑鬃鵝每日直送到店，分批即醃即燒，確保每隻都熱氣騰騰。招牌燒鵝分為全隻、半隻及不同部位發售，高峰期每日售出近百隻，若售罄便會提早關門。除了燒鵝，蜜汁叉燒、燒鴨、花雕醉雞和滷水等亦值得一試；店家更出售清熱的自製五花茶。

YUÈ (GOLD COAST)
粵 (黃金海岸)

Cantonese • Traditional
粵菜 • 傳統

It's not often one can enjoy Cantonese food surrounded by verdant scenery but here on the ground floor of the Gold Coast hotel that's exactly what you get as this comfortable restaurant looks out onto a delightful garden. The menu includes both traditional and more contemporary dishes and it's worth seeking out the chef's specialities such as barbecued pork and double boiled pork lung soup with almond milk and fish maw, and deep-fried chicken with shrimp paste.

位於黃金海岸酒店的地面層，優雅舒適的室內環境，與落地玻璃窗外的園林景致巧妙地配合起來。選擇豐富的餐單提供傳統懷舊及較創新的粵菜，廚師精選菜式如龍皇杏汁花膠燉白肺和星洲蝦醬炸雞件等，值得一試。邊品嘗美味的廣式點心，邊欣賞宜人的園林美景，實在是賞心樂事。

TEL. 2452 8668

LG, Gold Coast Hotel, 1 Castle Peak Road, Gold Coast, Tuen Mun

屯門黃金海岸青山公路1號
黃金海岸酒店低層

www.goldcoasthotel.com.hk

■ PRICE 價錢
Lunch 午膳
Set Menu 套餐 $ 150-200
À la carte 點菜 $ 200-1,000
Dinner 晚膳
Set Menu 套餐 $ 200-500
À la carte 點菜 $ 200-1,000

■ OPENING HOURS 營業時間
Lunch 午膳 11:30-15:00
Dinner 晚膳 18:00-22:30

NEW TERRITORIES 新界

STREET FOOD
街頭小吃

CHIN SIK
千色車仔麵

Typical Hong Kong-style cart noodles, with a selection of toppings such as squid and chicken wing tips.

典型港式車仔麵店，備有豬紅、魷魚、雞翼尖等多樣選擇。

49 Shiu Wo Street, Tsuen Wan
荃灣兆和街49號

PRICE 價錢: $ 30-60
OPENING HOURS 營業時間: 11:30-01:00

FORK EAT

Chicken from a local farm comes smoked, roasted or in a chicken broth. Homemade spicy chicken organs and chicken liver pate are also offered.

以自家農場供應的新鮮雞為主，有濃湯浸、煙燻或香烤做法，亦有售賣自家製麻辣雞雜和雞肝醬。

**Shop 10, GF, Yik Fat Building,
11-15 Fung Yau Street North, Yuen Long**
元朗鳳攸北街11-15號益發大廈10號舖

PRICE 價錢: $ 50-170
OPENING HOURS 營業時間: 12:00-21:00

NEW TERRITORIES 新界

SO KEE
蘇記燉蛋

Offers cooked-to-order double-steamed egg white with milk.

只售原味牛奶燉蛋白，以北海道牛乳及鮮蛋白燉製，即叫即做。

Shop 15, GF, Block A, Ho Shun Yee Building, 9 Fung Yau Street East, Yuen Long
元朗鳳攸東街9號好順意大廈A座地下15號舖

PRICE 價錢: $ 35

OPENING HOURS 營業時間: 15:30-22:30

ymgerman/iStock

HOTELS
酒店

HYATT REGENCY SHA TIN
沙田凱悅

Business • Contemporary

商務•時尚

Just a minute's walk from University Station is this 26-floor hotel, whose large, well-equipped bedrooms have either harbour or mountain views. It makes clever use of neutral colours and natural materials like stone and wood to create a soothing ambience. It's business-orientated during the week; the impressive leisure facilities appeal to families at weekends.

沙田凱悅於2009年開幕,從港鐵大學站前往僅需步行兩分鐘。酒店設計充滿時代感,巧妙運用中性色彩及天然物料如石材及木材製造出柔和融洽的感覺。酒店平日以接待商務旅客為主,到週末則以出色的休閒設施吸引家庭顧客。

TEL. 3723 1234
hyattregencyhongkongshatin.com
18 Chak Cheung Street, Sha Tin
沙田澤祥街18號

388 Rooms/客房 $ 950-2,800
174 Suites/套房 $ 2,150-5,700

MACAU

澳門

Ruchaneewan Togran/iStock

澳門
MACAU

G94

G94

嘉路米耶圓形地
Rotunda de
Carlos da Maia

大三巴牌坊
Ruins of St. Paul's

東望洋炮台
Guia Fortress

議事亭前地
Senado Square

漁人碼頭
Fisherman's Wharf

主教山小堂
Chapel of Our
Lady of Penha

觀音蓮花苑
Kun Iam
Ecumenical Centre

媽閣廟
A-Ma Temple

澳門旅遊塔
Macau Tower

R. do Alm. Sergio

Av. Dr. Sun Yat-Sen

Ponte da Amizade

友誼大橋

孫逸仙大馬路

河邊新街

嘉樂庇大橋 Ponte de Sai Van

SOUTH CHINA SEA

氹仔
TAIPA

Av. Wai Long

偉龍馬路

官也街
Rua do Cunha

龍環葡韻
Taipa House

路氹
COTAI

蓮花路 Estrada Flor de Lótus

路環
COLOANE

黑沙海灘
Hac Sa Beach

路環聖方濟各聖堂
Chapel of
St. Francis Xavier

澳門
MACAU

0   1 km

0   1 mile

anutr tosirikul/iStock

MACAU
澳門

MACAU 澳門

RESTAURANTS
餐廳

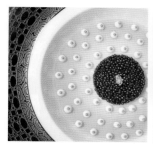

❀ ❀ ❀

ROBUCHON AU DÔME
天巢法國餐廳

French Contemporary • Luxury

時尚法國菜 • 豪華

Its lofty position atop the Grand Lisboa hotel lets diners take in breathtaking views over Macau and is a great setting for Joël Robuchon's renowned contemporary French cuisine. Choose the 7-course 'Menu Aux Crustacés' or an 8-course seasonal menu; the dishes are intricate, beautifully presented and deliver an array of intense flavours, with the stunning dessert trolley providing a fitting finale. The restaurant boasts one of the best wine lists in Asia.

Joël Robuchon的天巢法國餐廳位於新葡京酒店頂樓，大型水晶吊燈引人矚目，食客更能俯瞰令人屏息的360度澳門全景，是品味時尚法式美饌的絕佳舞台。可選擇七道菜的海鮮菜單或八道菜的季節菜單。菜式艷麗如畫，入口濃郁可口，各菜單均以精緻甜品作結。餐酒選擇過萬種，大概在亞洲數一數二。

🏛 ◑❙ ৬ ≾ ⇪ 👥 **P**

TEL. 8803 7878

43F, Grand Lisboa Hotel,
Avenida de Lisboa, Macau

澳門葡京路新葡京酒店43樓

www.grandlisboahotels.com

■ **PRICE** 價錢
Lunch 午膳
Set Menu 套餐 MOP 688-1,488
À la carte 點菜 MOP 1,300-3,500
Dinner 晚膳
Set Menu 套餐 MOP 2,488-3,388
À la carte 點菜 MOP 1,300-3,500

■ **OPENING HOURS** 營業時間
Lunch 午膳 12:00-14:30
Dinner 晚膳 18:30-22:00

MACAU 澳門

295

🍴 ⓞ 🚻 ♨ **P**

TEL. 8803 7788

**2F, Grand Lisboa Hotel,
Avenida de Lisboa, Macau**

澳門葡京路新葡京酒店2樓

www.grandlisboahotels.com

■ **PRICE 價錢**
Lunch 午膳
Set Menu 套餐 MOP 2,800
À la carte 點菜 MOP 400-3,000
Dinner 晚膳
Set Menu 套餐 MOP 2,800
À la carte 點菜 MOP 400-3,000

■ **OPENING HOURS 營業時間**
Lunch 午膳 11:30-14:30
Dinner 晚膳 18:30-22:30

✿ ✿ ✿

THE EIGHT
8餐廳

Cantonese • Luxury

粵菜 • 豪華

The lavish interior uses the traditional Chinese elements of the goldfish and the number eight to ensure good fortune for all who dine here. The cuisine is a mix of Cantonese and Huaiyang, but the kitchen also adds its own innovative touches to some dishes. Specialities include steamed crab claw with ginger and Chinese wine, and stir-fried lobster with egg, minced pork and black bean. At lunchtime, over 40 kinds of dim sum are served.

豪華的內部裝潢採用了傳統中國元素，如金魚及數目字「8」，寓意所有到訪的客人都會遇上好運。菜式融合了廣東及淮揚風味，部分美食更滲入了創新點子。推介菜式有薑米酒蒸鮮蟹拑及廣東式炒龍蝦。午餐時段供應逾四十款精美點心。

FENG WEI JU
風味居

Hunanese and Sichuan • Luxury

湘菜及川菜 • 豪華

Gold and red are the traditional festive hues for the Chinese and also the colour scheme of this opulent restaurant. Along with Sichuan classics, such as sautéed chicken with peanuts and chilli, are Hunanese favourites like steamed carp fish head with chilli. The hand-pulled noodles are also worth trying – watching the chefs pulling them in the display kitchen adds to the entertainment.

貫徹天花、餐桌至地氈的金黃色讓整個餐室給映襯得金光閃爍，加上大紅色的皮制椅子，視覺效果分外鮮明。紅色的裝飾就像與餐廳提供的湘川菜互相呼應似的，由剁椒魚頭到宮保雞丁，味道全都鮮辣刺激！多款手製麵條和餃子也值得一試，隔着玻璃，你還能夠看到廚師團隊製作麵條的過程。

TEL. 8290 8668
5F, StarWorld Hotel,
Avenida da Amizade, Macau
澳門友誼大馬路星際酒店5樓
www.starworldmacau.com

■ **PRICE** 價錢
À la carte 點菜 MOP 300-800

■ **OPENING HOURS** 營業時間
11:00-22:30

MACAU 澳門

✿✿

GOLDEN FLOWER
京花軒

Beijing Cuisine & Cantonese • Luxury
京菜及粵菜 • 豪華

TEL. 8986 3663

GF, Encore Hotel,
Rua Cidade de Sintra, NAPE, Macau

澳門外港新填海區仙德麗街
萬利酒店地下

www.wynnmacau.com

■ PRICE 價錢
Lunch 午膳
À la carte 點菜 MOP 300-2,000
Dinner 晚膳
Set Menu 套餐 MOP 1,880
À la carte 點菜 MOP 300-2,000

■ OPENING HOURS 營業時間
Lunch 午膳 11:30-14:15
Dinner 晚膳 18:00-22:15

■ ANNUAL AND WEEKLY CLOSING
休息日期
Closed Monday to Friday lunch and
Tuesday 週一至週五午膳及週二休息

(*Restaurant is temporarily closed due to COVID-19.*) The gold-and-orange colour scheme of the room evokes ethereal glamour and the semi-circular white leather booth seats are particularly inviting. The astute kitchen team use well-honed skills and superb ingredients to create Sichuan, Shandong, Tanjiacai and Cantonese fare. The strikingly-attired servers and the tea sommelier provide charming service.

（受疫情影響，餐廳於評審期間暫時停業。）京花軒的裝潢以金色和橙色為主調，讓這間位於萬利酒店內的中菜館典雅而別具貴氣。白色皮製卡座設計成圓形，方便三五知己談天說地。廚房選料上乘，俐落地烹調出川菜、魯菜、譚家菜和廣東菜。服務悉心周到，更設有調茶師為食客配搭茶品。

MACAU 澳門

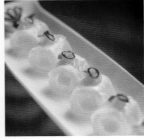

❀ ❀

MIZUMI (MACAU)
泓（澳門）

Japanese • Trendy
日本菜 • 前衛

The lucky colours of gold and red were incorporated into the decoration – and it's certainly a strikingly bright room. Three consultants are involved, including Chef Shimamiya from Sushi Zen in Hokkaido. The fish comes from Japan; the beef from a private ranch on Ishigaki Island, south of Okinawa. Go for the 'Taste of Mizumi'.

主餐室的地氈、牆身和裝飾均披上金、紅兩色，加上入口的銅鑄日本摺紙工藝雕塑，奪目且煥然一新。食物方面，不論是魚生、壽司、鐵板燒或天婦羅均選用高質食材，包括每週由日本運到的新鮮海產及精心搜購的沖繩和牛，加上精細的烹調，令人回味無窮。點選泓之風味套餐能一次品嘗各式料理。

《🍴 占 ⊕ ⊞ 🛏 🅿

TEL. 8986 3663

GF, Wynn Hotel,
Rua Cidade de Sintra, NAPE, Macau

澳門外港新填海區仙德麗街
永利酒店地下

www.wynnmacau.com

■ **PRICE 價錢**
Lunch 午膳
Set Menu 套餐 MOP 650-950
À la carte 點菜 MOP 500-1,800
Dinner 晚膳
Set Menu 套餐 MOP 890-2,490
À la carte 點菜 MOP 500-1,800

■ **OPENING HOURS 營業時間**
Lunch 午膳 12:00-14:30
Dinner 晚膳 17:30-23:00

■ **ANNUAL AND WEEKLY CLOSING**
休息日期
Closed Monday to Friday lunch and Wednesday
週一至週五午膳及週三休息

MACAU 澳門

MACAU 澳門

😊 🍷 ♿ 🏵 🎴 **P**

TEL. 8986 3663

**GF, Wynn Hotel,
Rua Cidade de Sintra, NAPE, Macau**

澳門外港新填海區仙德麗街
永利酒店地下

www.wynnmacau.com

■ **PRICE** 價錢
Lunch 午膳
À la carte 點菜 MOP 300-2,000
Dinner 晚膳
À la carte 點菜 MOP 500-2,000

■ **OPENING HOURS** 營業時間
Lunch 午膳 11:30-14:45
Dinner 晚膳 18:00-22:45

🙐 🙐

**WING LEI
永利軒**

Cantonese · Luxury
粵菜 · 豪華

Equally great for power lunches and friendly get-togethers, this strikingly lavish restaurant dominated by a crystal-pavé flying dragon isn't just about the looks. Cantonese classics and dim sum impeccably made with the best ingredients are what keep diners coming back. Steamed grouper fillet on egg white custard features 30-year-old dried tangerine peel and has a wonderful aroma. Lemon-scented pumpkin sponge cake roll is always a treat.

任何人來到永利軒，都會被標誌性的立體飛龍吸引。巨龍由九萬片水晶組成，璀璨奪目，盡顯豪華氣派，適合高級商務宴請。食物也毫不遜色，多款傳統粵菜選用優質食材用心製作，從前菜到甜品，皆予人非凡的體驗，尤其是午市的精美手工點心，不容錯過。推介之作包括三十年陳皮蛋白蒸星斑、香檸金瓜馬拉卷等。

✿

THE KITCHEN
大廚

Steakhouse • Contemporary Décor

扒房 • 時尚

Beef is the star of the show at this handsome, masculine dining room which also houses a sushi bar, a salad bar and a live fish tank. Choose from prime cuts from the U. S. and Wagyu from Kagoshima and Australia; then have it seared on an open flame to your desired 'doneness' and pair it with one of the 17,000-plus wine labels from around the world. Bread is baked daily and appetisers are made in the open kitchen à la minute.

融匯西式扒房、日式壽司吧及海鮮魚缸於一室，餐廳裝潢亦別樹一格。廚師會在開放式廚房即席製作麵包和各款頭盤，確保提供最新鮮的美食佳餚予食客。來自美國、澳洲及日本等地的頂級牛肉放於肉櫃內供挑選，食客可選取不同部位與分量，亦可從魚缸中點選新鮮海產。酒單備有逾萬款來自世界各地的名酒佳釀。

🏧 🍽 ⚘ ♿ ⛩ 🚗 🧺 **P**

TEL. 8803 7777

3F, Grand Lisboa Hotel, Avenida de Lisboa, Macau
澳門葡京路新葡京酒店3樓
www.grandlisboahotels.com

■ **PRICE** 價錢
Lunch 午膳
Set Menu 套餐 MOP 430-630
À la carte 點菜 MOP 500-1,800
Dinner 晚膳
Set Menu 套餐 MOP 980
À la carte 點菜 MOP 500-1,800

■ **OPENING HOURS** 營業時間
Lunch 午膳 11:30-14:30
Dinner 晚膳 18:30-22:30

MACAU 澳門

TIM'S KITCHEN
桃花源小廚

Cantonese • Traditional

粵菜 • 傳統

TEL. 8803 3682

**Shop F25, GF, East Wing,
Hotel Lisboa, 2-4 Avenida de
Lisboa, Macau**

澳門葡京路2-4號
葡京酒店東翼地下F25號舖

www.hotellisboa.com

■ **PRICE** 價錢
Lunch 午膳
À la carte 點菜 MOP 300-1,600
Dinner 晚膳
À la carte 點菜 MOP 300-1,600

■ **OPENING HOURS** 營業時間
Lunch 午膳 12:00-14:30
Dinner 晚膳 18:30-22:30

Hong Kong foodies make special pilgrimages here and it's easy to see why: the Cantonese dishes may appear quite simple but they are very skilfully prepared. Among the highlights are poached and sliced pork stomach in wasabi sauce, and sweet & sour pork ribs. Do make sure you try the crystal prawn and, during the winter, the tasty snake ragout. The restaurant is decorated with a variety of operatic costumes and photos.

香港食家喜歡專程到此朝聖，原因十分簡單：此食府的廣東菜看似簡單，卻實在是經過精心巧手炮製。推介菜式包括涼拌爽肚片及京都骨。此外，萬勿錯過玻璃蝦球及冬瓜蒸原隻蟹拑，而冬天的重點推介則離不開美味的太史五蛇羹。餐廳放滿戲曲照片和戲服裝飾，散發出淡淡的藝術氣息。

MACAU 澳門

CHEONG KEI
祥記

Noodles • Neighbourhood

麵食 • 親切

A family business since the '70s, this tiny noodle shop sticks to its roots and its thin, fine noodles are pressed by bamboo pole in its own little factory nearby. Their soup uses dried prawns and bonito and is cooked for 8 hours. The noodles with dried shrimp roe are great, but also try the wonton and deep-fried fish ball. Although it's handily placed on Rua de Felicidade, you'll need to weave round shoppers and stalls to get here.

這間家族經營的小麵店於七十年代開業，裝潢簡單且帶強烈的懷舊氣息。店家在鄰近自設小型廠房製造幼細竹昇麵，湯底以蝦乾和大地魚熬製八小時而成；蝦籽撈麵非試不可，雲吞及鯪魚球亦不容錯過。店內更有頂級蝦籽及秘製辣椒油發售。

TEL. 2857 4310

68 Rua de Felicidade, Macau

澳門福隆新街68號

■ **PRICE** 價錢
À la carte 點菜 MOP 35-50

■ **OPENING HOURS** 營業時間
11:30-23:30

MACAU 澳門

Ⓒ⛵ & ⟷ **P**

TEL. 8598 3077

**Pousada de Mong-Há,
Colina de Mong-Há, Macau**

澳門望廈山望廈迎賓館

www.ift.edu.mo

■ **PRICE** 價錢
Lunch 午膳
Set Menu 套餐 MOP 220
À la carte 點菜 MOP 300-700
Dinner 晚膳
Set Menu 套餐 MOP 390
À la carte 點菜 MOP 300-700

■ **OPENING HOURS** 營業時間
Lunch 午膳 12:30-14:00
Dinner 晚膳 19:00-21:30

■ **ANNUAL AND WEEKLY CLOSING**
休息日期
Closed weekends and Public
Holidays
週末及公眾假期休息

😀

IFT EDUCATIONAL RESTAURANT
旅遊學院教學餐廳

Macanese • Cosy

澳門菜・舒適

Being part of the Institute for Tourism Studies
means that while the head chef is a professional,
some of his brigade and front of house team
are students – and the pride they have in their
work is palpable. The menu is a mix of European
and Macanese dishes – presented in a modern
style using herbs from their own garden. There's
even the occasional Scandinavian touch (they
cure their own salmon). 3-course set menu and
tasting menu are offered at night.

這家旅遊學院教學餐廳的廚房由專業廚師主理，部分
團隊成員則由學生組成，供應多款歐陸及澳葡美食。
其特色是採用多種自家種植的有機香草和蔬菜作食
材，並以廚餘作肥料。晚市分別提供三道菜的套餐和
味覺體驗套餐。葡國雞和澳門土生炒兔治肉碎都是推
介菜式，別忘了試試甜品。團隊友善而專業，是遠離賭
場喧囂的用膳好去處。

LOK KEI NOODLES
六記粥麵

Noodles and Congee · Simple

粥麵 · 簡樸

This busy shop next to the pier still kneads the noodles with a bamboo pole just like old times and the flavourful broth is simmered with an array of seasonal fish. The owner's wife insists on making wonton wrappers and cooking noodles by herself and she's very specific about both the cooking time and the consistency of the noodles. Other popular dishes include crab congee, tossed noodles with dried prawn roe, and deep-fried wontons with crispy dace balls.

店子位於碼頭旁邊的街道上，廣受食客歡迎。第二代店主堅持以傳統手法製作竹昇麵，並由其太太親手烹煮，她對時間控制及麵條質感的要求十分嚴謹。湯底以時令的鮮魚熬製，鮮味十足；而雲吞皮更是手製。小小的餐牌上附有特色食品的照片，包括蝦籽撈麵、炸鴛鴦（炸雲吞及米通鯪魚球）及水蟹粥等。

TEL. 2855 9627
1-D Travessa da Saudade, Macau
澳門沙梨頭仁慕巷1號D

■ **PRICE** 價錢
À la carte 點菜 MOP 40-70

■ **OPENING HOURS** 營業時間
12:30-23:00

■ **ANNUAL AND WEEKLY CLOSING**
休息日期
Closed 4 days Lunar New Year
農曆新年休息4天

MACAU 澳門

LOU KEI (FAI CHI KEI)
老記 (筷子基)

Cantonese · Traditional

粵菜 · 傳統

If you're looking for a simple, good value supper, then Lou Kei may well fit the bill. Granted, it may not be in the centre of town, but every local and cab driver knows this lively place. For over 20 years, its sizeable selection of tasty noodles, congee and Cantonese dishes have won the hearts of countless diners. Sizzling Bombay duck with sand ginger delivers amazing 'wok hei'. Frogs' legs in claypot and crab congee are both highly recommended.

老記二十多年來供應傳統粥品麵食及廣東菜式,縱使並非位於市中心,但價廉物美的美食讓其在本地人之間早已遠近馳名。田雞腿煲及水蟹粥向來備受食客推崇;而以沙薑及生薑同煮的生啫九肚魚味道香濃,鑊氣十足,更是不容錯過。店內光潔潔淨,侍應親切有禮,更營業至凌晨,是不少夜貓子吃宵夜的好去處。

💲
TEL. 2856 9494

Shop H&M, GF,
12 Avenida Da Concórdia N, Macau

澳門和樂大馬路12號
宏基大廈第4座H及M舖

■ **PRICE** 價錢
Dinner 晚膳
À la carte 點菜 MOP 100-250

■ **OPENING HOURS** 營業時間
Dinner 晚膳 18:00-04:30

MACAU 澳門

99 NOODLES (MACAU)
99麵 (澳門)

Noodles • Friendly

麵食 • 友善

Noodle lovers will need a few visits to this stylish pit-stop at the Encore hotel to work their way through the huge choice of Chinese noodles – there's everything from Beijing la mian to Shanxi knife-shaved, tip-ended and one string noodles, all served with various broths and garnishes, along with specialities from Northern China. The colours of the room are vivid; the jumbo chopsticks on the walls are striking; and the atmosphere is buzzy.

細小的餐室以鮮艷的紅色作主調，牆上懸着一雙雙色彩繽紛的巨型筷子，華麗且充滿活力，與四周的賭場環境風格一致。顧名思義，這裏是嘗麵的好地方：北京拉麵、山西刀削麵、轉盤剔尖一根麵等多款麵食，配以各式湯底和澆頭，令人食指大動。餃子和北方點心當然也不能錯過。

TEL. 8986 3663

GF, Encore Hotel,
Rua Cidade de Sintra, NAPE, Macau

澳門外港新填海區仙德麗街
萬利酒店地下

www.wynnmacau.com

■ **PRICE** 價錢
Set Menu 套餐 MOP 150
À la carte 點菜 MOP 150-500

■ **OPENING HOURS** 營業時間
10:00-00:30

MACAU 澳門

MACAU 澳門

○⊪ &

TEL. 2831 3193

289 Rua do Almirante Sergio, Macau

澳門河邊新街289號

www.alorcha.com

■ **PRICE 價錢**
Lunch 午膳
Set Menu 套餐 MOP 98-128
À la carte 點菜 MOP 200-400
Dinner 晚膳
Set Menu 套餐 MOP 98-128
À la carte 點菜 MOP 200-400

■ **OPENING HOURS 營業時間**
Lunch 午膳 12:30-14:30
Dinner 晚膳 18:30-21:30

■ **ANNUAL AND WEEKLY CLOSING**
休息日期
Closed Tuesday 週二休息

¶○

A LORCHA
船屋

Portuguese • Friendly
葡萄牙菜 • 友善

Business is booming at this friendly restaurant near Barra Temple as regulars just can't get enough of the hearty food from a kitchen helmed by the owner's mother. Start with the obligatory salted cod fritter. Besides barbecue dishes cooked over a charcoal grill, the extensive menu includes specialities like sautéed pork and clams Alentejo style, mixed seafood rice, and Macanese coconut and turmeric chicken; all great choices to share.

餐廳位於媽閣廟附近,地點便利固然是吸引食客之處,但真正讓其大受歡迎的,是東主母親三十多年來一直親力親為炮製的葡國美食。食品質素一直保持水準,風味正宗,燒烤全以炭爐烹調。頭盤炸馬介休球值得一試,其他推介包括豬肉炒蜆、燴海鮮飯及葡國雞。菜式種類繁多,與三五知己共享可多嘗不同滋味。

CAFÉ ENCORE
咖啡廷

Macanese • Mediterranean

澳門菜 • 地中海風

(Restaurant is temporarily closed due to COVID-19.) An elegant restaurant on the ground floor of the Encore hotel. The look is that of a classic European café but one with a strong Italian accent. The menu offers a combination of Macanese and Portuguese cuisine, along with a separate menu of Cantonese dishes, but it is in the Macanese specialities that the kitchen particularly excels. Try dishes like crab curry and baked African spring chicken.

（受疫情影響，餐廳於評審期間暫時停業。）咖啡廷位於萬利酒店地下，格調高雅。餐廳設計以傳統歐洲餐館裝潢作藍本，並滲入大量意大利藝術元素。菜單以澳門菜與葡國菜為主，另設有粵菜菜單和每季更新的季節性菜式。不過最出色的還是地道澳門菜，例如咖喱蟹與焗非洲春雞。

TEL. 8986 3663

GF, Encore Hotel,
Rua Cidade de Sintra, NAPE, Macau

澳門外港新填海區仙德麗街
萬利酒店地下

www.wynnmacau.com

■ **PRICE** 價錢
À la carte 點菜 MOP 250-600

■ **OPENING HOURS** 營業時間
06:30-23:45

MACAU 澳門

IL TEATRO
帝雅廷

Italian • Friendly
意大利菜 • 友善

TEL. 8986 3663

1F, Wynn Hotel,
Rua Cidade de Sintra, NAPE, Macau

澳門外港新填海區
仙德麗街永利酒店1樓

www.wynnmacau.com

■ **PRICE** 價錢
Dinner 晚膳
Set Menu 套餐 MOP 980-1,580
À la carte 點菜 MOP 500-1,000

■ **OPENING HOURS** 營業時間
Dinner 晚膳 17:30-23:00

■ **ANNUAL AND WEEKLY CLOSING**
休息日期
Closed Monday 週一休息

The name, which means 'the theatre', makes perfect sense as you can watch the fire, water and light show from most tables in the restaurant. Equally spectacular is the family-style cuisine given a modern edge, which includes homemade pasta, pizza and seafood. Try their four cheese ravioli and make sure you save room for the divine Il Teatro tiramisu. The menu offers seasonal dishes which update every two to three months and service is slick and smooth.

餐廳大部分的座位都能飽覽表演湖景致，湖上每晚上演噴泉表演，音樂水柱與激光穿梭，蔚為奇觀。這兒主要提供帶現代元素的意大利家庭菜，如四式芝士雲吞及意大利軟芝士餅，亦有意粉、即製薄餅及高級海鮮可供選擇。餐牌上的時令菜式每兩至三個月會更新一次。年輕團隊服務殷勤周到。

MACAU 澳門

IMPERIAL COURT
金殿堂

Cantonese • Luxury

粵菜 • 豪華

On the same floor as the hotel's VIP lobby, this sleek and contemporary dining room wows guests with a vividly carved Chinese dragon coiling around a marble pillar. The head chef has over 20 years of experience and updates the menu regularly to include seasonal ingredients. Try his scrambled egg white with sea urchin and crabmeat, and barbecued duck liver and pork skewers. The impressive wine list includes over 2,000 labels.

如欲品嘗傳統廣東菜，金殿堂是尚佳選擇。餐廳格調高雅而不失時尚，氣勢十足的雕龍雲石柱更是標誌，巧奪天工值得駐足欣賞。經驗豐富的香港主廚上任以後，挑選優質時令食材，定時更新季節菜單。推介菜式包括海膽鮮蟹肉炒蛋白、大千爆蝦球，以及甚具特色的吊燒鴨肝金錢雞，不妨一試。

TEL. 8802 2361

GF, MGM Macau,
Avenida Dr. Sun Yat Sen,
NAPE, Macau

澳門外港新填海區孫逸仙大馬路
澳門美高梅酒店地下

www.mgm.mo

■ **PRICE** 價錢
Lunch 午膳
Set Menu 套餐 MOP 128-1,180
À la carte 點菜 MOP 200-800
Dinner 晚膳
Set Menu 套餐 MOP 1,180
À la carte 點菜 MOP 500-1,500

■ **OPENING HOURS** 營業時間
Lunch 午膳 11:00-15:00
Dinner 晚膳 18:00-23:00

MACAU 澳門

TEL. 8793 3821

2F, Grand Lapa Hotel,
956-1110 Avenida da Amizade,
Macau

澳門友誼大馬路956-1110號
金麗華酒店2樓

www.grandlapa.com

■ **PRICE 價錢**
Lunch 午膳
Set Menu 套餐 MOP 488-628
À la carte 點菜 MOP 200-1,000
Dinner 晚膳
Set Menu 套餐 MOP 488-628
À la carte 點菜 MOP 200-1,000

■ **OPENING HOURS 營業時間**
Lunch 午膳 11:00-14:15
Dinner 晚膳 18:00-21:30

■ **ANNUAL AND WEEKLY CLOSING**
休息日期
Closed Tuesday 週二休息

KAM LAI HEEN
金麗軒

Cantonese • Classic Décor
粵菜 • 經典

(Restaurant is temporarily closed due to COVID-19.) The dining room exudes understated elegance thanks to its eye-catching lights and subtle Chinese design motifs. The long-standing kitchen team attracts a loyal Macanese following thanks to its classic Cantonese dishes prepared in traditional ways. An array of exquisitely crafted dim sum are on offer, along with other signature dishes.

（受疫情影響，餐廳於評審期間暫時停業。）酒店大堂的上方正是金麗軒所在之處，餐室天花上的燈飾華麗奪目，配以牆上富中國韻味的圖案和裝飾，格調高貴優雅。廚師團隊經驗十足，烹調手法熟練，精於傳統技法同時亦不忘為菜式注入本土元素。菜單上除了一系列富澳門特色的粵菜，亦不乏經典的廣東菜餚及點心。

🍴○

LUNG WAH TEA HOUSE
龍華茶樓

Cantonese • Traditional

粵菜 • 傳統

Little has changed from when this old-style Cantonese tea house, up a flight of stairs, opened in the 1960s: the large clock still works, the boss still uses an abacus to add the bill and you still have to refill your own pot of tea at the boiler. The owner buys fresh produce, including chicken for their most popular dish, from the market across the road. Get here early for the freshly made dim sum.

這家有一列樓梯的傳統廣東茶樓自1962年開業以來，變化不大，古老大鐘依然在擺動，老闆依然用算盤結算帳單，你依然要自行到熱水器前沖茶。店主從對面街市選購新鮮食材烹調美食，包括茶樓名菜蔥油雞。建議早上前來享用新鮮點心。

💳 🚫🍴

TEL. 2857 4456

3 Rua Norte do Mercado Aim-Lacerda, Macau

澳門提督市北街3號

■ **PRICE** 價錢
À la carte 點菜 MOP 50-150

■ **OPENING HOURS** 營業時間
07:00-14:00

■ **ANNUAL AND WEEKLY CLOSING**
休息日期
Closed 4 days Lunar New Year
農曆新年休息4天

MACAU 澳門

NAAM

灆

Thai · Friendly

泰國菜 · 友善

TEL. 8793 4818

**GF, Grand Lapa Hotel,
956-1110 Avenida da Amizade,
Macau**

澳門友誼大馬路956-1110號
金麗華酒店地下

www.grandlapa.com

■ **PRICE** 價錢
Lunch 午膳
Set Menu 套餐 MOP 188
À la carte 點菜 MOP 350-850
Dinner 晚膳
À la carte 點菜 MOP 350-850

■ **OPENING HOURS** 營業時間
Lunch 午膳 12:00-14:30
Dinner 晚膳 18:00-22:00

The name of Grand Lapa's Thai restaurant translates as 'water', which seems appropriate as it overlooks the pool and tropical garden and features a small fountain in the middle of the room, which adds to the calm and peaceful atmosphere. The majority of the kitchen and service team are Thai and the food is attractively presented and the spicing is well-judged. The menu also features a section of Royal Thai cuisine dishes.

Naam在泰文中是水的意思，正與餐廳的環境互相呼應──位於泳池旁邊，中央位置設有一個水池，天然光線從其頂上透射而下，整個環境寧靜而優雅。這兒的泰國菜味道較為柔諧，賣相精緻美觀，更設有一系列宮廷菜式，友善的泰籍侍應亦會給予客人合適的推介。

MACAU 澳門

🍴🍽

NGAO KEI KA LEI CHON (MACAU)
牛記咖喱美食 (澳門)

Noodles and Congee • Simple

粥麵 • 簡樸

Don't judge a book by its cover because the simple neon signs outside do not reflect the quality of food and service at this friendly, well-run noodle shop. The key draw is the swimmer crab congee – crabs are dressed à la minute and burst with seafood flavours, while the creamy congee imparts a rich aroma of rice. Other recommendations include braised E-fu noodles with crab roe, beef brisket in clear broth, and curry chicken with coconut milk.

位於大街一角的小巷內，這小小的粥麵店被老舊的建築物包圍，卻不減其吸引力，全因店家管理有序，職員態度友善，服務使人稱心滿意。店子以水蟹、蟹黃燜伊麵和蟹粥聞名，所用的蟹均即叫即劏；粥底香綿且帶蟹肉鮮甜味。此外，清湯牛腩、牛筋麵和椰汁咖喱雞也值得一試。

💵 🍽

TEL. 2895 6129

GF, 1 Rua de Cinco de Outubro, Macau

澳門十月初五街1號地下

■ **PRICE** 價錢
À la carte 點菜 MOP 40-90

■ **OPENING HOURS** 營業時間
08:00-00:30

■ **ANNUAL AND WEEKLY CLOSING**
休息日期
Closed 3 days Lunar New Year, Mid-autumn Festival and National Day
農曆新年3天、中秋節及國慶日休息

MACAU 澳門

MACAU 澳門

🍽

TEL. 2837 2248

308-310A Rua do Campo, Macau

澳門水坑尾街308-310號A

www.wongkun.com.mo

■ **PRICE** 價錢

À la carte 點菜 MOP 50-120

■ **OPENING HOURS** 營業時間

10:00-22:00

🍴🍽

WONG KUN SIO KUNG (RUA DO CAMPO)

皇冠小館 (水坑尾街)

Noodles and Congee • Simple

粥麵 • 簡樸

Owner Mr. Cheng, who is native Macanese, has over 30 years of experience when it comes to making noodles using the traditional bamboo pressing method. His shop opened back in 2000 but such was its popularity that he later expanded into next door. A selection of traditional Cantonese dishes is offered but most come here for the sea crab congee and the bamboo noodles with dried shrimp roe (which is also sold in bottles in the shop).

澳門土生土長的東主鄭先生，已有逾三十年以傳統竹竿手打方法製麵的經驗。餐廳早於2000年開業，大受歡迎下擴充至隔鄰鋪位。他的店子提供一系列傳統廣東美食，但慕名而來的食客，通常會點遠近馳名的竹昇蝦籽撈麵及海蟹粥。店內亦有出售瓶裝蝦籽及辣椒油。

Paul_Brighton/iStock

MACAU 澳門

STREET FOOD
街頭小吃

CHONG SHING
昌盛

Cantonese dim sum and steamed buns. Sponge cakes and sticky rice rolls are recommended.

供應多款熱騰騰的粵式點心及包點，推介馬拉糕和糯米卷。

GF, 11 Tomé Pires, Macau
澳門新橋道咩啤利士街11號地下

PRICE 價錢: MOP 10-20
OPENING HOURS 營業時間: 07:00-20:00

KIKA

Japanese gelato. It specialises in matcha flavour with different levels of richness.

售賣日式雪糕，抹茶雪糕有不同濃度可供選擇。

GF, 11A Travessa da Sé, Macau
澳門大堂巷11A號地下

PRICE 價錢: MOP 30-130
OPENING HOURS 營業時間: 10:00-22:00

MACAU 澳門

MACAU 澳門

LEONG HENG KEI
梁慶記全蛋麵食（大排檔）

Offers springy egg noodles freshly made each day. Topping with braised beef brisket makes a satisfying and economical meal.

全蛋麵每日鮮製，麵質煙韌，爽滑帶蛋香。配上筋腩俱備的柱侯牛腩，價廉物美。

GF, 51 Rua de Cinco de Outubro, Macau
澳門十月初五日街51號地舖

PRICE 價錢: MOP 25-35

OPENING HOURS 營業時間: 07:00-18:00
Closed 7 days Lunar New Year
農曆新年休息7天

SEI KEE CAFÉ
(RUA DA PALHA)
世記咖啡（賣草地街）

Serves pork chop buns, deep-fried à la minute. The bun is crispy while the meat is tender and juicy.

秘製豬扒包外層鬆脆，塗上適量牛油美味非常；豬扒即叫即炸，肉味香濃且鬆軟多汁。

15D, Patio da Palha, Rua de Palha, Macau
澳門賣草地街乾草圍15號D

PRICE 價錢: MOP 15-30

OPENING HOURS 營業時間: 11:00-19:00
Closed 3 days Lunar New Year, National Day and Tuesday
農曆新年3天、國慶日及週二休息

VING KEI (MACAU)
榮記荳腐（澳門）

Apart from the signature cold or hot tofu pudding, it also provides tofu products, squid and noodles.

除了招牌冷、熱豆腐花，還有各式小食如豆腐、白灼鵝腸、魷魚和麵食等。

GF, 47 Rua da Tercena, Macau
澳門果欄街47號地下

PRICE 價錢: MOP 20-40

OPENING HOURS 營業時間: 08:00-18:30

YI SHUN (MACAU)
義順鮮奶（澳門）

A longstanding shop offering traditional desserts, such as pineapple with crushed ice and lotus seed sweet soup with egg. Milk custard stands out.

老字號甜品店，提供椰汁雪糕冰、菠蘿冰、蓮子燉雞蛋等傳統甜品，其中雙皮奶為招牌。

381 Avenida de Almeida Ribeiro, Macau
澳門新馬路381號

PRICE 價錢: MOP 30-40

OPENING HOURS 營業時間: 11:00-21:00

321

HOTELS
酒店

ENCORE
萬利

Grand Luxury • Contemporary
奢華・時尚

For VIPs wanting an even more exclusive resort experience than the Wynn, there is Encore – their luxury brand. The word 'standard' certainly does not apply here as the choice is between suites or villas, all of which are lavishly decorated. You also get an exceptional spa offering bespoke treatments and Bar Cristal: as small as a jewellery box and just as precious.

欲享受比永利更獨特尊貴的服務，可考慮同集團旗下更豪華的萬利。酒店提供豪華套房及渡假別墅，兩者均以紅色與金色裝潢，特顯富麗堂皇。貴賓級水療中心為你提供身訂造的療程，酒店內的Bar Cristal一如其名，像珠寶盒般嬌小高貴。賭場內附設多間貴賓娛樂房。

  ♿ ✧ ⇪ ☯ ⌇ ⌂ 📶 🛁 🅿️ 🚗

TEL. 2888 9966
www.wynnmacau.com

Rua Cidade de Sintra, NAPE, Macau
澳門外港新填海區仙德麗街

410 Suites/套房 MOP 2,700-7,900

Recommended restaurants/推薦餐廳:
Café Encore 咖啡廷 ⅃○
Golden Flower 京花軒 ✿✿
99 Noodles (Macau) 99麵(澳門) ⅃○

GRAND LISBOA
新葡京

Grand Luxury • Elegant
奢華 • 典雅

Impossible to miss, the Grand Lisboa can be seen from miles away with its eye-popping, brightly-lit lotus design atop a shining diamond. Opulent soundproofed bedrooms feature Asian paintings, and offer grand sea or city vistas. If you have a corner room or a suite, you'll get the added bonus of a sauna; if you have neither, you can make use of the sumptuous spa.

2008年開幕的新葡京外形像一片耀目的黃蓮葉，坐落於一顆閃爍的鑽石之上，遠處可見。客房隔音設備完善，擁有典型的棕色牆壁、紅色扶手椅和亞洲油畫，並坐擁豪華海景或澳門的秀麗風光。角位客房及套房設有桑拿設施，其他客房亦可享用豪華的水療設備。

TEL. 2828 3838
www.grandlisboahotels.com

Avenida de Lisboa, Macau
澳門葡京路

381 Rooms/客房 MOP 2,400-3,200
50 Suites/套房 MOP 4,500-48,000

Recommended restaurants/推薦餐廳:
Robuchon au Dôme 天巢法國餐廳 ✳✳✳
The Eight 8餐廳 ✳✳
The Kitchen 大廚 ✳

MGM MACAU
澳門美高梅

Grand Luxury • Elegant

奢華 • 典雅

Its iconic, wave-like exterior makes MGM one of Macau's more instantly recognisable hotels. The interior is pretty eye-catching too: topped by a vast glass ceiling, the Grande Praça covers over 1,000 square metres and is where you'll find an assortment of bars and restaurants. Spread over 35 floors, bedrooms are suitably luxurious and have glass-walled bathrooms.

標誌性的波浪形建築設計讓美高梅成為澳門最矚目酒店之一。店內設計同樣出色：巨型玻璃天幕下的天幕廣場佔地逾一千平方米，設有多間酒吧和餐廳。如果看膩了浮華的裝潢，不妨前往恬靜的水療中心。酒店有35層，客房華麗得恰到好處，景觀優美，浴室採用玻璃間隔，感覺寬敞。

TEL. 8802 8888
www.mgm.mo

Avenida Dr. Sun Yat Sen, NAPE, Macau
澳門外港新填海區孫逸仙大馬路

468 Rooms/客房 MOP 1,600-6,000
99 Suites/套房 MOP 4,100-18,000

Recommended restaurants/推薦餐廳:
Imperial Court 金殿堂 ⅰ○

MACAU 澳門

TEL. 2888 9966
www.wynnmacau.com

Rua Cidade de Sintra, NAPE, Macau
澳門外港新填海區仙德麗街

460 Rooms/客房 MOP 1,900-7,300
134 Suites/套房 MOP 4,000-9,500

Recommended restaurants/推薦餐廳:
Il Teatro 帝雅廷 ⌁
Mizumi (Macau) 泓（澳門） ❀❀
Wing Lei 永利軒 ❀❀

WYNN
永利

Grand Luxury • Contemporary
奢華 • 時尚

The Wynn's easy-on-the-eye curving glass façade is enhanced by a lake and dancing fountains, while the classically luxurious interior includes Murano glass chandeliers, plush carpets and much marble. An attractively landscaped oasis pool forms the centrepiece to corridors lined with famous retail names. Comfortable bedrooms display a considerable degree of taste.

弧形的玻璃外牆十分奪目，更設有表演湖及噴水池。酒店內部散發着古典豪華氣息：穆拉諾穆玻璃吊燈、豪華的地氈，觸目所及皆是大理石。走廊中心設有一個造型迷人的綠洲池，而兩旁滿是名店。客房融合了傳統與現代兩種設計風格，盡顯卓越品味。其吉祥樹同樣令你印象深刻。

MACAU 澳門

MANDARIN ORIENTAL
文華東方

Luxury • Elegant

豪華・典雅

The Mandarin Oriental is a non-gaming hotel but that's not the only reason it stands out – it is also a model of taste and discretion. Local artists' work adds a sense of locale to the bedrooms which come in muted, contemporary tones and offer great views – even from the tub! Those in search of further relaxation can choose between a very serene spa and a slick bar.

於2010年開業的澳門文華東方，除了不經營賭場外，更是品味的典範。本地藝術家的創作，為色調柔和和時尚的客房添上韻味，即使在浴室裏也能欣賞醉人景觀。想進一步放鬆身心，可到幽靜的水療中心或雅致的酒吧。此外，服務質素保持極高水準。

TEL. 8805 8888
www.mandarinoriental.com/macau

945 Avenida Dr. Sun Yat Sen, NAPE, Macau
澳門外港新填海區孫逸仙大馬路945號

186 Rooms/客房 MOP 2,100-15,000
27 Suites/套房 MOP 3,600-19,000

TEL. 2838 3838
www.starworldmacau.com

Avenida da Amizade, Macau
澳門友誼大馬路

465 Rooms/客房 MOP 1,500-2,400
40 Suites/套房 MOP 2,900-4,700

Recommended restaurants/推薦餐廳:
Feng Wei Ju 風味居 ❀❀

STARWORLD
星際

Traditional · Modern
傳統·現代

Opened in 2006, StarWorld Macau is a comfortable, well-managed hotel in a good location. Its bedrooms are bright and contemporary and the bathrooms are smart and well-equipped. Along with various restaurants and assorted gaming, the hotel also offers comprehensive entertainment and leisure facilities and these include a bar with live music every night.

在2006年開業的星際酒店地點便利之餘,亦是一間管理完善的酒店。光猛的房間設計風格前衛,時髦的浴室設施相當完備。渡假人士所需完全不假外求,除了各式餐館和娛樂場所外,酒店內還附設各種休閒設施,例如每天晚上都有現場音樂演奏的酒吧。

LISBOA
葡京

Traditional · Classic

傳統 · 經典

Thanks largely to its 1970s style façade, The Lisboa sports a relatively sober look for Macau, and so stands in stark contrast to the glitzier Grand Lisboa. There are ten types of guestroom available and the decoration is a mix of Chinese and Portuguese styles; it's worth asking for a Royal Tower room, as these are larger and more luxurious than those in the east wing.

仍然保留着七十年代外觀的葡京酒店，帶出澳門較為樸實的一面，與閃閃生輝的新葡京酒店可謂相映成趣。酒店共有十種客房，其陳設融合了中葡兩國的風格與特色；當中尊尚客房比東翼的客房更大更豪華。酒店設有多家餐廳，提供多國菜式。

TEL. 2888 3888
www.hotellisboa.com

2-4 Avenida de Lisboa, Macau
澳門葡京路2-4號

860 Rooms/客房 MOP 1,000-2,400
66 Suites/套房 MOP 1,750-7,300

Recommended restaurants/推薦餐廳:
Tim's Kitchen 桃花源小廚 ✿

MACAU 澳門

font83/iStock

COLOANE & TAIPA
路環及冰仔

RESTAURANTS
餐廳

✿ ✿ ✿

JADE DRAGON
譽瓏軒

Cantonese • Elegant

粵菜 • 典雅

This lavish room is a destination in itself – Chinese art, ebony, crystal, jade, gold and silver are all used to great effect but they don't outshine the food. The head chef has a passion for recipes deeply rooted in Cantonese traditions, but jazzed up with modern techniques and exotic ingredients from around the world. Besides the double-boiled tonic soups with herbal medicine, seasonal offerings such as roasted prime rib with chilli are also a delight.

裝潢糅合了現代設計與中式美學，豪華而不失格調，無論是透明酒窖還是玉雕筷子座，都給人留下深刻印象。歐陽師傅帶領的團隊在傳統粵菜的基礎上，巧妙配搭世界各地的材料，把食材發揮得淋漓盡致，並孜孜不倦研發新菜式。除了荔枝木燒味、應季滋補燉湯外，多款時令菜式亦風味十足，其中以香辣牛肋骨額外出色。

🏧 🍽 ♿ 🛗 👔 **P**

TEL. 8868 2822

2F, The Shops at the Boulevard, City of Dreams, Estrada do Istmo, Cotai

路氹連貫公路新濠天地新濠大道2樓

www.cityofdreamsmacau.com

■ **PRICE** 價錢
Lunch 午膳
Set Menu 套餐 MOP 880-1,280
À la carte 點菜 MOP 400-2,000
Dinner 晚膳
Set Menu 套餐 MOP 1,680
À la carte 點菜 MOP 400-2,000

■ **OPENING HOURS** 營業時間
Lunch 午膳 12:00-14:15
Dinner 晚膳 18:00-22:15

COLOANE & TAIPA 路環及氹仔

COLOANE & TAIPA 路環及凼仔

TEL. 8868 3432

3F, Morpheus, City of Dreams,
Estrada do Istmo, Cotai

路氹連貫公路新濠天地摩珀斯3樓

www.cityofdreamsmacau.com

■ **PRICE** 價錢
Dinner 晚膳
Set Menu 套餐 MOP 2,688
À la carte 點菜 MOP 1,450-2,150

■ **OPENING HOURS** 營業時間
Dinner 晚膳 18:00-21:30

■ **ANNUAL AND WEEKLY CLOSING**
休息日期
Closed Monday 週一休息

ALAIN DUCASSE AT MORPHEUS
杜卡斯

French Contemporary • Elegant

時尚法國菜 • 典雅

You'll find renowned French Chef Alain Ducasse's first restaurant in Macau on the third floor of the architecturally striking Morpheus hotel. Water, glass and atmospheric mood lighting are used to great effect to create a unique environment that is both stylish and intimate. Dishes are intensely flavoured, perfectly balanced and sophisticated. Those who know his other restaurants around the world will recognize some of the signature dishes.

法籍廚師Alain Ducasse在澳門的首間餐廳，選址別具型格的摩珀斯酒店三樓。室內設計巧妙運用水、玻璃及燈光，營造出高雅而親密的格調，與其所在的酒店同樣令人難以忘懷。食物也沒有令人失望，味道濃烈而恰到好處，簡單中盡顯不平凡。在此食客能細味廚師在全球各地的招牌菜。

SICHUAN MOON
川江月

Sichuan • Elegant

川菜 • 典雅

(Restaurant is temporarily closed due to COVID-19.) Supervised by celebrity chef André Chiang, Sichuan Moon is the total package – theatrical décor, detailed service, and creative cooking. The 15-course tasting menu that subverts all pre-conceptions about Sichuanese food never fails to surprise. The exquisite appetiser platter and Ma Po tofu in a bay leaf basket qualify as works of art. Hot and sour soup assembled at the table is as spectacular as it is tasty.

（受疫情影響，餐廳於評審期間暫時停業。）餐廳對食物品質一絲不苟，廚師曾到四川考察，深得當地飲食文化的精髓。由前菜開始盡顯團隊創意：新鮮醃製的老罈泡菜，以及88富貴涼菜，激活了大家的味蕾。再來一道錦繡酸辣湯，以蘿蔔皮包裹多樣材料，如花似錦，顛覆傳統酸辣湯的概念。十五道菜的套餐完美展現新派川菜的魅力。

TEL. 8889 3663

GF, North Esplanade, Wynn Palace, Avenida da Nave Desportiva, Cotai

路氹體育館大馬路
永利皇宮北名店街地面層

www.wynnpalace.com

■ **PRICE** 價錢
Dinner 晚膳
Set Menu 套餐 MOP 1,688-3,268

■ **OPENING HOURS** 營業時間
Dinner 晚膳 17:30-21:30

■ **ANNUAL AND WEEKLY CLOSING**
休息日期
Closed Wednesday 週三休息

COLOANE & TAIPA 路環及氹仔

LAI HEEN
麗軒

Cantonese • Luxury

粵菜 • 豪華

TEL. 8886 6712

51F, The Ritz-Carlton, Galaxy, Estrada da Baia da Nossa Senhora da Esperança, Cotai

路氹城望德聖母灣大馬路
銀河綜合渡假城麗思卡爾頓酒店51樓

www.ritzcarlton.com/macau

■ **PRICE** 價錢
Lunch 午膳
Set Menu 套餐 MOP 528-2,188
À la carte 點菜 MOP 300-800
Dinner 晚膳
Set Menu 套餐 MOP 2,288-2,688
À la carte 點菜 MOP 500-1,500

■ **OPENING HOURS** 營業時間
Lunch 午膳 12:00-14:30
Dinner 晚膳 18:00-22:30

If you're looking to impress then you can't fail with this Cantonese restaurant on the top floor of the Ritz-Carlton hotel. The stunning room is richly decorated and supremely comfortable, as are the numerous private dining rooms which can be opened out and enlarged. Chef Ho has many years of experience in Cantonese cooking and he and his team create tasty dishes presented in a modern aesthetic, a match for the sumptuous surroundings.

位處麗思卡爾頓酒店51樓，居高臨下，盡賞窗外秀麗景色。富麗堂皇的裝潢與造型精緻的傳統粵菜，同時滿足視覺與味覺的需求。館內設有五間裝飾華美的私人廂房，適合舉行大小宴會。專業的服務團隊態度親切，令食客有賓至如歸之感。主廚有多年中餐經驗，繼續帶領團隊提供高品質粵菜。

❀

8 1/2 OTTO E MEZZO - BOMBANA

Italian • Fashionable

意大利菜 • 時髦

(Restaurant is temporarily closed due to COVID-19.) Chef Umberto Bombana offers the same menu here as he does at the Hong Kong original; the wine list – of mostly Italian and French bottles – is also of equal breadth and depth. The kitchen team have been meticulously preparing every course here, including the terrific pasta courses. Service is attentive and thoughtful, and the elegant, chic dining room comes with a striking central bar.

（受疫情影響，餐廳於評審期間暫時停業。）與香港店同由意籍廚師Bombana帶領，餐單及食物風格亦與香港店如出一轍。廚師團隊使出品維持一貫的高水準，從頭盤到甜品每一道都經精心烹調，讓人回味無窮，意粉尤其不能錯過。酒單羅列眾多來自意大利及法國的佳釀。室內佈置美輪美奐，位於餐廳中央的雞尾酒吧也甚為吸引。

❀ ◎¶ & ⇔ 🍴 **P**

TEL. 8886 2169

Shop 1031, 1F, The Promenade,
Galaxy, Avenida de Cotai, Cotai

路氹路氹城大馬路
澳門銀河綜合渡假城1樓1031號舖

www.ottoemezzobombana.com

■ **PRICE** 價錢
Dinner 晚膳
Set Menu 套餐 MOP 1,598-2,280
À la carte 點菜 MOP 1,050-1,350

■ **OPENING HOURS** 營業時間
Dinner 晚膳 18:00-22:30

■ **ANNUAL AND WEEKLY CLOSING**
休息日期
Closed Wednesday 週三休息

COLOANE & TAIPA 路環及氹仔

TEL. 8865 6560

Shop 2111, 2F, Star Tower,
Studio City Hotel, Estrada do Istmo,
Cotai

路氹連貫公路新濠影滙酒店
巨星滙2樓2111號

www.studiocity-macau.com

■ **PRICE** 價錢
Lunch 午膳
Set Menu 套餐 MOP 1,080-1,880
À la carte 點菜 MOP 350-1,300
Dinner 晚膳
Set Menu 套餐 MOP 1,080-1,880
À la carte 點菜 MOP 350-1,300

■ **OPENING HOURS** 營業時間
Lunch 午膳 12:00-14:30
Dinner 晚膳 18:00-22:30

PEARL DRAGON
玥龍軒

Cantonese · Elegant
粵菜 · 典雅

No expense has been spared at this elegant
and luxurious Cantonese restaurant on the 2nd
floor of Studio City. The menu offers a range
of refined Cantonese dishes with lychee wood
barbecue being a speciality. Other highlights
are stir-fried Brittany lobster with mushroom
and lily bulbs; and traditional sweet and sour
pork. The tea counter offers a choice of over 50
premium teas.

這家位於新濠影滙酒店的粵菜餐廳裝潢時尚高雅，細
節中盡顯心思。香茗選擇逾五十款，酒櫃內放滿陳年
佳釀，餐桌上的擺設及用具以龍和珍珠設計，別致而
雍雅豪華。菜單選擇繁多，招牌菜包括果木燒烤，百合
珍珠菌法國藍龍蝦及懷舊咕嚕肉均值得一試。貼心周
到的服務，令用餐過程更添美滿。

THE GOLDEN PEACOCK
皇雀

Indian • Exotic Décor

印度菜 • 異國風情

(Restaurant is temporarily closed due to COVID-19.) It's in the vast Venetian complex so you may need a map to find this contemporary Indian restaurant. The chef is a native of Kerala but the menu covers all parts of India. Spices are ground in-house and everything from paneer to pickles is made from scratch. At lunch they offer an extensive buffet; come for dinner and you'll experience dishes that are flamboyant in presentation and rich in flavour.

（受疫情影響，餐廳於評審期間暫時停業。）嚴謹認真的印度主廚會自製各種醬料、乳酪、芝士、腰果蓉等，加上每週由印度空運而到的食材和新鮮研磨的香料，炮製出色香味俱全的印度美食。石榴烤雞肉串、洋葱燴羊小腿和各款素菜均值得一試。店內陳設簡約時尚，以印度國鳥孔雀作裝飾，具濃濃的印度風情。

TEL. 8118 9696

Shop 1037, 1F, The Venetian Resort, Estrada de Baia de Nossa Senhora da Esperança, Taipa

氹仔望德聖母灣大馬路威尼斯人酒店
大運河購物中心1樓1037號舖

www.venetianmacao.com

■ **PRICE** 價錢
Lunch 午膳
Set Menu 套餐 MOP 208
Dinner 晚膳
À la carte 點菜 MOP 300-700

■ **OPENING HOURS** 營業時間
Lunch 午膳 11:00-15:00
Dinner 晚膳 18:00-22:30

COLOANE & TAIPA 路環及氹仔

WING LEI PALACE
永利宮

Cantonese · Design

粵菜 · 型格

TEL. 8889 3663

GF, West Esplanade, Wynn Palace, Avenida da Nave Desportiva, Cotai

路氹城體育路大馬路永利皇宮
西名店街地面層

www.wynnpalace.com

■ **PRICE 價錢**
Lunch 午膳
Set Menu 套餐 MOP 480-980
À la carte 點菜 MOP 400-1,000
Dinner 晚膳
Set Menu 套餐 MOP 980-1,680
À la carte 點菜 MOP 600-1,500

■ **OPENING HOURS 營業時間**
Lunch 午膳 11:30-14:45
Dinner 晚膳 17:30-22:15

The appointment of chef Tam led to a rejuvenation of Wing Lei Palace, with many of his signature and seasonal dishes added to the menu. Don't miss the lychee wood roasted meats or braised fish broth with fish maw and vegetables. At lunch, dim sum options are also available. The room features spacious table settings and floor to ceiling windows which also provide fantastic views of the Performance Lake show.

金碧輝煌的餐室以碧玉及孔雀為題，一邊以落地玻璃環繞，讓食客享受美食的同時能欣賞窗外的音樂噴泉表演。行政總廚譚師傅為菜單加入了不少巧手菜式及時令佳餚。萬勿錯過各款以荔枝木炮製的燒味，以及精緻味美的花膠魚蓉羹。中午時段不妨點選各式精美點心。

COLOANE & TAIPA 路環及氹仔

YING
帝影樓

Cantonese • Elegant

粵菜 • 典雅

Ying is much-loved by locals for its sweeping harbour views, striking décor and most importantly, the well-executed Cantonese classics. The head chef fares well with traditional techniques that bring out the best in every ingredient. Signatures such as flambéed Iberico pork char siu, and steamed minced pork patty with salted fish are unmissable. Dim sum at lunch also show exquisite craftsmanship and astute judgment.

坐擁海港及澳門景色，帝影樓的位置得天獨厚，難怪一直深得本地人歡迎。室內設計風格絢麗，飾有金鶴和水晶樹圖案的珠簾使裝潢更添神采。來自廣東的大廚把傳統粵菜發揮得淋漓盡致，午市供應的點心盡顯手藝，更有部分菜式融入了新口味。果木火焰黑豚叉燒和馬友鹹魚蒸手剁肉餅均具水準。專業的服務令人稱心滿意。

TEL. 2886 8868

11F, Altira Hotel,
Avenida de Kwong Tung, Taipa
氹仔廣東大馬路新濠鋒酒店11樓
www.altiramacau.com

■ **PRICE** 價錢
Lunch 午膳
À la carte 點菜 MOP 300-1,000
Dinner 晚膳
À la carte 點菜 MOP 500-2,000

■ **OPENING HOURS** 營業時間
Lunch 午膳 11:00-14:45
Dinner 晚膳 18:00-22:15

COLOANE & TAIPA 路環及氹仔

♨ ♿ ♻ 🚿 🅿

TEL. 2881 8888

GF, Four Seasons Hotel, Estrada da Baia de Nossa Senhora da Esperanca, Cotai

路氹望德聖母灣大馬路四季酒店地下

www.fourseasons.com/macau

■ **PRICE 價錢**
Lunch 午膳
Set Menu 套餐 MOP 1,800-3,000
À la carte 點菜 MOP 300-2,000
Dinner 晚膳
Set Menu 套餐 MOP 1,800-3,000
À la carte 點菜 MOP 500-2,000

■ **OPENING HOURS 營業時間**
Lunch 午膳 12:00-14:15
Dinner 晚膳 18:00-22:15

ZI YAT HEEN
紫逸軒

Cantonese • Traditional

粵菜 • 傳統

This spacious, elegant yet intimate restaurant boasts a glass-clad wine cellar at its centre. The chef champions a cooking style with reduced amounts of seasoning so as to allow the true flavours of the first-rate ingredients to come through. Recommendations include baked stuffed crab shell, baked lamb chops in coffee sauce and egg white milk custard with sweetened mashed taro.

巨型玻璃餐酒庫佔據餐廳的正中位置，具空間感的設計令紫逸軒洋溢着高雅格調。精於烹調傳統粵菜的廚師着重選材用料，堅持採用最新鮮食材與最少的調味料，經他處理的菜式鮮味清新，推介有傳統的焗釀鮮蟹蓋和具創意的咖啡汁焗羊排；甜品芋蓉燉鮮奶更是不容錯過。

CHAN SENG KEI
陳勝記

Cantonese • Simple

粵菜 • 簡樸

This semi open-air restaurant has stood next to an ancient church for over 70 years and the 3rd generation of the family still focus on traditional Cantonese cooking. Seafood is the highlight as the owner works closely with local fishermen to secure the best catch – he prefers wild-caught fish about 500 to 600g for their tender flesh. Also try stewed duck with tangerine peel which takes more than 10 hours to make, with only a few available each day.

開業至今已傳至第三代,以傳統粵菜和海鮮菜式馳名,半開放式餐室非常樸實,數棵老榕樹見證着飯店逾七十載歷史。由於老闆跟漁民有緊密聯繫,能夠每天取得新鮮海產。其中,海魚只取十四兩至一斤,大小適中,取其肉質嫩滑。招牌菜陳皮鴨工序繁複,製作需時,屬限量供應菜式。梅菜扣肉及生炒骨也值得一試。

TEL. 2888 2021
21 Rua Caetano, Coloane
路環計單奴街21號

■ **PRICE** 價錢
À la carte 點菜 MOP 150-350

■ **OPENING HOURS** 營業時間
12:00-22:30

■ **ANNUAL AND WEEKLY CLOSING**
休息日期
Closed 2 days Lunar New Year
農曆新年休息2天

COLOANE & TAIPA 路環及氹仔

DIN TAI FUNG (COD)
鼎泰豐 (新濠天地)

Shanghainese • Friendly
滬菜 • 友善

☎ & ♿ P

TEL. 8868 7348

SOHO, 2F, City of Dreams, Estrada do Istmo, Cotai
路氹連貫公路新濠天地2樓蘇濠
www.dintaifung.com.hk

■ **PRICE 價錢**
Lunch 午膳
Set Menu 套餐 MOP 170-190
À la carte 點菜 MOP 150-350
Dinner 晚膳
Set Menu 套餐 MOP 180-200
À la carte 點菜 MOP 150-350

■ **OPENING HOURS 營業時間**
Lunch 午膳 12:00-16:00
Dinner 晚膳 17:30-22:00

The second floor of COD plays host to a plethora of casual eateries – and in the corner you'll find this sizeable branch of the international chain. Din Tai Fung is rightly known for its exquisite xiao long bao but also special here is the steamed crab roe and pork dumpling. Other notables from the 70-odd Shanghainese dishes on offer include the excellent braised beef noodle soup. To finish, try the red bean glutinous rice cake.

這是鼎泰豐的第一間澳門分店，位於新濠天地的蘇濠區內，特高的樓底配搭一貫的雅淨裝潢。菜單包羅逾七十款涼菜、麵食、小炒、湯品及甜點等，焦點是玲瓏的小籠包，香濃味美的紅燒牛肉麵會給你不少驚喜，正宗上海甜點如赤豆鬆糕亦不容錯過。

344

O CASTIÇO

Portuguese • Neighbourhood

葡萄牙菜 • 親切

Ownership of this simple, unassuming little place with just five tables has now passed down to the late owner's son – though his spirit is still honoured in the atmosphere of the restaurant, which is as friendly and as intimate as it ever was. The food is also just as good – the home-style dishes are authentic and carefully prepared, with recommendations being the stewed pork with clams and the oven-roasted bacalhau with potatoes.

這家隱藏於氹仔舊城區大街附近的小店陳設簡約樸實，只有五張餐桌。店子由已故葡籍廚師的兒子掌管，女友則負責掌廚。從清早到深夜，她就在細小的開放式廚房，以原店主的食譜繼續烹調家庭式葡國美食。店家待客如親人、收費合理的作風貫徹不變，推介菜有豬肉粒炒蜆。

TEL. 2857 6505

65B Rua Direita Carlos Eugénio, Taipa

氹仔施督憲正街65號B

■ **PRICE** 價錢
À la carte 點菜 MOP 130-250

■ **OPENING HOURS** 營業時間
11:00-22:30

■ **ANNUAL AND WEEKLY CLOSING** 休息日期
Closed Thursday 週四休息

COLOANE & TAIPA 路環及氹仔

TEL. 2882 1519

**G-H, GF, Block 5,
Edf. Nam San Garden, 154A and
154B Avenida de Kwong Tung, Taipa**

氹仔廣東大馬路154A及154B號
南新花園第5座地下G、H座

■ **PRICE** 價錢
Lunch 午膳
Set Menu 套餐 MOP 98
À la carte 點菜 MOP 200-300
Dinner 晚膳
Set Menu 套餐 MOP 150
À la carte 點菜 MOP 200-300

■ **OPENING HOURS** 營業時間
Lunch 午膳 12:00-15:00
Dinner 晚膳 18:00-22:00

BANZA
百姓

Portuguese • Cosy
葡萄牙菜 • 舒適

Located in a huge apartment complex, Banza boasts a green and white dining room which exudes country chic. The fish dishes are the hero items on the menu, while the popular choices among regulars include clams 'Banza-style' in a spicy tomato, onion and bell pepper sauce. Feel free to ask about their selection of Portuguese wine. The cosy mezzanine seats about six. Set menus only available on weekdays.

位於氹仔的大型屋苑內，餐廳四周環境寧靜，室內裝潢以白、綠色調為主，感覺休閒舒適。菜單上眾多的美食中以魚類最受歡迎，另推介配以甜椒洋葱蕃茄汁的百姓炒蜆。餐廳亦備有多款精心挑選的葡萄牙美酒，嗜杯中物者不容錯過。套餐僅於週一至五供應。

BEIJING KITCHEN
滿堂彩

Beijing Cuisine • Family
京菜・溫馨

'Dinner and a show' at Beijing Kitchen means one and the same, as the cooking is divided between four lively show kitchens which will hold your attention. There's a dim sum and noodle area; a duck section with two applewood-fired ovens; a wok station; and a dessert counter whose bounty is well worth leaving room for. Northern China provides many of the specialities. Ask for one of the tables under the birdcages suspended from the ceiling.

餐廳內有四個開放式廚房：點心與粉麵區、烤鴨區、明爐小炒區和甜品區；食客在進餐之餘還能欣賞現場烹飪表演，稱得上集用膳與娛樂於一身。廚房團隊來自北京，招牌菜以北方菜為主。烤鴨區廚房內懸掛着兩座燃木窯爐，甚具特色，因此絕不能錯過這兒的果木烤鴨。

TEL. 8868 1930

**1F, Grand Hyatt Hotel,
City of Dreams, Estrada do Istmo,
Cotai**

路氹連貫公路新濠天地君悅酒店1樓
www.grandhyattmacau.com

■ **PRICE** 價錢
Lunch 午膳
Set Menu 套餐 MOP 200-500
À la carte 點菜 MOP 300-1,400
Dinner 晚膳
Set Menu 套餐 MOP 400-800
À la carte 點菜 MOP 300-1,400

■ **OPENING HOURS** 營業時間
Lunch 午膳 11:30-14:30
Dinner 晚膳 17:30-23:15

COLOANE & TAIPA 路環及氹仔

BI YING

碧迎居

Cantonese & Sichuan • Cosy

粵菜及川菜 • 舒適

An ideal pit-stop if you need a quick break from the gaming tables – and its name is a homophone for 'sure win' in Chinese. The centre of attention of this buzzy, busy 24-hour operation is the show kitchen where the noodles are hand-pulled. The chef, with over 30 years of experience, may hail from Sichuan, but his menu features a wide array of classic Cantonese dishes, with wood-roasted dishes standing out. Finish with Lingzhi herbal jelly.

廿四小時提供大江南北美饌，近年由擁三十多年經驗的主廚接任，但菜單變動不大，繼續以粵川味道留住客人。無論是川式脆椒炒肉蟹、古法醬燒琵琶鴨，或是南北點心，都帶來無比滿足。不妨試試招牌燒味，並以靈芝龜苓膏或花旗參冰糖燉官燕作結。開放式廚房設有果木燒烤爐，更有機會觀賞手拉麵條的製作過程。

TEL. 8865 6650

Shop 1182, 1F, Casino at Studio City, Estrada do Istmo, Cotai

路氹連貫公路新濠影滙娛樂場
1樓1182號舖

www.studiocity-macau.com

■ **PRICE** 價錢
À la carte 點菜 MOP 200-500

■ **OPENING HOURS** 營業時間
24 hours 24小時

COLOANE & TAIPA 路環及氹仔

DYNASTY 8
朝

Cantonese • Traditional

粵菜 • 傳統

Inspired by the eight dynasties of ancient China, the intricately carved wood chairs, red lanterns and classic Chinese eaves provide plenty of old-world charm. From a menu that changes every six months come traditional Cantonese dishes made with top-quality gourmet ingredients. It's worth pre-ordering their double-boiled soups in smoked coconut. A variety of dim sum is available at lunch and wine lovers will want to check out the cellar.

雕花木椅、木地板、紅燈籠，濃濃中國古風的裝潢意念來自中國古代八個皇朝，亦與店名同出一轍。餐廳選用名貴高質的新鮮食材，製作出一道道色香味美的傳統廣東小菜。特別推介原個椰皇燉湯，選用新鮮原個椰皇燉製逾四小時，建議預訂。餐牌菜式每半年會更換一次，午市亦有點心供應；另設有酒窖，適合愛酒人士。

TEL. 8113 8920

1F, Conrad Hotel, Estrada do Istmo, Cotai

路氹連貫公路康萊德酒店1樓

www.sandscotaicentral.com

■ **PRICE** 價錢
Lunch 午膳
Set Menu 套餐 MOP 168-688
À la carte 點菜 MOP 250-1,250
Dinner 晚膳
Set Menu 套餐 MOP 688
À la carte 點菜 MOP 250-1,250

■ **OPENING HOURS** 營業時間
Lunch 午膳 11:00-14:45
Dinner 晚膳 18:00-22:45

COLOANE & TAIPA 路環及氹仔

☎📶
TEL. 2888 2226
8 Rua das Gaivotas, Coloane
路環水鴨街8號

■ **PRICE** 價錢
Lunch 午膳
Set Menu 套餐 MOP 88-100
À la carte 點菜 MOP 250-500
Dinner 晚膳
Set Menu 套餐 MOP 88-100
À la carte 點菜 MOP 250-500

■ **OPENING HOURS** 營業時間
Lunch 午膳 12:00-15:00
Dinner 晚膳 18:30-22:00

■ **ANNUAL AND WEEKLY CLOSING**
休息日期
Closed Wednesday 週三休息

🍴⭕

ESPAÇO LISBOA
里斯本地帶

Portuguese • Cosy
葡萄牙菜 • 舒適

The owner has created a homely 'Lisbon space' within this two-storey house in this Chinese village. The decorative style comes straight out of Portugal, as do the influences behind many of the home-style dishes. Don't miss the presunto pata negra and if you fancy something a little different then try the African chicken from Mozambique with its coconut flavour. Ask for a table on the veranda when the weather is right.

Espaço意謂空間，店主有意在東方這臨海小鎮營造一個充滿葡國情調的空間。不論是鋪地板的石塊、擺設以至烹調用的陶缽，全部從葡國運抵。葡籍廚師用家鄉材料與傳統食譜炮製多款家常菜。源自莫桑比克食譜的非洲雞，啖啖椰汁香，美味無窮；風味絕佳的黑蹄火腿亦不能錯過。

FIVE FOOT ROAD
蜀道

Sichuan • Elegant

川菜 • 典雅

Guests are greeted by an elegant tea saloon at the entrance, while the main dining room is serenely enveloped in ink mural art. The experienced chef from Sichuan excels in specialities such as marinated abalone, and braised crab with dried chilli and Sichuan pepper, to be paired with your choice from a wine list of over 1,500 labels. Live daily performances at 1pm and 8pm feature long-spout teapots and Bianlian theatre.

英文名源於古人在狹窄的絲綢之路的貿易往來，室內設計同樣帶有傳統氣息。大家可以在茶廊品嘗功夫茶，以及一系列特色茶製酒釀。來自四川的主廚經驗豐富，選用優質食材，烹調多款正宗川菜。招牌菜包括川味油鹵鮮鮑、回味無窮香辣蟹。配搭逾千款餐酒，更顯滋味。特定時段更有變臉等文化表演。

TEL. 8806 2358

GF, MGM Cotai, Avenida da Nave Desportiva, Cotai

路氹體育館大馬路美獅美高梅地下

www.mgm.mo

■ **PRICE** 價錢
Lunch 午膳
Set Menu 套餐 MOP 268-1,280
À la carte 點菜 MOP 200-800
Dinner 晚膳
Set Menu 套餐 MOP 880-1,280
À la carte 點菜 MOP 400-1,000

■ **OPENING HOURS** 營業時間
Lunch 午膳 11:00-14:45
Dinner 晚膳 18:00-22:45

COLOANE & TAIPA 路環及氹仔

🍴○

FOOK LAM MOON
福臨門

Cantonese • Classic Décor

粵菜 • 經典

🔲 ⓒ🍴 ♿ ⌂ 🛏 🅿

TEL. 2888 0888

Shop 2008, 2F, Galaxy Macau Phase 2 Shopping Mall, Estrada da Baia de Nossa Senhora da Esperança, Cotai

路氹城望德聖母灣大馬路
澳門銀河綜合渡假城二期商場
2樓2008號舖

www.fooklammoon-grp.com

■ **PRICE** 價錢
Lunch 午膳
À la carte 點菜 MOP 200-500
Dinner 晚膳
À la carte 點菜 MOP 500-1,000

■ **OPENING HOURS** 營業時間
Lunch 午膳 11:00-14:30
Dinner 晚膳 18:00-22:30

■ **ANNUAL AND WEEKLY CLOSING**
休息日期
Closed Monday 週一休息

(Restaurant is temporarily closed due to COVID-19.) A Hong Kong restaurant brand celebrated for its traditional Cantonese menu. With its clientele of high-rollers and decision makers, it is no surprise that a branch eventually appeared in Macau. You'll find local lobster on the menu, along with their famous crispy chicken; many regulars opt for the chicken stuffed with bird's nest – even though it isn't always listed on the menu.

（受疫情影響，餐廳於評審期間暫時停業。）門外的對聯和橢圓形的水晶吊燈為餐廳營造了別具一格的氣派。福臨門於香港享負盛名，熟客都懂得預訂餐牌上沒有的鳳吞燕，當紅炸子雞則是廚師得意之作，此外，桂花干貝炒花膠和各款精緻點心亦值得一試。食客更可向品酒師請教配搭美酒佳餚的心得，專業的服務態度讓人賓至如歸。

COLOANE & TAIPA 路環及氹仔

🍴

LEI GARDEN
利苑酒家

Cantonese • Traditional

粵菜 • 傳統

A smart restaurant set amongst the canals of this vast hotel's third floor. A comprehensive range of traditional Cantonese dishes are delivered by an efficient and well-organised team of servers. The best place to be seated is in one of the cosy booths. Pre-order the popular crispy roasted pork and various double-boiled soups. Reservations are highly recommended.

餐廳設於三樓,佔據此大型酒店運河旁的位置,雄據地利。翻新過的餐室以橘紅色座椅配搭杏色牆身,簡潔明亮。服務團隊的效率非常高,但以這家餐廳的受歡迎程度,食客到此用膳,預先訂座無疑比較明智。熱門菜式如冰燒三層肉及各款燉湯均值得一試,不妨提早預訂。

◎🍴 ⇔ **P**

TEL. 2882 8689

Shop 855, 3F, Grand Canal Shoppes, The Venetian Resort, Estrada da Baia de Nossa Senhora da Esperança, Taipa

氹仔望德聖母灣大馬路威尼斯人酒店大運河購物中心3樓855號舖

www.venetianmacao.com

■ **PRICE 價錢**
Lunch 午膳
À la carte 點菜 MOP 200-1,000
Dinner 晚膳
À la carte 點菜 MOP 250-1,000

■ **OPENING HOURS 營業時間**
Lunch 午膳 11:30-14:15
Dinner 晚膳 18:00-22:15

■ **ANNUAL AND WEEKLY CLOSING**
休息日期
Closed 3 days Lunar New Year
農曆新年休息3天

TEL. 2882 7571

90 Rua de Femão Mendes Pinto, Taipa

氹仔飛能便度街90號

■ **PRICE** 價錢
Lunch 午膳
À la carte 點菜 MOP 150-350
Dinner 晚膳
À la carte 點菜 MOP 150-350

■ **OPENING HOURS** 營業時間
Lunch 午膳 12:00-14:30
Dinner 晚膳 18:00-21:30

■ **ANNUAL AND WEEKLY CLOSING**
休息日期
Closed Wednesday 週三休息

MANUEL COZINHA PORTUGUESA
阿曼諾葡國餐

Portuguese · Exotic Décor
葡萄牙菜 · 異國風情

Authenticity and hospitality are what draw customers to this cosy little corner restaurant. Newcomers will find themselves welcomed by the owner-chef just as warmly as if they were regulars. His traditional Portuguese cooking uses quality ingredients and many of the dishes are cooked in the old-fashioned barbecue way. He makes his own cheese and the two specialities of which he is most proud are grilled codfish, and fried rice with squid ink.

離開氹仔舊城區的熱鬧街道，從施督憲正街向飛能便度街方向走，便會找到位於路口這家小店。在這兒你能吃到美味正宗的葡國菜。葡籍店東兼主廚親切好客。他堅持選用本地和葡國優質食材，且以炭火燒烤食物，還在店內自製芝士。燒馬介休和墨魚汁炒飯是他最引以為傲的菜式。

TENMASA
天政

Japanese • Minimalist
日本菜 • 簡約

This outpost of its renowned namesake in Tokyo that opened in 1937 boasts a sushi bar, a tempura counter, a tatami area, and decked walkways over golden pebble filled ponds that connect to the private rooms. Two Japanese chefs take turns to make tempura with fresh, seasonal ingredients. Besides watching the culinary magic unfold, you can also enjoy dazzling firework displays from the restaurant.

天政總店早於1937年在東京開業,澳門店則位於新濠鋒酒店內,榻榻米地板、鋪板走廊和金石水池使人感覺猶如身處日本!天婦羅料理採用新鮮時令食材,由兩位日籍大廚輪替為客人炮製;廚師就在眼前大顯身手,視覺同時得到滿足。餐廳設有壽司吧、天婦羅櫃枱及私人廂房,臨窗的座位有機會觀賞到煙花美景。

TEL. 2886 8868

11F, Altira Hotel,
Avenida de Kwong Tung, Taipa
氹仔廣東大馬路新濠鋒酒店11樓
www.altiramacau.com

■ **PRICE 價錢**
Lunch 午膳
Set Menu 套餐 MOP 338-900
À la carte 點菜 MOP 450-950
Dinner 晚膳
Set Menu 套餐 MOP 688-1,780
À la carte 點菜 MOP 450-950

■ **OPENING HOURS 營業時間**
Lunch 午膳 11:00-14:15
Dinner 晚膳 18:00-22:15

TERRAZZA
庭園
Italian • Mediterranean
意大利菜 • 地中海風

The menu covers the culinary traditions of every region in Italy and is updated every three months to keep it fresh. Guests get to see how the food is prepared through the glass wall. Pizza dough, tagliatelle, ravioli and tagliolini are made from scratch in-house and the extensive wine list is well worth exploring. Add in exceedingly comfy chairs and warm, welcoming service and you have a great place for a relaxing meal.

室內設計古典優雅、加上柔軟舒適的座椅、友善熱情的服務，使你身心放鬆；透過玻璃窗看看廚房團隊的烹調過程更是饒有趣味。菜單涵蓋意大利全國美食，且不時變更菜式，讓饕客保持新鮮感。個別食材是自家製，包括薄餅及部分意粉。飯後不妨一試席前製作的提拉米蘇。餐酒單種類繁多，更是使人驚喜。

TEL. 8883 2118

**Shop 201, 2F, Galaxy Hotel,
Estrada da Baia de Nossa Senhora
da Esperanca, Cotai**

路氹城望德聖母灣大馬路
澳門銀河綜合渡假城
銀河酒店2樓201號鋪

www.galaxymacau.com

■ **PRICE** 價錢
Dinner 晚膳
À la carte 點菜 MOP 350-700

■ **OPENING HOURS** 營業時間
Dinner 晚膳 18:00-23:00

COLOANE & TAIPA 路環及氹仔

🍴○

THE RITZ-CARLTON CAFÉ
麗思咖啡廳

French • Friendly

法國菜 • 友善

Tiles, mirrors and marble are used to great effect in this bright, lively French brasserie with an all-day dining concept. It prides itself not only on its friendly service, but also the array of classic French food on offer. Besides the daily special, steak is big on the menu with many prime cuts to choose from. Seafood lovers should try freshly shucked oysters. Round out your dinner with the spectacular tableside Grand Marnier flambéed crepes.

意大利白色雲石地板、真皮沙發和雲石餐桌,再加上典雅的水滴形吊燈、精緻的長鏡,營造出高貴舒適的環境。食品方面,提供多款經典法國菜,亦包括新鮮生蠔、牛扒,以及不同主題的是日特色菜單。在悠閒的午後,可以細細品嘗色彩斑爛的甜品。就算是晚餐時段,也不要忘記留點空間,以醉人的橙酒火焰班戟作結。

○🍴♿🛆🅿

TEL. 8886 6712

GF, The Ritz-Carlton, Galaxy, Estrada da Baia da Nossa Senhora da Esperança, Cotai

路氹城望德聖母灣大馬路
澳門銀河綜合渡假城
麗思卡爾頓酒店地下
www.ritzcarlton.com/macau

■ **PRICE 價錢**
Lunch 午膳
Set Menu 套餐 MOP 258-888
À la carte 點菜 MOP 350-1,000
Dinner 晚膳
Set Menu 套餐 MOP 258-1,528
À la carte 點菜 MOP 350-1,000

■ **OPENING HOURS 營業時間**
Lunch 午膳 11:30-14:15
Dinner 晚膳 17:30-22:15

COLOANE & TAIPA 路環及氹仔

357

♿ 🍴 **P**

TEL. 8868 3436

3F, Morpheus, City of Dreams, Estrada do Istmo, Cotai

路氹連貫公路新濠天地摩珀斯3樓

www.cityofdreamsmacau.com

■ **PRICE** 價錢
Lunch 午膳
Set Menu 套餐 MOP 178-208
À la carte 點菜 MOP 300-1,600
Dinner 晚膳
À la carte 點菜 MOP 300-1,600

■ **OPENING HOURS** 營業時間
Lunch 午膳 12:00-14:30
Dinner 晚膳 18:00-22:30

🍴

VOYAGES BY ALAIN DUCASSE
風雅廚

French • Design

法國菜 • 型格

Famed chef Alain Ducasse's dining concept takes you on gastronomic voyage to France, thanks to its classic bistro food. The young and talented head chef was on board in early 2020. Must-tries include Lucien Tendret's traditional pâté en croûte, and roasted French corn-fed chicken from Les Landes. The seasonally changing tasting menu is a good way to sample the breadth and depth of her repertoire.

位於摩珀斯酒店三樓,顧名思義,是法國廚師Alain Ducasse名下的餐廳。裝潢時尚,附設酒吧,氣氛輕鬆。新任主廚致力為餐廳炮製優質傳統法國菜。雖然菜單會按季節轉換,但酥皮鴨肝肉批及燒焗法國雞等招牌菜一直長駐,讓食客可一嘗經典滋味。若是首次到訪,建議選擇嘗味套餐,完整體驗美食之旅。

WONG KUN SIO KUNG (BROADWAY)

皇冠小館（百老匯）

Noodles and Congee · Simple

粥麵 · 簡樸

(Restaurant is temporarily closed due to COVID-19.) If you're looking for a quick bite after watching all the street entertainment on Broadway then try this simple noodle and congee shop. The menu is slightly smaller than the original branch but it still has the same focus on handmade noodles using the traditional bamboo method and served with dried shrimp roe. The congee is smooth and satisfying and has a delicate aftertaste.

（受疫情影響，餐廳於評審期間暫時停業。）百老匯酒店後面的食街，雲集多間澳門本地知名食店，非常熱鬧。作為本地代表之一，皇冠小館以古法竹竿炮製的彈牙麵配大頭蝦籽，及以新鮮原隻海蟹及瑤柱熬製的蟹粥馳名。另外還有其他粥麵小食和數款小炒。環境簡樸乾淨。

♿ 🅿️

TEL. 8883 1877

Shop A-G017, Broadway Food Street, Broadway Macau, Avenida Marginal Flor de Lotus, Cotai

路氹城蓮花海濱大馬路澳門百老匯百老匯美食街A-G017舖

www.broadwaymacau.mo

■ **PRICE** 價錢
À la carte 點菜 MOP 150-300

■ **OPENING HOURS** 營業時間
11:00-23:45

COLOANE & TAIPA 路環及氹仔

🕐 ♿ ⟨ ⊟ 🚇 🍽 **P**

TEL. 8883 5127

28F, Hotel Okura, Galaxy, Galaxy, Avenida Marginal Flor de Lotus, Cotai

路氹城蓮花海濱大馬路
澳門銀河綜合渡假城
大倉酒店28樓

www.hotelokuramacau.com

■ **PRICE** 價錢
Lunch 午膳
Set Menu 套餐 MOP 580
À la carte 點菜 MOP 400-3,000
Dinner 晚膳
Set Menu 套餐 MOP 1,680
À la carte 點菜 MOP 400-3,000

■ **OPENING HOURS** 營業時間
Lunch 午膳 12:00-14:30
Dinner 晚膳 17:30-21:30

■ **ANNUAL AND WEEKLY CLOSING**
休息日期
Closed Monday 週一休息

🍴🍽

YAMAZATO
山里

Japanese • Elegant
日本菜・典雅

(Restaurant is temporarily closed due to COVID-19.) A few contemporary flourishes are enough to make this minimalist dining room warm and welcoming. The Japanese and Macanese kitchen team has been working with the hotel group for years and is well-versed and well-honed in a variety of Japanese cooking styles, from sashimi and sushi, to tempura, grill and even shabu shabu... almost any Japanese dish you can think of.

（受疫情影響，餐廳於評審期間暫時停業。）除了壽司和刺身兩款主打食物外，山里還提供應各式日本料理：懷石料理、天婦羅、燒物、日本火鍋⋯⋯應有盡有。廚師團隊來自日本及澳門本土，曾於大倉集團服務多年，經驗十足。金黃色的牆身、時尚的水晶吊燈和淺啡色的木製傢具，瑰麗雅致，巨幅玻璃窗讓你盡賞動人園景。

🍽️

YI
天頤

Chinese Contemporary • Design

時尚中國菜 • 型格

Located on a Sky Bridge on the 21st floor, Yi's impressive position is matched by stunning views, impressive architecture and exotic interiors. The menu is a unique blend of authentic and modern Chinese cuisine, with sommeliers providing tea-pairing suggestions. Along with local ingredients, you can also expect Australian Wagyu, Vietnamese prawns, Hakka chili and Chiu Chow Puning sauces from China.

天頤位於摩珀斯二十一樓的高架天橋，食客不單被迷人景色環抱，更可從另一角度欣賞酒店獨特的建築風格。包含六或八道菜的品嘗菜單以廚師發辦形式上場，主廚按當日新鮮材料構思菜式，並糅合全球各地和中國各省份的特色食材及調料，菜式兼具創意和精緻賣相。更設茶藝師為客人配對茶飲。用餐區內的龍形屏風閃閃生輝，別具氣派。

📞🚻♿🅿️

TEL. 8868 3443

21F, Morpheus, City of Dreams, Estrada do Istmo, Cotai

路氹連貫公路新濠天地摩珀斯21樓

www.cityofdreamsmacau.com

■ **PRICE** 價錢
Dinner 晚膳
Set Menu 套餐 MOP 1,388-1,888

■ **OPENING HOURS** 營業時間
Dinner 晚膳 18:00-22:30

COLOANE & TAIPA 路環及氹仔

STREET
FOOD
街頭小吃

🍴○

FONG KEI
晃記餅家

A longstanding shop offering Chinese cakes and biscuits. The almond cakes and egg rolls stand out.

歷史悠久的餅店，提供各種中式餅食，杏仁餅和蛋捲尤具水準。

14 Rua do Cunha, Taipa
氹仔官也街14號

PRICE 價錢: MOP 30-50
OPENING HOURS 營業時間: 09:00-21:00

🍴○

LORD STOW'S BAKERY (RUA DO TASSARA)
安德魯餅店（戴紳禮街）

Opened for over 30 years, the store prides itself on its Portuguese egg tarts that have a crisp shell and silky smooth filling.

開業逾30年，其鬆脆而香甜軟滑的葡撻深受歡迎。

1 Rua do Tassara, Coloane Town Square, Coloane
路環市中心戴紳禮街1號

PRICE 價錢: MOP 20-30
OPENING HOURS 營業時間: 07:00-22:00

🍴◯

MOK YEE KEI
莫義記

Offering Serradura pudding and ice cream. The signature durian ice cream comes with Musang King, D24 and Mon Tong choices.

提供木糠布甸及不同口味的雪糕,其中榴槤雪糕有頂級貓山王、D24及金枕頭等多款選擇。

9 Rua do Cunha, Taipa
氹仔官也街9號

PRICE 價錢: MOP 25-70
OPENING HOURS 營業時間: 09:00-22:30

S. Grandadam/age fotostock

COLOANE & TAIPA 路環及氹仔

HOTELS
酒店

BANYAN TREE
悅榕庄

Spa and Wellness • Personalised
水療及保健・個人化

Forming part of Galaxy Macau, this luxurious resort comprises 246 suites, as well as 10 villas which come with their own private gardens and swimming pools. The very comfortable bedrooms all have large baths set by the window and the array of services includes a state-of-the-art spa – the biggest in the group. Guests enjoy full access to all of Galaxy's facilities.

作為路氹城澳門銀河綜合渡假城的一部分及毗鄰澳門國際機場，澳門悅榕庄共有246間套房和10間擁有私人花園和泳池的別墅。所有寬敞套房內均設有私人悅心池，酒店提供一系列貼心服務，當中包括集團最大及最頂級的水療中心。住客更可享用銀河綜合渡假城內所有設施。

TEL. 8883 6888
www.banyantree.com/en/china/macau

Galaxy Macau, Avenida Marginal Flor de Lotus, Cotai
路氹城蓮花海濱大馬路
澳門銀河綜合渡假城

246 Suites/套房 MOP 2,800-7,900

COLOANE & TAIPA 路環及氹仔

🏨

FOUR SEASONS
四季

Palace · Classic
宮殿 · 經典

TEL. 2881 8888
www.fourseasons.com/macau

Estrada da Baia de Nossa Senhora
da Esperanca, Cotai
路氹望德聖母灣大馬路

276 Rooms/客房 MOP 1,900-8,900
84 Suites/套房 MOP 3,200-14,300

Recommended restaurants/推薦餐廳:
Zi Yat Heen 紫逸軒 ❀

The luxurious Four Seasons fuses East and West by blending Colonial Portuguese style with Chinese traditions. The lobby acts as a living room, with its fireplace, Portuguese lanterns and Chinese lacquer screens. The hotel also has a luxury shopping mall and connects to The Venetian and Plaza Casino. If you want peace, simply escape to the spa or one of the five pools and the charming garden.

2008年開幕的四季酒店融合了東西方元素,將葡萄牙風格與中國傳統融為一體。大堂設有壁爐、葡國燈籠和中國雕漆屏風,猶如置身家中客廳。酒店設有豪華購物商場,直通威尼斯人酒店及百利沙娛樂場。想離開五光十色稍作喘息,可享用酒店的水療設備和五個泳池,還有迷人的花園。

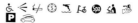

MORPHEUS
摩珀斯

Luxury • Design
豪華 • 型格

This hotel, part of the City of Dreams, is set to become a landmark in Cotai. It's architecturally stunning exterior was designed by the late Dame Zaha Hadid. Its interior is no less striking with a rooftop pool, a spa and numerous eateries, including two restaurants from Alain Ducasse. Bedrooms are luxurious, beautifully styled and equipped with the latest technology.

摩珀斯由已故建築師札哈·哈蒂女爵士設計，其縱橫交錯的外觀別樹一格，目光難以從中移離，勢成為區內的地標建築。客房同樣時尚奢華，先進科技設施應有盡有。酒店餐飲選擇良多，包括兩家法國大廚Alain Ducasse名下的餐廳，以及各式環球美食。欲肆意享受，怎能錯過天台泳池及水療設施？

TEL. 8868 8888
www.cityofdreamsmacau.com

City of Dreams, Estrada do Istmo, Cotai
路氹連貫公路新濠天地

582 Rooms/客房 MOP 3,000-31,800
178 Suites/套房 MOP 4,000-81,000

Recommended restaurants/推薦餐廳:
Alain Ducasse at Morpheus 杜卡斯 ❀❀
Voyages by Alain Ducasse 風雅廚 ⌁◎
Yi 天頤 ⌁◎

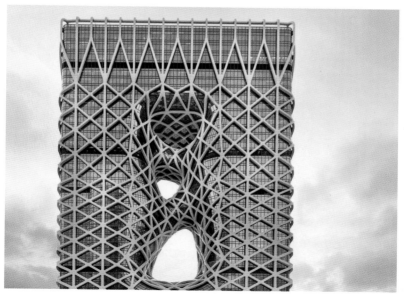

COLOANE & TAIPA 路環及氹仔

TEL. 8886 6868
www.ritzcarlton.com/macau

Galaxy Macau, Estrada da Baia de Nossa Senhora da Esperança, Cotai

路氹城望德聖母灣大馬路
澳門銀河綜合渡假城

242 Suites/套房 MOP 2,600-8,600

Recommended restaurants/推薦餐廳:
Lai Heen 麗軒 ❀
The Ritz-Carlton Café 麗思咖啡廳 ❀

THE RITZ-CARLTON
麗思卡爾頓

Luxury • Classic
豪華 • 經典

All bedrooms are suites at the exclusive Ritz-Carlton hotel, which is located on the upper floors at Galaxy Macau. They are impeccably dressed and come with particularly luxurious marble bathrooms. They also provide great views of Cotai, as does the outdoor pool. Along with a state-of-the-art spa is an elegant bar and stylish, very comfortable lounges.

講究的裝潢、精緻的藝術擺設、舒適的座椅,甫踏進設在51樓的接待處,心已給融化!風格典雅的套房除了設有舒適奢華的大理石浴室外,還能俯瞰欣賞銀河渡假村景觀及遠眺市內風光。與接待處同層的麗思酒廊設計優雅,且能飽覽氹仔景致,是與摯愛親朋把酒談心的好地方。

WYNN PALACE
永利皇宮

Luxury • Modern
豪華 • 現代

Opened in 2016, with a striking flower motif and impressive pieces of art scattered around the vast hotel. Luxurious bedrooms are uncluttered, large and bright, with a Mandarin, Peacock or Gold colour theme; the caramel-coloured suites are also impressive. There's a host of dining choices, from noodles to steaks; show kitchens are a feature of several of the restaurants.

於2016年開業，以上萬朵花卉製作的巨型花卉雕塑、隨處可見的藝術作品，寬敞的酒店，典雅高貴。以柑橘、孔雀和金作主題陳設的豪華客房感覺整潔、寬敞及明亮，橙棕色作主調的套房尤為使人印象深刻。酒店內餐廳種類很廣，從簡單的麵食到高級的牛扒，一應俱全，開放式廚房似乎是這裏的餐廳特色。

COLOANE & TAIPA 路環及氹仔

TEL. 8889 8889
www.wynnpalace.com

Avenida da Nave Desportiva, Cotai
路氹體育館大馬路

836 Rooms/客房 MOP 2,400-13,900
861 Suites/套房 MOP 2,900-15,900

Recommended restaurants/推薦餐廳:
Sichuan Moon 川江月 ❋❋
Wing Lei Palace 永利宮 ❋

ALTIRA
新濠鋒

Luxury • Modern
豪華•現代

TEL. 2886 8888
www.altiramacau.com

Avenida de Kwong Tung, Taipa
氹仔廣東大馬路

188 Rooms/客房 MOP 1,700-17,300
24 Suites/套房 MOP 2,300-21,000

Recommended restaurants/推薦餐廳:
Tenmasa 天政 ⑩
Ying 帝影樓 ❁

High quality design, a serene atmosphere and wondrous peninsula views produce something quite spectacular here. Guests arrive at the stylish lobby on the 38th floor and the luxury feel is enhanced by a super lounge and terrace on the same level. Bedrooms face the sea and merge tranquil tones with a contemporary feel. There's also a great spa and a pool-with-a-view.

酒店設計獨特，舒適典雅，位置優越，澳門半島的環迴美景盡入眼簾。38樓的大堂時尚尊貴，同層的天宮備有室內酒廊及露天陽台，豪華瑰麗。客房位於較高的樓層，海景一望無際，寧靜的環境與現代設計相互交織，氣派超凡。顧客享用附設的豪華水療設施時可飽覽美景。

MGM COTAI
美獅美高梅

Luxury • Contemporary

豪華・時尚

Sister to MGM Macau, this hotel boasts the world's largest indoor LED wall, which is part of its impressive central atrium. As well as shops it offers a comprehensive choice of dining options. Take a break from the casino and relax by the appealing pool or be invigorated in Tria spa. Gaze over Cotai from Resort bedrooms that offer luxury and all the latest technology.

澳門美高梅的姊妹酒店，附設獨立購物商場及娛樂場所，多家餐廳讓你能盡享各地美饌，從牛扒到川菜，以至澳門首間日式秘魯菜餐廳，應有盡有。酒店中庭的視博廣場設有全球最大型室內LED牆，帶來不同感官藝術體驗。客房極盡奢華，備有先進科技設施，滿足住客需求；亦可到泳池或禪澇水療放鬆身心。

TEL. 8806 8888
www.mgm.mo

Avenida da Nave Desportiva, Cotai
路氹體育館大馬路

1257 Rooms/客房 MOP 1,300-6,000
106 Suites/套房 MOP 3,800-11,000

Recommended restaurants/推薦餐廳:
Five Foot Road 蜀道 ⑪○

COLOANE & TAIPA 路環及氹仔

TEL. 8865 6868
www.studiocity-macau.com

Estrada do Istmo, Cotai
路氹連貫公路

977 Rooms/客房 MOP 1,300-11,000
621 Suites/套房 MOP 2,100-16,000

Recommended restaurants/推薦餐廳:
Bi Ying 碧迎居 ⊄
Pearl Dragon 玥龍軒 ⊛

STUDIO CITY
新濠影滙

Resort • Contemporary
渡假勝地•時尚

Even by Macau standards, this immense, art deco styled hotel made quite a statement when it opened in 2015. It aims to offer the complete leisure experience and that means extensive gaming facilities, a 5,000-seater arena, a 4D Batman experience, a magic show, shopping malls, spas, numerous restaurants and a nightclub! Bedrooms have floor-to-ceiling windows and good views.

這家耗資逾三十億美元興建、裝飾派藝術風格的酒店於2015年開業,目標是提供一站式的綜合娛樂,設有娛樂場、大型表演場地、4D影院、購物商場、水療中心等等,還有號稱高度冠絕全球、達130米的8字形摩天輪,讓你流連忘返。時尚而設備完善的客房分佈於兩幢大樓內,落地玻璃窗外是金光大道的醉人景致。

OKURA
大倉

Traditional • Minimalist

傳統•簡約

Looking for sanctuary from the outside world? Try this tasteful, discreet and elegant hotel, which is part of Galaxy Macau resort. Charming staff provide excellent service; bedrooms are up-to-the-minute; and all suites have private saunas and steam showers. Dining options include Japanese and international fare.

酒店位處銀河綜合渡假城內，裝潢典雅與品味並重，讓賓客感覺如遠離了凡塵的一切。身穿日本和服的服務員親切貼心，時尚的酒店客房寬敞舒適，套房配備私人桑拿及蒸氣浴設施，足不出戶亦能一洗疲累。餐飲方面，除了日本餐廳，尚有中國和其他菜系選擇。

TEL. 8883 8883
www.hotelokuramacau.com

Galaxy Macau, Avenida Marginal
Flor de Lotus, Cotai
路氹城蓮花海濱大馬路
澳門銀河綜合渡假城

429 Rooms/客房 MOP 1,400-3,000
59 Suites/套房 MOP 2,600-4,200

Recommended restaurants/推薦餐廳:
Yamazato 山里

COLOANE & TAIPA 路環及氹仔

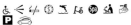

TEL. 2882 9000
www.conradmacao.com

Estrada do Istmo, Cotai
路氹連貫公路

430 Rooms/客房 MOP 1,400-7,000
229 Suites/套房 MOP 2,000-7,600

Recommended restaurants/推薦餐廳:
Dynasty 8 朝 🍴

CONRAD
康萊德

Luxury • Contemporary
豪華 • 時尚

The largest of all the Conrad hotels is on the Cotai Strip and its guests have access to an abundance of shopping, gaming, dining and entertainment opportunities. The Himalayan and Chinese inspired décor creates a relaxing environment; anyone requiring extra stress reduction should book a restorative session in one of the ten treatment rooms in the luxurious spa.

坐落於路氹金光大道上的康萊德,是該集團規模最大的酒店,這裏有為數不少的購物、餐飲及娛樂場所。陳設靈感取材自喜瑪拉雅和中國地區,感覺悠閒舒適。豪華水療中心內設有十間套房,客人可盡情享受水療服務,令壓力和疲勞一掃而空。客房空間寬敞,設計時尚。

THE VENETIAN
威尼斯人

Palace · Themed

宮殿 · 主題

One thing you'll need at Asia's largest integrated resort is a map to find your way around. Expect vast shopping malls and even canals with singing gondoliers; there are frescoes, colonnades and sculptures everywhere – it's easy to get caught up in the sheer scale and exuberance of it all. Identikit luxury is assured in a towering bedroom skyscraper with 3,000 rooms.

你需要一張地圖才能環遊這間全亞洲最大型綜合渡假酒店！在這裏你會找到大型購物商場，更有貢多拉船夫一邊撐船一邊唱歌。遍佈各處的壁畫、柱廊和雕塑裝飾，具規模且色彩繽紛，令人目不暇給。高聳的摩天大樓設有三千間套房，全都寬敞舒適。

TEL. 2882 8888
www.venetianmacao.com
Estrada da Baia de Nossa Senhora da Esperança, Taipa
氹仔望德聖母灣大馬路

3000 Suites/套房 MOP 1,600-8,650

Recommended restaurants/推薦餐廳:
Lei Garden 利苑酒家 ⬤
The Golden Peacock 皇雀 ✿

COLOANE & TAIPA 路環及氹仔

377

INDEX
索引

INDEX OF RESTAURANTS
餐廳列表

🅝 New entry in the guide 新增推介

N Restaurant promoted to a Bib Gourmand or Star 評級有所晉升的餐廳

HONG KONG 香港

MACAU 澳門

STARRED RESTAURANTS
星級餐廳

ⓃNew entry in the guide 新增推介
N Restaurant promoted to a Bib Gourmand or Star 評級有所晉升的餐廳

HONG KONG 香港

🏵🏵🏵

🏵🏵

🏵

MACAU 澳門

✿ ✿ ✿

✿ ✿

✿

STARRED RESTAURANTS 星級餐廳

BIB GOURMAND
必比登美食推介

Ⓝ New entry in the guide 新增推介

N Restaurant promoted to a Bib Gourmand or Star 評級有所晉升的餐廳

HONG KONG 香港

MACAU 澳門

RESTAURANTS BY CUISINE TYPE
餐廳 — 以菜式分類

HONG KONG 香港

CANTONESE/粵菜

BALINESE/峇里菜

BARBECUE/燒烤

BEIJING CUISINE/京菜

CANTONESE ROAST MEATS/燒味

CHINESE CONTEMPORARY/時尚中國菜

CHIU CHOW/潮州菜

DIM SUM/點心

DUMPLINGS/餃子

EUROPEAN CONTEMPORARY/時尚歐陸菜

FRENCH/法國菜

FRENCH CONTEMPORARY/時尚法國菜

FUJIAN/閩菜

SEAFOOD/海鮮

SHAANXI/陝西菜

SHANGHAINESE/滬菜

SHUN TAK/順德菜

SICHUAN/川菜

SINGAPOREAN AND MALAYSIAN/星馬菜

STEAKHOUSE/扒房

SUSHI/壽司

MACAU 澳門

CANTONESE/粵菜

BEIJING CUISINE/京菜

CHINESE CONTEMPORARY/時尚中國菜

FRENCH/法國菜

FRENCH CONTEMPORARY/時尚法國菜

HUNANESE/湘菜

INDIAN/印度菜

RESTAURANTS BY AREA
餐廳 — 以地區分類

N New entry in the guide 新增推介
N Restaurant promoted to a Bib Gourmand or Star 評級有所晉升的餐廳

HONG KONG 香港

HONG KONG ISLAND 香港島

Admiralty 金鐘

Causeway Bay/銅鑼灣

Central/中環

Mong Kok/旺角

Prince Edward/太子

Sham Shui Po/深水埗

Tai Kok Tsui/大角咀

Tsim Sha Tsui/尖沙咀

RESTAURANTS BY AREA 餐廳 — 以地區分類

NEW TERRITORIES EAST 新界東

Sai Kung/西貢

Sha Tin/沙田

Tai Wai/大圍

NEW TERRITORIES WEST 新界西

Sham Tseng/深井

Tuen Mun/屯門

Yuen Long/元朗

RESTAURANTS BY AREA 餐廳 — 以地區分類

TAIPA 氹仔

INDEX OF STREET FOOD
街頭小吃

INDEX OF HOTELS
酒店列表

HONG KONG 香港

MACAU 澳門

INDEX OF HOTELS 酒店列表

CREDITS:

Page 4: ansonmiao/iStock (top) - Wenbin/iStock (bottom) – **Page 5:** (from top to bottom): Nikada/iStock – bushton3/iStock - Yongyuan Dai/iStock - Ruchaneewan Togran/iStock - pilesasmiles/iStock - **Page 18-19:** BlueOrange Studio/Shutterstock.com - Nikada/iStock - Nikada/iStock - trusjom/iStock - PamelaJoeMcFarlane/iStock (center) - Doug Armand/Shutterstock.com - J. Warburton-Lee/Photononstop

All other photos by Michelin or by the kind permission of the establishments mentioned in this guide.

MICHELIN TRAVEL PARTNER
Société par actions simplifiées au capital de 15 044 940 €
27 Cours de L'Île Seguin - 92100 Boulogne Billancourt (France)
R.C.S. Nanterre 433 677 721

© **2021 Michelin Travel Partner - All rights reserved**
Legal Deposit : 11-2020
Printed in China: 11-2020

No part of this publication may be reproduced in any form without the prior permission of the publisher.

Although the information in this guide was believed by the authors and publisher to be accurate and current at the time of publication, they cannot accept responsibility for any inconvenience, loss or injury sustained by any person relying on information or advice contained in this guide. Things change over time and travellers should take steps to verify and confirm information, especially time sensitive information related to prices, hours of operation and availability.